Hopeful Realism
in Urban Ministry

Hopeful Realism
in Urban Ministry

Critical Explorations and Constructive
Affirmations of Hoping Justice Prayerfully

Barry K. Morris

FOREWORD BY
Tim Dickau

WIPF & STOCK · Eugene, Oregon

HOPEFUL REALISM IN URBAN MINISTRY
Critical Contributions and Constructive Affirmations of Hoping Justice Prayerfully

Copyright © 2016 Barry K. Morris. All rights reserved. Except for brief quotations in critical publications or reviews, no part of this book may be reproduced in any manner without prior written permission from the publisher. Write: Permissions, Wipf and Stock Publishers, 199 W. 8th Ave., Suite 3, Eugene, OR 97401.

Wipf & Stock
An Imprint of Wipf and Stock Publishers
199 W. 8th Ave., Suite 3
Eugene, OR 97401

www.wipfandstock.com

PAPERBACK ISBN: 978-1-4982-2143-6
HARDCOVER ISBN: 978-1-4982-2145-0

Manufactured in the U.S.A.

To that cloud of steadfastly faithful witnesses—also, alas, those who have fumbled and stumbled along the way as even fragmentary partakers of "the Way" with and for urban ministries—you are the salt of the earth: your flavor sustains.

Contents

Foreword by Tim Dickau · xi
Preface and Acknowledgements · xiii

Chapter 1—Proposal of Hopeful Realism · 1
    On Realism: Finitude, Ignorance and Sin · 2
    On Hope: Pressing the Limits · 4
    Hope and Realism Combined: Leaven of a Just Realm beyond
        Our Eager but Meager Strivings · 5
    Hopeful Realism for Urban Ministry: Animating Contrast Awareness · 7
    Framing Urban Ministry via a Triad: Grounded, Hopeful Realism · 10
    Discerning Key Elements in Urban Ministries · 12

Chapter 2—Urban Ministry and Theology's Enduring Themes · 16
    Survey of the Field and Actors · 16
    Anthologies, Urban Training and Action Research · 22
    Smouldering Embers · 29
    Critical and New Faithful Responses · 31
    Summary Conclusion · 32

Chapter 3—Urban Ministry Dynamics and Triad Intimations · 34
    In the Midst of Despair, Hope Intimated · 35
    In the Midst of 'Endless' Charity, Justice Intimated · 37
    In the Midst of 'Heroic' Weariness, Prayer Intimated · 38
    Search for Theological Containers and Anchorages · 40
    Venture of Crossovers and Hybrids · 45
    Inspiring, Sustaining and Renewing Themes · 47
    Triad, Critical Responses and Hopeful Realism · 50
    Summary · 52

Chapter 4—Hope via Moltmann and Urban Ministry Intimations · 54
    Introduction · 54
    Moltmann's Theology toward Hope · 55
    What Brought Moltmann to Hope · 57
    Long-Haul Resources via Moltmann's Theology of Hope · 58
    Hoping Justice Prayerfully Intimations and Urban Ministry Implications · 60
    Summary · 65

Chapter 5—Justice via Niebuhr and Urban Ministry Intimations · 67
   Introduction · 67
   Niebuhr's Understanding and Implications of Justice · 69
   Love Is Not Enough: What Brought Niebuhr to Justice · 71
   Long Haul Resources for What Kept Niebuhr Committed to Justice · 73
   Praying Justice Hopefully, Intimations, and Urban Ministry Implications · 78
   Summary · 82

Chapter 6—Prayer via Merton and Urban Ministry Intimations · 83
   Merton's Theology of Prayer · 84
   Long Haul Resources for Merton's Theology of Prayer · 88
   Just Prayer Hopefully, Triad Intimations and Urban Ministry Implications · 93
   A Summary Triad: Grounding Reflection · 97

Chapter 7—Longhouse Ministry and Networking · 100
   Introduction · 100
   Indispensable Networks · 101
   On Cases: Intrinsic and Instrumental · 107
   Enduring Responses and the Help of Response Ethics' Criteria · 109
   Longhouse Ministry Nourishment · 110
   The Triad, Realism, and the Longhouse · 112
   Longhouse Ministry and Network Comparisons · 113
   Triad's Conjunctive in the Service of Hopeful Realism · 119
      If Only Justice Is Present · 120
      If Only Prayer Is Present · 121
      If Only Hope Is Present · 122
      If Two Discipline Terms Are Present but Not the Third · 123
   Summary Conclusion · 126

Chapter 8—Summary Considerations and Conclusions · 127
   Introduction · 127
   A Singular Prayer in Focus · 130
   The Original Serenity Prayer Clause-by-Clause · 131
   Grace Hi-lighted · 135
   Conclusion · 137

Appendix A: The Merton and New Monasticism Check and Balance · 141
   The New Monastics' Vocation and Challenge · 141
   Probing a Constructive Criticism · 143
   The Praying Justice Hopefully Triad · 145
   Steadfast Insights and Guidance · 147

Appendix B: Networks' Viva Voce Testimonies and Inducing Central
        Story Line · 150
    From the Streams of Justice (SoJ) network's co-founders: · 150
    From Metro Vancouver Alliance (MVA): · 152
    From A Community Aware (ACA) by way of co-founder
        Terry Patten, with Mary Etey and Ken Lyotier: · 153
    A Concluding note from FNSP student researcher Andrea Reid: · 155
    Inducing a compact story-line via a brief application of grounded theory · 156

Bibliography · 159

Index · 185

Foreword

URBAN MINISTRY, ESPECIALLY WHEN it is going "well", can often be exhilarating and exciting. Sticking with urban ministry through congregational, neighborhood, and cultural transition, when the church is struggling for survival, is often painstaking and tedious. With thankful exceptions, most books on urban ministry seem to be written by those for whom things are going "well", for folks who seem to be a cut above other practitioners in their entrepreneurial and charismatic leadership. Most of those books leave the rest of us in urban ministry feeling less of ourselves and our churches.

This book is different. This book is written by a man who has persisted in a three-decade long obedience while being honest about his own struggles. This book is written by someone who has continued to pursue a hopeful and prayerful justice in the face of numerous obstacles. This book is written by someone who has continued to look outwards, learning from and synthesizing into his own ministry the challenging vision of theologians and cultural critics. This book is written to encourage you.

Barry and I began working in our neighboring parishes at about the same time. I have watched, observed, admired, confided in, complained to and collaborated with Barry over the years. What I appreciate most about Barry is that he continues to work with what is in front of him. He starts where his church and neighbours are at, rather than where they are not. In that sense, he has modeled for all these years the realism of which he writes. Yet, he does so with hope—a hard-wrung hope that keeps working for the personal, corporate, and systemic transformation that the Biblical story calls us towards. And no doubt the reason that he persists in this mission journey is that he continues to pray and contemplate the divine. Without this practice he wouldn't be here today. The three main writers whom he draws upon for his ministry and whose thought he elucidates in this book—Niebuhr, Moltmann and Merton—are not only his mentors, they have become companions in the work of urban ministry.

Another reason to read this book is that it gives new imagination for ways that we can partner with others in urban ministry. One of the strengths of the church Barry pastors, the Longhouse, is that it looks for common ground to build upon with others. On this path, both Barry and the Longhouse reflect these three mentors and companions. On a personal level, I believe it is part of the reason why he can pray monthly with the local Pentecostal, Charismatic, and Reformed pastors; why he can work for social change with Catholics, Baptists and trade unions; and why he can offer hope for those struggling with addiction by working alongside psychiatrists and counselors. What he offers in this book is a vision for how justice and love, the two-sided shape of Christ's mission, can be integrated. Given that the groups he partners with have often separated them, this is good news for urban ministry today.

You don't have to be with Barry long to see why this model of urban ministry that he espouses is compelling; it is nestled deeply within his life and ministry. Barry lives amid the stark realities of poverty, and often peppers his speech with gruff words depicting this reality, yet he does not forsake hope. Hope keeps seeping out of his speech too, like antibodies fighting disease. As he engages the world in the divine name, he continues reflecting, ruminating, and forgiving—he continues to pray. For almost three decades now, we have walked the streets of East Vancouver, he mostly along Hastings Street, I along Commercial Drive. I trust him. You can trust him too. And you can trust that his vision for ministry will give you courage to confront what is in front of you, hope to embrace God's renewed future, and desire to bring all of this before the One who groans with us and leads us towards new life.

My proposal is this: Read this book, because if you do, I believe that you will wake up the next day ready to go back to work in the place and parish God has called you with a realistic, prayerful hope. . . .

. . . Tim Dickau

Preface and Acknowledgements

FOR YEARS, THEN DECADES, and now generations, I have wondered what makes and keeps an urban ministry—any ministry, really—pastorally *and* prophetically faithful for the long hauls. How is it possible to discern in the service of ministry a comprehensive and compelling perspective? Thankfully there have been and are earnest contributions to this field of research. But the field and task remain incomplete and imperfect. Ministry in the city, which always includes more than merely the inner-city or urban core of the city given the pervasive pressures of "urbanism as a way of life",[1] has been engaged by practitioners, participant-observers, and academics for generations. The best models are likely those based on reflection and action—or action, then reflection on it—and finally, further revised reflections. I have long felt that urban ministry and theology models feel particularly helpful when both ministry and theology are combined—as with the 1948-1968 East Harlem Protestant Parish or the likes of an intergenerational urban theologian such as Kenneth Leech.

My work and writing has also been shaped by community-based initiatives—such as A Community Aware (ACA), the group noted in Chapter 7—which is effective at bridging the gap between the theoretical and the practical aspects of community, as they provide space for intellectual development in the context of one's experiences and emotions. The following thoughts were expressed by Andrea Reid, a former First Nations Studies Program student who did research with the Longhouse Ministry. Her words speak to the importance of bridging the gap between the theoretical and personal in the practical aspects of urban ministry.

> It is so easy to judge someone based on the way that they look or come across, without considering that person as a unique human being with an amazing set of experiences, struggles, and insights that you could not have previously imagined. Although this is something that I have always known on a theoretical

---

1. See Louis Wirth's classic manner of describing urban reality as *a way of life*, featuring numbers, density and heterogeneity—to which one would add the currently fierce pressures of gentrification and concomitant urban inequalities. See Wirth's "Urbanism as a Way of Life", 21-33. Also, Camacho, *God Loves Gentrification*.

level, I am now incorporating that realization into my life more fully and consciously. I am truly humbled and amazed by people and their struggles. Often, people do not realize how much they have to share and offer based on their unique life experiences. Through our relations with others, we have the possibility to open up to so much more than is possible in isolation. Together, we can work to realize a world that is rich in diversity, creativity, and compassion.[2]

Even though there have been many earnest contributions, the interpretive task to provide a compelling perspective on urban ministry remains incomplete and imperfect. This book is a reflection on the biblical and classical virtues of justice, hope, and prayer, considering how they might assist an urban ministry to be both faithfully public and prophetic over the long haul. For we need a disciplined commitment that extends beyond the initial and enthusiastic inspiration to get involved and moves towards long-term dedication. Such discipline is not a ready-made roadmap, but rather comes as we live out our convictions.[3] As we share those convictions with others along the way, seeking both encouragement and revision, we also need to discover resources of renewal and bold modesty for when weariness sets in and we are tempted by self-righteousness and despair.

As an urban minister in several center and inner-city zones for forty years, I have wondered how urban ministry might be grounded in both comprehensive theory and compelling and realistic practice that acknowledges the formidable limits, vulnerabilities, and fragilities of the human condition and the struggles of urban core city living.[4] I began inner-city ministry with the simple thrill of just hearing the varied sounds of life on the streets and in backyards (for those who have them) and came to appreciate on tenement roof-tops cooler summer breezes amid sizzling, humid weather. As I got to work within the city core areas, I became acutely aware of churches that had followed their parishioners to the suburbs. But I also became aware of the East Harlem influence on the Toronto Christian Resource Centre. These ministries returned to the inner-city before and even as professionals moved back, seeking the convenience of proximity

2. Andrea Reid, when a FNSP student researcher at U.B.C., personal correspondence, April 2013.

3. See Merton, *Contemplation in a World of Action:* "The real function of discipline is not to provide us with maps, but to sharpen our own sense of direction, so that when we really get going we can travel without maps", 126–7.

4. Martha Fineman and Martha Nussbaum are important contemporary contributors on the central realities of, respectively, vulnerability, and fragility. We would do well to attend to such.

to work or studies and perhaps recently to exercise a semblance of climate responsibility. Alas, such migration has brought with it mixed blessings: dilapidated or even abandoned housing units were retrieved and restored, at high prices, while the resident welfare and working poor scrambled for any kind of remaining rental stock. Living where I work has been a central motif of my privilege to work in urban ministry and hence engage in a lot of hopefully consistent ways and means of being available—easier said than done, despite the witness of others. Sensing an ending that is sooner rather than later—ending as both *finis* and as *telos*, as one's mortality and yet as a purposeful completion—I felt nudged to reflect on the years and places, and now the decades. I have always longed for my predecessors to actually reflect and pass on their memoirs as encouraging legacies, though few have been able. *The Word on the Street: An Invitation to Community Ministry in Canada* marked a welcome exception, as eighteen of us gathered for a solid week in mid-country Winnipeg for disciplinary sharing, recording and writing, followed by a year of further culling and editing. Other examples are duly noted in later chapters.

My modest efforts to date consist of:

a. wrestling with "radicalism as a way of life" via a Chicago Theological Seminary B.D. (now, MDiv.) thesis;

b. *The Word on the Street* (1990) anthology by practicing community or urban ministers who represented a dozen Canadian cities at the time. These professionals, several of us full-time at part-time pay, engaged for a week and earnestly shared via their nudging, creative writing coach (the late Don Bailey) with plenty of follow-up editing;

c. a Master of Theology thesis which endeavored to analyze several case studies by engaging grounded theory in a perspective that took realistic notice (to employ four "A's") of what urban ministries *animate* out of the given *availability* of people and concerns—as well as what these ministries press for *alternatives* while almost always confessing to states of *anguish*, given the fierce limits of the human condition and our projections onto city living and struggles; and,

d. once laboring towards a PhD thesis on a conjunctive triad of the biblical and classical virtues of *justice, hope,* and *prayer,* a project which examined what these terms mean for an urban ministry that is faithfully public and prophetic for the long haul.

I remain focused on the last of these four research endeavors, continuing to be grateful for those people and ministries in my life, reading, and practice, past and present. I desire to pass on bits and pieces of hindsight—inspired by one of the President John Kennedy's confessions that experience is that which we learn from our mistakes. I seek to summarize the gist of urban ministry in the combined term and spirit of a hopeful realism. My work is indebted to three time-tested theologians: systematic, historical, and autobiographical theologian, Jürgen Moltmann; pastoral and social ethicist theologian, Reinhold Niebuhr; and poet, priest and spiritual monastic, Thomas Merton.

Moltmann's, Niebuhr's and Merton's legacies offer rich themes for urban ministries and ministers themselves. Their messages arise from each of the virtue disciplines that they engage (respectively hope, justice, and prayer). These virtue disciplines arise from their work and reveal some of their opposite conditions: disillusionment and despair; the indignities and inequalities of powerlessness; and the temptation of a compartmentalized self-righteousness to counter a passive timidity, an inevitable weariness if not a helpless burn-out. With lots of grace-grounded help—including the inspiration and courage of Moltmann, Niebuhr and Merton, wisdom of my elders,[5] and encouragement of many friends—I have concluded that it is a hopeful realism rooted in prayerful justice that provokes, nourishes, critiques, and constructively sustains urban ministries' missions to bear a faithful, public, and prophetic witness.

A note on the persistent use of the virtue and discipline terms of prayer, justice, and hope is in order. That they are virtues is attested in the theological and ethical literature, and from the classics to the three theologians described, especially in Chapters 4, 5 and 6. That they are disciplines, more than convenient affirmations of abstract themes, is attested in the vast literature on urban ministry; their examples and practices are noted especially in Chapters 2 and 3—as well as the Longhouse Ministry case study and related networks elaborated in Chapter 7 (and both appendices). That the terms form an interactive, conjunctive triad is attested by the light that they shed together on what makes for an integrated and vital balance over the long-haul in urban ministry endeavors. The order of the three terms in the text is varied according to the requirements for emphasis in the context. Grammatically speaking, the terms could be ordered, and sometimes are, in

---

5. With my book reviews of personal elders, such as University of Winnipeg professor emeritus John Baderstcher's *Fragments of Freedom* and V.S.T. professor emeritus Terence Anderson's *Walking the Way,* there is a profile for *Touchstone,* for the October 2016 issue, on the late Bob Lindsey, a prophet, pastor, administrator, and irrepressible circuit-rider par excellence for otherwise scattered and perhaps lonely urban and community ministers. *Touchstone* is a University of Winnipeg quarterly journal emphasizing heritage and ministry, chiefly United Church of Canada but also ecumenical.

a manner where a preposition such as "for" separates them, as in "hoping (for) justice prayerfully". In the absence of a preposition, I appeal to the reader for understanding for the sake of strengthening the triad. A further word on the use of "hope" is important. Hope is employed as a term of virtue and discipline, as above; it is also employed in creative tension with the realities of life in the cities, sometimes harsh and often involving limited or forced options, and thus with the realism that urban ministries encounter and have to engage. This is discussed especially in Chapters 1 and 8. Put otherwise, as part of the conjunctive triad, hope is part of the content of that which provides the interpretative framework of the book, while hope is further that which interacts with and qualifies the harsh realities of urban life and ministries and dares to address and even contribute to changing such realities.

Future considerations arise from the texts that are worth flagging. There is first the enduring concern—more than a mere single issue—regarding the pervasive influence of socio-economic class interests. Such interests shape, finance, and limit the scope and depth of urban ministries. To a modest degree the concern of class interest is referenced in the chapter on Niebuhr's theology for justice (Chapter 5) and what influenced him during his early urban pastorate and numerous fellowships, the earliest intentionally focused on wedding the Christian Faith to socialism. There are precedents and cautions from the social gospel era and the critical emergence of Christian realism, duly noted later. Among many works there is Richard Sennett's *The Hidden Injuries of Class* (with Jonathan Cobb). There is the trilogy he has been writing, including *The Craftsman*; *Together: The Rituals, Pleasures and Politics of Cooperation*, and a future work on the making of the city. One could further look to works of the American Academy of Religion's recent *Class, Religion and Theology* group, but more concretely to the contributions of the new monasticism and the broad-based organizations linked to the Industrial Areas Foundation. To the extent that these bold endeavors practice ways and means to move beyond mere charity responses to urban poverty—to actually discern and employ the principles and practices of justice making and keeping—then there is a measure of hope that charity need not remain a substitute for justice (and, alas, a pretext for withholding it).

A second future consideration is the question of what makes for a "successful" ministry in the city (which I hope to contribute via a M Phil thesis undertaking). Indeed, how may an urban ministry extend to the whole of the city, its ecology, and not merely its urban core or once "inner-city" scope of understanding? Success is fraught with ambiguity. Do we seek to measure success by numbers of people, size of the budget, length of time it exists and endures, and the publicity it enjoys though often ephemeral? Or, do we more modestly employ criteria such as a ministry's faithfulness for the long haul, faithfulness to such biblically core credos as Micah 6:8's doing justice, loving kindness or integrity, and walking humbly with the Creator, Sustainer and Redeemer of all?[6] Tucked within these considerations is the creative tension noted throughout the book yet still remaining open-ended. The tension of charity versus justice is basic and is often a vexing challenge to urban ministry practitioners. There are currently several fresh attempts to illumine this tension[7]—adding philanthropy and variations such as "philanthrolocalism" to the vocabulary[8]—but it is my conviction that no one prophetically addresses this challenge as well as Niebuhr and his legacy.

Thirdly, there is the friendly challenge of "letting go" of the desire if not compulsion to control people's lives. These considerations arise from recent and poignant reflections on a "theology of the cross" as well as avid interests in the practices of meditation, contemplation, and centering prayer (or Christian meditation). There is also a hunger for spiritual direction and even healing. This is touched on in the discussion of the Merton's grounding prayer (Chapter 6) and is a component of the *hoping justice prayerfully* triad. What would be hopeful is the willingness to summon the likes of Douglas John Hall and his seminal, successor sources of influence (thinking of Pamela McCarroll's works, especially *Waiting at the Foot of the Cross* as well as *The End of Hope—the Beginning*). How this really relates to the practices of ministry and the necessity for a comprehensive, compelling, and social ethic is a challenge to engage. "Pacefulness" is surely key throughout the book and its conclusion, including the grace-based serenity prayer. Letting go is one thing. The question of to whom and for what to let go is a life-long challenging other! A generation ago, theologians engaged a socio-theology of letting go. Now a fourth consideration, outside of the scope of this book, is the compelling imperative related to the crisis of global warning and its challenges to our very existence.[9]

---

6. In Trothen's *Winning the Race?* from social ethical reflections on what makes for success, she evokes the three criteria of faithfulness, solidarity with the marginalized, and a capacity to love, 120.

7. See Lupton's companion volumes *Toxic Charity* and *Detox Charity*. See also Scott Bessenecker, *OverTurning Tables: Freeing Missions from the Christian-Industrial Complex*, IVPress, 2014.

8. See Beer, *The Philanthropic Revolution*, 85–112. But see challenges such as Finn and its instructive subtitle "Shortcomings of Philanthropy: Bigger Crumbs from the Tables of the Elite Are Not Enough".

9. See Sr. Neal, *A Socio-Theology of Letting Go* and Ruether, "A US Theology of Letting Go". Currently Canadian sources include David Suzuki and the independently funded foundation, the Canadian Centre for Policy Alternatives' work, Klein's *This Changes Everything: Capitalism versus the Climate* body of work. American sources include Martha

I acknowledge and give thanks for some editorial assistance from Karen Hollenbeck and toward the end for the gifts of their indispensable and editing labors of friendship, add Michele Lamont, Ryan Leamont-Koldewijn and Mike Glanville—also, Lori Gabrielson for timely help on indexing. For valuable input on drafts for another body of work that I have drawn on for parts of this book, there are Deb Cameron Fawkes, Michael Welton, David Tracy, and Bruce Alexander. I am indebted to Vancouver School of Theology professor emeritus of social ethics, Terry Anderson and to the Thomas Merton Society for their long, passionate interests respectfully in Reinhold Niebuhr and Merton. I am grateful for the earnest dedication of the indispensable urban networks depicted and drawn upon—particularly the Diewerts and their extended family/friends for Streams of Justice and Terry Patten and Bruce Alexander for A Community Aware (including Ken Lyotier, Kate Andrews, Gurvinder Parmar, Ross Banister, Doug Hetherington, and others mentioned in Appendix B). To the Metro Vancouver Alliance I am grateful for the earliest interested and dedicated persons who tirelessly toiled when it all seemed gloom and doom. I am thinking especially of the late (Franciscan) Sister Elizabeth Kelliher as well as David Dranchuk, Bob Doll, Sheila Paterson, Lane Walker, Bill Saunders, Margaret Marquardt, Fr. Clarence Li, Fr. Ken Forster, Doug Peterson, and numerous lay people whose convictions for broad-based community organizing for justice remain crucial. Finally, I want to thank long-time on-site Longhouse Ministry volunteer Daniel Wieb. He is a genuine new monastic and freed me more than he realized for my bouts and bursts of work for this book. Of course without the Longhouse Ministry itself, he and I could not have a supportive base for life-in-ministry together with original and sustaining elders, such as Jim White, Ruby Cranmer, Betty Traverse, Effie Njootli and the late Vince Shea (and his thoughtful widow, Janet). Though not all, I want to thank veteran Grandview Calvary Baptist pastor Tim Dickau, a Vancouver virtual animator for the new monasticism cause (and the author of the foreword to this book) and the late Douglas Graves, whose Holy Week 2016 death leaves us with thermal current memories and a bequeathed legacy.

Fineman's compelling reflections as part of Emory University's "Vulnerability and the Human Condition Initiative". There is Canadian David Tracey's *Earth Manifesto: Saving Nature with Engaged Ecology*. Finally, there are Michael Northcott's UK writings, all the more valuable for his background in urban theology studies. *Inter alia*, see his *A Political Theology of Climate Change* an edited *Systematic Theology and Climate Change: Ecumenical Perspectives,* and recently, *Place, Ecology and the Sacred: The Moral Geography of Sustainable Communities.*

Chapter 1—Proposal of Hopeful Realism

> Now I'm not one to lose hope. I keep on hoping. I still have faith in the future. But I've had to analyze many things over the last few years and, I would say, over the last few months. I've gone through a lot of soul searching and agonizing moments, and I've come to see that we have many more difficult days ahead. And some of the old optimism was a little superficial, and now it must be tempered with a solid realism. And I think the realistic fact is that we still have a long, long way to go.[1]
> —Martin Luther King Jr.

THERE ARE PERVASIVE PRESSURES, fierce forces, and competing interests confronting urban ministries today. Hitting brick walls and encountering forced options come to mind.[2] How often a ministry runs into a virtual dead-end and faces the dire possibilities of having to end the whole mission or admit that the actual options of a ministry are a lot more constrained than those touted during a year end fund-raising campaign. There is also the issue of weariness and for some of us, an eventual burnout. As one veteran urban ministry commentator has frankly noted, there come times when there are obvious signs of "success" although outcomes are less than predictable, shortcut temptations are rife, and the possibilities of falling into weariness and cynicism are close at hand. Barbara Brown Taylor expressed it well:

> Those of us in urban ministry read and hear a lot about professional burnout, that creeping deadness of the soul that narrows our vision and extinguishes our energy until it is all that we can do to get out of bed in the morning. We are sitting ducks for it

---

1. NBC News interview with Sander Vanocur 1967.
2. "Forced Options" is a term I first encountered in Christian realist, Roger Shinn's writings. See *Forced Options: Social Decisions for the 21st Century*, 1982, 3, where he states: "A forced option, says James, is a decision that allows no escape. Any efforts to delay for long, to sit it out, to compromise indefinitely are themselves decisions—as surely as is the deliberate choice of one of the alternatives." Shinn cites from William James' "The Will to Believe," 34.

[. . .] for at least four reasons: 1) our jobs are never done; 2) our results are hard to measure; 3) our expectations are high—not to mention the expectations others have of us; and 4) most of us do not get to choose whom or even how we will serve.[3]

In what follows there are reflections on realism, then hope, and finally a commentary on the combination of hope and realism and its illumining value for a steadfast urban ministry in the service of a faithful public and prophetic ministry. These reflections provide an interpretive framework for this book.

On Realism: Finitude, Ignorance and Sin

Human beings are finite, ignorant, and sinful, and hence we are certainly vulnerable; these characteristics provide the parameters and contours for the meaning of realism. Being finite, we are limited—limited by space, time, activities, influence, and the incapacity to control outcomes. Being ignorant, we do not know enough on any one subject to present all of the material on that subject. Being sinful, we think and act with our flaws, failures, and competing self-interests, rooted as these are in our egocentricity. Pretension is another way to name the propensity of human sinfulness. Pervading these realities, there is also the plain vulnerability of the human condition and the vulnerable institutions we create and that in turn, shape us.[4] The first two of the above, which depict realism, are readily accepted by urban ministry practitioners, but further elaboration on sin is necessary.

Sin can be generally understood as the human inclination to be more concerned about the self than about others and the health or fate of the earth and its support systems. More particularly, theologians have depicted sin as rooted in a primal act of mistrust and ensuring disobedience of the Creator/Redeemer. Niebuhr among others has depicted sin fundamentally as undue pride or arrogance and has related it to a pretentious if not willful disregard of human finiteness, of pretending to be more than what we really are. He relates the latter to the former: we are mortal, that is our fate; we pretend not to be mortal, that is our sin.[5] When we act as if we are less than

---

3. Taylor, "Looking for God in the City" with its intentional subtitle: "A Meditation," 8.

4. Ibid, 8. See also Fineman, "The Vulnerable Subject and The Responsive State" and "The Vulnerable Subject" with its instructive subtitle: "Anchoring Equality in the Human Condition."

5. Niebuhr, *Beyond Tragedy*, 28–29.

our human nature, sin may be manifested and depicted as sensuousness, apathy, or perhaps, *acedia*.[6]

In terms of urban ministry principles and practices, sin might be evidenced in the ministry's charitable acts and services. That is, if/as charity is used as a guise behind which to hide or deny a ministry's or church's relations to power in society, then the sin of withholding justice by the substitute action or service of charity is operative. This will be found in the writings of Augustine and Niebuhr.[7] When society and the planet's massive imbalances and resulting inequalities are rationalized as if they are givens and must remain so, then sin is operative. Some urban ministry practitioners have named this phenomenon as "toxic" charity.[8] When urban ministers deny their limits or pretend in some incidents that such limits can be defied, then we court an eventual bone-weariness and unnecessary burnout.[9]

All of the above could well lead to the sad conclusion that there is little point to embracing and engaging the practices of hope since the realistic limits and sins of one's ministry are confined to the status quo with little room for serious changes. To risk change is to risk a loss of support from and marginalization by one's peers, volunteers, board members and most threatening of all, one's funders. Year end and Christmas time funding appeals draw upon the seasonal sensitivities of their supporters and attempt to attract new supporters. The year end is also a last chance for charitable giving to be eligible for current year tax receipts. The Christmas season is timely because it ties the supporter to an appeal to practice some level of incarnation. As Merton aptly expressed it: "the time of the end is no room in the inn."[10] In any case, charitable giving might well mask the avoidance of any challenge to those in power to initiate and practice a deeper and wider change that could reduce if not eliminate the very need for Christmas season charity as substitutes for justice withheld. It is, of course, not only organized religion that engages in this practice. Mass media such as my city's *Vancouver Sun* newspaper also reminds its readers of serious need and of its own Adopt-a-School program appeals for funding to make up

---

6. Niebuhr, *Nature and Destiny of Man*, Vol. I, 228–40; also, Cox, *On Not Leaving It to the Snake*, xi–xix. See Don Grayston's recent work, fully elaborating Merton's experiences of the range of acedia, especially as restlessness, in "Thomas Merton and the Noonday Demon: The Camaldoli Correspondence," Eugene, OR: Cascade, 2015.

7. See Augustine for this basic distinction and caveat. www.brainyquote.com/quotes/quotes/s/saintaugus148531.html.

8. See Lupton *Toxic Charity*, 1–30 and passim.

9. See, Taylor, op. cit.

10. Merton, "Time of the End is No Room in the Inn," 65–78.

for government cutbacks to poor students needing food and transportation tickets to attend school.[11]

On Hope: Pressing the Limits

The practices of hope suggest a wide and deep range of inter-disciplinary activity or even a sensible relaxation of activity for the sake of pacefulness and restored harmony. The linking of meditation, contemplation, and/or prayer to the spheres of being active in ministry has come of age though it has been present in and among the monastic traditions for centuries. Not alone, the new monasticism has retrieved and compellingly given fresh expressions.

A basic phenomenological rendering of what hoping engages in is the following. When one hopes, one shows up, and gives of one's time, energy, money, and surely patience. As one stays involved in a cause or a ministry, near or distant, there is evidence of perseverance, a bearing under the strains and burdens of what it means to remain dedicated and committed to a cause or ministry.[12] Such perseverance or endurance attracts, in turn, the presence of helpers or helpmates. Hope on its own, students aptly discern, is not an absolute but is relative to what is being hoped for, with whom, and the kind and range of help that hoping needs and thus invites.[13] The activity of hope discloses an element of adventure, what one spiritual writer names as the "hop" in hope.[14] The nature and content of hope illustrates the presence of disciplines through which there is provided the framework for being steadfast for the long haul. The very act of summoning mentors or leaning into inspirational figures or ministries themselves mirrors the presence of desire, and desire recently has been given its due exegesis in the service of accounting for that which spurs or sparks one or a ministry to arise to respond to a crisis situation both in the moment and for the long haul.[15]

Apart from the frank realities of despair, hope could be a mere abstract consideration. When confessed to be part of the conditions that give rise to and break through serious and sustained despair, there is a far-reaching understanding of the meaning of hope that seems possible. Indeed the combination of hope with despair is indispensable in and for Jürgen Moltmann's

---

11. See Bellett, "High School Reeling from Severe Budget Cuts: . . . Leaving Needy Students Hungry," A10.

12. See Bonhoeffer, "The Secret of Suffering March 1938," 291.

13. See Lynch, *Images of Hope*, 23–25, passim.

14. See Norris, *Acedia and Me*, 217–22.

15. Respectively, see Farley, *The Wounding and Healing of Desire*, xviii, 2; and Caputo, *The Weakness of God*, 36. Their contributions are duly noted also in chapter 3.

theology of hope, from his early work, *Theology of Hope*, to his recent, steadfast reflections: *In the End—the Beginning: the Life of Hope* and *Ethics of Hope*. Hope is also engaged in Pamela McCarroll's 2014 writings, *Waiting at the Foot of the Cross* and *The End of Hope—The Beginning*. Addressing the despair in a lack of a basis for hope also evokes or invites the helpmates of prayer and justice. Chapters 2 and 8 focus on this utterly basic triad of terms. As virtues, hope, prayer, and justice are more than mere "terms" or concepts or ideas. They are discipline virtues which have stood the tests of time and, when in a conjunctive relationship, intimate a power greater than when only on their own.[16]

Hope and Realism Combined: Leaven of a Just Realm beyond Our Eager but Meager Strivings

To approach combining hope with realism is to ask of each virtue discipline what it contributes and challenges—each on its own and with a consistent mutual inter-penetration. What does hope critically and constructively offer to realism? What is hopeful about realism is that hope protests the givens in any status quo situation, lest they be rendered a resigned fate. Hope strains and stretches to seek meaning by way of a firm grounding in even despair, since "despair is suffering without meaning."[17] Hope is what qualifies tragedy and realism and is what challenges temptation to mere wishful thinking, with little foundation in reality.[18] By pressing the premature limits—an assumed once-and-for-all fate—of a poverty situation or a system of assumed inequalities, the practices of hope open up fresh and further options, and more inclusive possibilities. It is what theologians and ministers affirm to be the prophetic and not only the pastoral function of ministry. A genuine restlessness is felt and honored—what Moltmann further depicts as an "unquenchable hope" due to ministers remaining unreconciled with what is.[19] There is the promise and lure of professing the biblical God with whom all will be all, and which cannot rest until all is fulfilled and until peace with justice with dignity for all is included.[20] There is also the critical penchant of realism to press the profession of hope for its actual basis, that its practice be more or other than that of mere wishful thinking. If it

16. See Anderson, *Walking the Way*, 135, 246–47; Wilson, *Gospel Virtues*, 41, 97, 196 notes 5 and 6; Kuile, *The Virtues of a Christian Realist*, passim.
17. Frankl, "Finding Meaning in Difficult Times: Interview with Victor Frankl."
18. See Frankl, "The Case for a Tragic Optimism," 161-79.
19. See Moltmann, *Theology of Hope*, 21–22.
20. See I Cor. 15:26–28 and Hammarskjöld, *Markings*, 35.

is wishful thinking or ungrounded aspirations that reign, then the "dashed hopes" of disillusionment are inevitable.

What becomes realistic about hope, thus, is that with the check and balance of realism there would be an analysis of the phenomenon of hope that disciplines one to look for the grounds of hope and the contributing field force conditions for its realization or at least its further approximation. Among still other ingredients, there are the agents and/or agencies by means of which the goals of hope are earnestly and patiently pursued.[21] Indeed as one commentator and student of hope professes:

> . . . all hopes—whether ultimate or penultimate, whether regarding eschatological futures or tomorrow's weather—are characterized by (a) formal structure of a hoper, who intends something in the future, as that which is hoped for, on the basis of a particular ground of hope. If any element is missing, we are without hope.[22]

Theological and Christian writers on hope—and biblical and possibly spiritual writers in general—are wont to ground the basis of their hope and the possibilities of its fulfillment in God. Moltmann, we will see, attests to this especially—as do a host of other thoughtful writers. However, there is not space to elaborate on a full discussion of combing and applying hope and realism. Suffice it to note that Reinhold Niebuhr was not alone in affirming the centrality of realism. In addition to John Bennett there were also the existential and phenomenological influences of European theology and philosophy. Representatively, Paul Tillich wrote of *belief-ful realism*, wherein an intuited, philosophical and biblical sense of hope was twinned with taking seriously and fully the given situations under scrutiny and engagement—" . . . that is an unconditioned acceptance of our concrete situation in time and of the situation of time in general in the presence of eternity."[23] The translator of this volume, Reinhold's younger brother H. Richard Niebuhr, adds in the book's preface:

> By the connection of belief-ful and realism the most fundamental of all dualisms is called into question and if it is justly called into question it is also overcome. Faith is an attitude which transcends every conceivable and experienceable reality; realism is

---

21. See Anderson, *Walking the Way*, 130–32.

22. J. K. Smith, "Determined Hope: A Phenomenology of Christian Expectation," 210, see also 225–27. Cf. McCarroll, *The End of Hope–The Beginning*, 24–33, for similar and necessary foundations, objects or aims, and agencies for hope, including "waiting and receptivity," for hope to be no mere wishful thinking or shadow boxing.

23. Tillich, *The Religious Situation*, 116.

an attitude which rejects every transcending of reality, every transcendency, and all transcendentalizing [. . .] Evasion is possible in one of two directions, either [. . .] a beliefless realism or in the direction of idealism.[24]

Hopeful Realism for Urban Ministry: Animating Contrast Awareness

There are helpful reflections on the meaning of hope and realism combined. Douglas Ottati writes a whole book by the title of *Hopeful Realism*. Therein he asserts

> (T)his practical stance and attitude [. . .] refuses both easy optimisms and cynical pessimisms [. . .] that we do not really know ourselves when we concentrate on our abilities apart from our limits and our faults [. . .] that we do not truly know ourselves when we consider our limits and our faults apart from our abilities, and apart from the traces of true communion in community that we encounter in God's world.[25]

For our purposes hope and realism are summoned to support the pervasive need of urban ministries to take note of what is happening in their ministries in the city, with all of the rough and tough conditions of survival, coping, facing the same old oppressive and lonely situations upon release from prison, hospital, or any of a number of post-recovery challenges following a short or long-term stay in treatment facilities. Hope and realism are combined to gain the fuller force of synergism, the uncovering and release of perhaps neglected and even repressed energies for change. Hence Ottati prefaces the above perspective of hopeful realism with this theological summary:

> . . . (I)nterlocking symbols, such as God's sovereign reign or dominion, creation, sin, providence, and redemption, yield a particular picture of life-before-God-and-God-before-life. They support an outlook that encourages us to participate in God's world; to recognize that we are fitted for true communion with God in community with others; to acknowledge our

---

24. H.R. Niebuhr, 14.

25. Ottati, *Hopeful Realism*, 3. There are others of course, who engage realism and hope in their own disciplined ways. See Fineman's rich descriptions of the realities of vulnerability and further, resilience as a major mark of hope in human nature and our finite and flawed institutions, "The Vulnerable Subject and The Responsive State."

significant but limited and dependent powers and capabilities; to expect diminishment, estrangement, conflict, fragmentation, and death; but nevertheless to look for enlargement, reconciliation, and life.[26]

It is not only at the level of analysis or a detached reflection that a hopeful realism can be professed. Prayer offers the complementary if not deeper and wider resources of confession. That is, confessing the limits of one's own and one's ministerial situation along with and grounded in the catalyst of recognizing and willingly honoring a contrast-awareness arousal—an awareness that takes negative experiences, especially of indignities and inequalities, seriously and persistently as to be resolved, with a socially just outcome. I know not of a more articulate statement describing this core concept than that of the late Catholic theologian and biblical scholar, Edward Schillebeeckx. Worthy of elaboration, he professes:

> The contrast experiences of the two World Wars, the concentration camps, political torture, the color-bar, the developing countries, the hungry, the homeless, the underprivileged and the poor in countries where there is so much potential wealth, and so on—all these experiences make people suddenly say: 'This should not and must not go on' [. . .] When we allow (the) Christian factor to play in human experience, particularly in contrast experiences whence the new moral imperatives spring forth, it becomes clear that the protest prompted by negative experiences ('this cannot go on') is also the expression of the firm hope that things *can* be done differently *must* improve and *will* get better through our commitment. The prophetic voice that rises from the contrast-experience is therefore protest, hope-inspiring promise and historical initiative [. . .] what makes the protest and the historical decision possible is the actual presence of this hope, for, without it, the negative experience would not prompt the contrast-experience and the protest [. . .] it is only when people become *aware* of the fact that a better existence than the 'established' one is possible and indeed seen as realizable that protest appears and the need for historical decisions is sensed. Because of the continuity in man's consciousness, where preflexive experience and reflective analysis meet in a complex unity, we can roughly distinguish two phases in these contrast experiences: first, that of the negative experience itself [. . .] where the moral demand for changes and improvements develops [. . .] secondly, the phase where the message of the Gospel

---

26. Ibid.

matures through a combination of theology and the scientific analysis of a particular situation into a responsible and more concrete plan of social and political action.[27]

There is also the well-known and frequently cited confessional and professing prayer rooted in Reinhold Niebuhr's theology and practice of ministry. It is really a praxis evolving from years of urban ministry, teaching of social ethics, circuit riding in the university and social justice networks, and organizing of social action journals to give voice to actual fellowships for expressing the need for and resources of change (see Chapter 5). Of all the Niebuhr prayers, it is the original grace-based serenity prayer that invites a full study. It integrates the combination of realism and hope and evokes the need to nurture and practice a faithful public-prophetic witness by way of opting for justice prayerfully. Thus: "O God, grant us the grace to accept with serenity the things we cannot change; the courage to change the things we ought to; and the wisdom to distinguish the one from the other."[28]

Anticipating later elaborations, there are three key distinctions of this original version of the prayer to note. It is in the first person plural, not merely "me"; it names the courage to change to be normative, not content to change merely what can be; and finally, it invites and includes a fourth theme of "grace." Compared to the popular version the prayer, this version is more inclusive, normative, and rooted in a specific acknowledgement of the presence of God's gift of grace. Importantly, it means that this prayer embodies that creative balance of realism and hope, and the latter's affinity with and need for the helpmate of justice. Not surprisingly, the author of the prayer, Niebuhr, is the key theologian this book summons to unpack the depth and range of the meaning of justice and its implications for urban ministry.

---

27. Schillebeeckx, *God the Future of Man*, 158–59, cited in Morris, *The Radicalization Process*, 118–19, n. 55. Cf. Schillebeeckx's later *Christ the Experience of Jesus as Lord*, 713. See also *The Schillebeeckx Reader*, especially 18, 45, 54–59. Therein, Schreiter comments: "This (contrast experience) moment reveals the difference between what is and what ought to be or will be. The *power of this moment* [. . .] is in its negation of that difference; that is, moving away from what ought not to be (suffering in the present) toward what ought to be (a full sense of humanity, or humanum, in the future)," 45. See also Appendix B and Hessel, *Time for Outrage Indignez-vous!* especially 26–29, combining hope and resistance in fighting fascism in WW II and since. (italics added).

28 Sifton, *The Serenity Prayer*, 7–14.

Framing Urban Ministry via a Triad: Grounded, Hopeful Realism

The purpose of naming realism and hope is for their interpretive—heuristic—value. Urban ministries could tidily be summarized in terms of a singular, dominant purpose and mission; that is, the biblical term of "shalom" or the oft-cited prophetic triad of Micah 6:8 that a ministry is called to do justice, love kindness, and walk humbly or modestly with thy God.[29] My own United Church of Canada denomination, by way of its B.C. Conference, cites three chief mission purposes, the third of which illustrates a major perspective. Thus a faithful public witness refers to loving one's neighbor along with God and the self—in addition to rendering effective leadership and maintaining healthy congregations and ministries.[30] When "public" is aptly combined with "prophetic" to read a "faithful, public, and prophetic ministry", then an urban ministry is commissioned with a wide and deep mandate pithily representative of Micah's triad.

However, a hopeful realism speaks to the need to combine analysis with mission, to leaven the analysis of the forces and pressures of city life with the patterns and processes of doing justice and praying for it, and to balance this with hope. The heuristic value of the term "hopeful realism" is in providing guidelines as to what to look for in a ministry in the city. It dovetails with what response ethics employs in its general disposition to exercising responsible ministry—disposition along with responsibility, being the way that John Bennett applies the concept of realism to societal ministry and social ethics.[31] Hence, a ministry asks what is going on in this situation; then, what are the responses already being made by other ministries or agencies; and finally, what is discerned to be a pertinent or fitting response.[32] The importance of realism in the first question is to help assure that the ministry situation is honestly and adequately assessed and continually so. Because self-interests and power are at play in virtually any ministry situation and that of its actors or board members, analysis needs to be shrewd and subject to a checks and balances to minimize the undue or unfair influence of interest. The importance of realism in response to the second question (fitting responses of urban ministries to their situations) twins with and builds on discerning the presence of hope in ministry situations and the "process (and processes) by which to facilitate hope." Pamela

---

29. Among many, see Brueggemann et al., *To Act Justly, Love Tenderly, Walk Humbly*.
30. See further http://www.bc.united-church.ca/content/mission-and-vision.
31. Bucher, "Christian Political Realism after Niebuhr," 53.
32. See Ogletree, *Hospitality to the Stranger*, 97–126.

McCarroll aptly asserts these two guides based on her descriptive definition of hope. To wit, "Hope is the experience of the opening of horizons of meaning and participation in relationship to time, other human and nonhuman being, and/or the transcendent."[33]

Hope counterbalances the tendency and temptation to cynicism as realism checks and counters the temptation and tendency to naïve optimism in urban ministries. Christian or theological realists have long held such tendencies in balance and sought to be aware of the temptations to veer off to one side or the other.[34]

Christian realism, in modern and postmodern theology, is chiefly located and reflected in Reinhold Niebuhr's early and mature thought. How he came to the disposition or perspective of realism is elaborated later for it is instructive for urban ministry. Among others (and especially in The Niebuhr Society), John Bennett, Larry Rasmussen, Robin Lovin, and Gary Dorrien represent early and continuing lines of thought. Dorrien has written extensively of realism, especially in his several works on historical roots and trends in liberal progressive theology in the late 19th and 20th centuries—albeit, he is sometimes tempted to be dismissive of Christian realism as being anything much more than Niebuhr's life and thought.[35] The origins of these realists basically arise from disillusionment with the social gospel, painful encounters with the 1930s and 1940s when depression and world wars chastened church views of what had been thought to be optimistically possible and now, plainly, was not. Realism also arose out of disillusionment with grand schemes of viewing society and international progress, specifically with communism and its once-sweeping hopes of transforming society by combining economics with politics. Nevertheless, the enduring tenets of theological realism are attested to be: ". . . history has its tragic dimensions and human beings their finitude and sin, individuals have a capacity for fair-mindedness and selflessness which nations do not, and political and social power offer temptation and responsibility."[36]

---

33. McCarroll, *The End of Hope—The Beginning*, 48–50.

34. Among others, see Lovin, *Christian Realism and the New Realities*, 81–83; Fackre, *The Promise of Reinhold Niebuhr*, 59–68; and of course, Niebuhr, *Christian Realism and Political Problems*, 119–46.

35. See Dorrien, "Society as the Subject of Redemption" in *Economy, Difference, Empire*, 5; though Dorrien's many summaries and reflections on Niebuhr, his peers, and their era convey the influence of Niebuhr to be vast and certainly more than individualistic, as Chapter 3 of this same volume attests, "The Niebuhrian Legacy," 46–65.

36. Bucher on Bennett, op. cit, 53.

Discerning Key Elements in Urban Ministries

One could employ[37] sophisticated qualitative research methods such as that of grounded theory or thematic analysis to discern what it is going on when comparing ministry cases or networks. Suffice it here to ask what leads to the very origins and formation of a dedicated ministry. It is surely out of a response to urgently felt needs or out of a long held concern that something be done—likely by us or no one at all—that a move is made. Whether quickly or by way of much conversation and deliberation, a need is identified arising out a realization that the way and level we live and work is in sharp contrast to what before us beckons. This situation is what we have referred to above as contrast awareness. It is what aroused and inspired the earliest formation of the Toronto Christian Resource Centre (CRC), The Open Door in Victoria (now a part of Our Place Society), and Vancouver's Streams of Justice network (SoJ). It has formed the precedents out of which these ministries arose—the East Harlem Protestant Parish for the CRC and Grandview Calvary Baptist Church for SoJ. It is what has inspired and sustained the Metro Vancouver Alliance (MVA)—and any Industrial Areas Foundation local community organizing venture—and the more interim Coalition for Migrant Worker Justice (C4MWJ). Similarly, it accounts for the rise and maintenance of the network of A Community Aware (ACA). To be sure, more examples abound.

New or revised ministries could not likely develop without the arousal impetus of contrast-situations. It is the awareness of such contrasts that fuels the passion to engage in the ministry of change. It is the same contrast awareness that animates transition from a mere interest, however initially important, to a more detailed awareness of the causal conditions for the inequality and indignities of the situation. And then, to move from awareness to an involvement, with sensitivity to organizing the means and resources to pursue with resolve a meaningful response with what is needed. If it is passion that animates the contrast awareness condition, then it is also a controlled anger and plain hard work as well as a sustained dedication that are needed to harness the ways and means to respond to the inequalities and indignities. As interesting, even exciting, as the origins to a dynamic urban ministry are, there is no substitute for this continuous combination of elements: awareness, sensitivity, resolve and animating ways and means to practice the nourishing and sustaining or revitalizing of a ministry's mission and its processes.

---

37. See Morris, *Engaging Urban Ministry,* Appendix C.

The Toronto CRC was initiated and sponsored in the 1960s out of an affluent area of the city known as Rosedale. One of the key Rosedale United Church lay-persons, Don Cameron recalled: "It bothered me that so little was being done, especially for children and young people—in spite of our general affluence"[38] Cameron was aware that the status quo for the church at that time was to do virtually nothing. But this time, there emerged a different response.

> He talked to some colleagues who shared both his faith and his business or professional interests; they decided to harness the latter to the former. They had heard about New York City's East Harlem Protestant Parish and its major ecumenically endowed engagement and re-embrace of the inner-city. The core committee of Rosedale United "went to New York and saw what the EHPP had been doing for many years and wondered why nothing like it had been started in Canada. 'Our slums are not as big as Harlem—but they're just as bad in their own way,' they said."[39]

Fellow parishioner, Ian Jennings, a construction engineer and chair of the Rosedale United Church board, had had actual mining experiences during the depression years and grasped that difficulties were not always due to one's own "faults."

> The need is so obvious [. . .] Our Rosedale people live in conditions at the extreme opposite to those in the inner-city and we feel under obligation to help'" adding, 'I am interested because it is something out of the usual and I guess I am a non-conformist [. . .] Our job is to help people regain their dignity and open up resources through personal contacts—enabling them to participate more meaningfully in society as a whole.[40]

Further, there are this book's three summoned theologians and their authoritative teachings which attest to the animating presence of contrast awareness. This is evident whether this be Niebuhr on how he came to justice and how and why he stayed there, Moltmann on how he came to hope and how and why he engages that central theme, or Merton on how he came to contemplative prayer and how and why he abided with that core conviction, including that of how and why conflict or contradiction is basic to his prayer life and writings. One could further add to the Niebuhr legacy—and similarly for those in the Merton and Moltmann legacies—recent theologians

---

38. Crysdale, *Churches Where the Action Is*, 23.
39. Ibid., 23–24.
40. Jennings, in Crysdale, *Churches Where the Action Is*, 24.

as Beverley Wildung Harrison, and in turn, her former student and present Emmanuel/T. S.T. theologian, Marilyn Legge. They both attest to how and why the struggles they attend to and their animating passion for justice arises and remains central. Further, one could add the whole body of Industrial Areas Foundation (IAF) and its Vancouver expression, the MVA. Their community organizing experiences and their teaching strategies express *the world the way it is*, in sharp contrast over against and in sharp tension with *the way that the world ought to be*. This leads to contrast-awareness-arousing experiences; it evokes and provokes a desire to do justice (or, if necessary, be converted to the disciplined witness and work of justice). Some of this is covered in chapters 7, 8 and again, in Appendix B.

A *hoping justice prayerfully* conjunctive triad provides significant content for the work of long-haul or steadfast ministry. The effects of despair, injustices and self-righteous or smug indifference could provoke a move to desire hope, justice and prayer.

> Far from leading us away from the pain (desire) leads us through the demon-haunted wilderness that blocks us from the courage to love the world, to feel compassion for its aches, and to delight in its beauty [. . .] We are not reconciled to life as it is given to us: [. . .] Our actual experience and our capacities for understanding or satisfaction remain achingly incommensurate. *Desire resides in this gap.*[41]

The acceptance of and attending to such desire requires patience and persistence—patience to stay the course in ministry for the long haul and persistence in order that a meaningful resilience evolves. The ingredients of prayer, justice, and hope relate to and contain aspects of the other two virtue disciplines. Were this triad not explicit, implicitly each would intimate or intuit the others in any event. As noted later, each of the three theologians chosen to ground and elaborate the triad terms also intimate and illumine the presence of the other two virtues.

It is time, however, to first depict the dynamics of ministry, those circumstances to which urban ministries seek to respond and in which they are immersed. We will also retrieve some key precedents that inform and shape the responses of urban ministry students and practitioners. In doing so, we will note the leaven of hope and the disrupting tendencies of realism, and the reverse, when hope may disrupt the tendencies of realism to be too consistently pessimistic or " . . . to obscure the residual moral and social sense even in the most self-regarding men and nations."[42]. Secondly,

---

41. Farley, *The Wounding and Healing of Desire*, xviii, 2. Italics added.
42. See Niebuhr, *On Man's Nature and His Communities*, 31. An earlier elaboration

the book notes new and critical urban ministry responses of which any contemporary ministry would want to take serious cognizance. Thirdly, we return to the proposition that the working triad of *hoping justice prayerfully* is indispensable for the practice of making a hopeful realism work but needs a thorough grounding so that it stands the burdens and tests of rough and tough ministry in the city for the long haul. Finally, we return to elaborate on this opening chapter's affirmation of incorporating and combining hope, justice and prayer, steadfastly dedicated to the service of a realistic ministry.

---

professes: "A realism becomes morally cynical or nihilistic when it assumes that the universal characteristic in human behavior must be regarded as normative. The biblical account of human behavior, upon which Augustine bases his thought, can escape both illusion and cynicism because it recognizes that the corruption of human freedom may make a behavior pattern universal without making it normative. Good and evil are not determined by some fixed structure of human existence," Niebuhr, *Christian Realism and Political Problems*, 130.

Chapter 2—Urban Ministry and Theology's Enduring Themes

At least two questions help to frame a survey of literature on urban ministry and theology. First, what do major urban ministry and theology writers express about the way the city is, and what do they prescribe to make it what it ought to be? A second query relates to the scope of the literature in urban ministry and theology: where does it fall short of providing workers in the field as well as students or scholars of ministry in the cities with a necessary perspective for a faithful public and prophetic witness for the long haul? A hopeful realism aspires to be a faithful ministry but is grounded in that which contributes to making the ingredients of hope realistically operative.

Survey of the Field and Actors

Of import are those writers who reflect and write out of their context, who write of the city and its poor, the injustices and their contributing causes. They do so biblically, theologically, pastorally, and prophetically. They do so in traditional, historical, and interdisciplinary ways—personal and anthologized writings. Further, they describe and critique the way the city is and what the city ought to be, akin to what response ethics does when it asks, "What is going on?" and then seeks an appropriate response. These writers include, *inter alia*, American social ethicists Beverley Harrison, James Gustafson, and Thomas Ogletree; Canadians like Terence Anderson, John Baderstcher, and Marilyn Legge; and in the United Kingdom, the late Kenneth Leech and the Church of England's Board of Social Responsibility writers for *Crucible*.[1] They identify the gaps in what has been done to date

---

1. Harrison *Making Connections* and *Justice in the Makings*; Gustafson, *Ethics from a Theocentric Perspective*, respectively, Vol. 1, "Theology and Ethics" and Vol. 2, "Ethics and Theology"; Ogletree, *Hospitality to the Stranger*; Anderson, *Walking the Way*; see Legge's contributions to *Justice in the Making* and Badertscher's comments in Morris' *Engaging Urban Ministry*, Appendix C-3. Leech's writings are representatively found in *Prayer and Prophecy*.

CHAPTER 2—URBAN MINISTRY AND THEOLOGY'S ENDURING THEMES

and identify what needs to be done, by ministries and city planners/politicians themselves. These authors identify the limits of what presently can be done, given the pressures of urban politics and the economic pressures of globalization. Urban ministry writers summon fresh—even if retrieved—beginnings while affirming the need to endure faithfully, given the urgency of engaging urban issues.

Liberals and conservatives, progressives and new evangelicals connect through engaging the issues. In the 40th anniversary *Sojourners* issue, Jim Wallis named three battles, all discerned from the test of "how society treats the poor, the vulnerable, and the stranger." He notes faith as more than a private matter. He critiques claims of the then-new "Religious Right" (only sexual issues are worth the fight). Finally, he calls *Sojourners* to "the nature of the society that God wants" and the need to retrieve, affirm, and advocate the common good, since "the next battle for Sojourners is to preach that vision and to practice that ethic, to seek the common good in an age of selfishness."[2] Helpful to urban ministries, *Sojourners'* publications practice a consistent attention to ministries in the city and theological education germane to urban issues.[3]

There are several American, British and Canadian writers who convey the nature of urban ministry possibilities—and thus hope—in the context of city forces and pressures. Harvey Cox's *The Secular City* (1965) depicted an earlier portrait of the dynamics of city living as he surveyed such characteristics as diversity, mobility, rapidity, isolation, compartmentalization, and anonymity. To this we would add at least the pressures of gentrification and for the vulnerable in my city of Vancouver, the realities of "reno-viction" (when one is forced out for renovation purposes by the owner or buyer and then the property is often flipped for another handsome profit). Cox also felt the sheer drama of city living and provided a faithful public witness role for the urban church. Some urban sociologists of the previous decades of the Chicago School have been criticized for conveying fairly dry if not banal descriptions of city life.[4] Cox, however, offered a Biblical theology and adult educational manner of interpreting these times again, dramatically

---

2. Wallis, "From a Shoebox to a Movement: For 40 yrs, Sojourners Has Been Fighting the Good Fight. Where Do We Go from Here?," 18, 20, adding: "which will surely challenge the ideologies and idolatries of both the Right and the Left."

3. See the September–October 2013 *Sojourners* issue with articles with instructive subtitles by Stetzer, "The world as God Intends: New survey Data on Pastors and Social Justice," 30–33, and Boulton, "The City of God and the City of Cain: How Taking It to the Streets Is Changing Theological Education," 34–37 respectively.

4. See Badertscher's letter to B. K. Morris, *Engaging Urban Ministry*, Appendix C-3's collated survey responses. Cf. Sennett, "Introduction" on "The Chicago School," 13–19.

affirming that God was, indeed, involved in secular forces and patterns. The volume's subtitle suggests: "A celebration of its liberties and an invitation to its disciplines." In *The Secular City's* twenty-fifth anniversary edition (1990), Cox emphasized two themes. He selected urbanisation and secularization as being central amid the critical pressures and patterns he observed. While these conditions did not indicate the arrival of the "anti-Christ," they all represented, he contended, a "dangerous liberation. The (urban circumstance) raises the stakes, vastly increasing the range of both human freedom and of human responsibility. It poses risks of a larger order than those it displaces. But the promise exceeds the peril, or at least makes it worth taking the risk."[5] In turn, these forces of secularization and urbanisation contributed to the dethroning influence of the once-established, dominant churches in the city. Cox challenges academia to connect concretely with grass-roots laity in the churches: "I like to think that *The Secular City* helped create the climate that forced church leaders and theologians to come down from their balconies and out of their studies and talk seriously with the ordinary people who constitute 99 percent of the churches of the world."[6]

Over the intervening generation, Cox dug deeper and ventured wider into the nature of human sin to account for apathy—passively resigned to life without challenge, or to a fateful existence—as well as the traditional human frailties masked by pride or arrogance as in *On Not Leaving It to the Snake* (1967). He drew attention to some saints of the time, naming Catholic Worker founder Dorothy Day, German Christian martyr Dietrich Bonhoeffer, Columbian guerrilla priest Camilo Torres, and Martin Luther King, Jr. He affirmed that faithfulness invited risk-taking decisions, bordering even on adventurism, similar to the more recent writings of new monastics like Kathleen Norris.[7] Cox noted that sloth is rooted in "*Acedia* [which] comes from the Greek words not caring (*a*-not; *kedos*-care)."[8] He further noted that traits once considered as virtues, such as obedience, self-abnegation, docility and forbearance, "can be expressions of sin"; whereas, the actions of the above leaders or virtual saints as "protest, scepticism, anger, and even insubordination can also be expressions of the gospel."[9] And again, as in *The Secular City*, Cox professed that the God of Justice is evoked when those bearing a faithful public witness engage with the victimized poor. He added with pertinence that "(God) has taught us that we must be

---

5. Cox, "The Secular City 25 Years Later," 1029.
6. Ibid.
7. Among her other writings, see Norris, *On Acedia and Me*.
8. Cox, *On Not Leaving It to the Snake*, xv.
9. Ibid., xiv.

willing to disappear, to see our buildings, our property, and our institutional safeguards threatened and even destroyed so that an authentic link with the people can be fashioned."[10]

These human realities of finiteness and sin along with the urban realities of sheer size, density, diversity and gentrification—accompanied by indignant inequalities—present persistent challenges to the church. Theologically, this has been expressed in Canadian theologian Douglas John Hall's earlier of two trilogies, namely: *The Reality of the Gospel* and *The Unreality of the Churches* (1975), *Has the Church a Future?* (1980), and *The Future of the Church: Where Are We Headed?* (1989). Hall has become Canada's most prolific, elder theologian, writing a second, more academic trilogy in the 1990s: *Thinking the Faith*, *Professing the Faith*, and *Confessing the Faith*. More recently, Hall has summarized his influential legacies. Even he has become a virtual legacy for contemporary theologians and practitioners (especially in Canada where we long for useable legacies even as we question them).[11] Gibson Winter also gave fresh interpretations for the urban ministry challenges of the 1960s and 1970s. Not as popular a writer as Hall but an academic as Cox, Winter has made two salient contributions; *The New Creation as Metropolis* accompanied his *The Suburban Captivity of the Church*.[12] Both volumes draw attention to the deepening and widespread realities of secularism and technology. The author notes an alienation of religious institutions from key decision-making spheres of influence. Rather than lament, Winter affirms that the "Metropolis, as a complex process of planned interdependence of life, is evolving a new form of the Church—the servanthood of the laity."[13] Tempted to mere "piety," the laity is becoming an indispensable key to the future of the urban church as the traditional roles of the professional clergy of once mainstream or dominant churches tend to retreat from serious urban involvements as they decline. Prophetic proclamation is noted as the appropriate response: "the task of proclamation [. . .] is one of evoking the Church, awakening authentic Christianity to consciousness in the midst of metropolitan struggle."[14] Winter equates the servant Church with the Church as a prophetic fellowship. These

10. Cox, "The Secular City 25 Years Later."

11. See thus, Hall's own reflections on legacy as *Remembered Voices*, and those indebted to him, e.g. McCarroll's *Waiting at the Foot of the Cross*, with a preface by Hall.

12. There are also later Winter volumes such as *Elements for a Social Ethic* and *Liberating Creation: Foundations of Religious Social Ethics*, as elaborated by Dorrien, *Social Ethics in the Making* with its subtitle purpose: *Interpreting an American Tradition*, 549–63; see also Winter and Witmar "The Problem of Power in Community Organizing."

13. Winter, *The New Creation as Metropolis*, 11.

14. Ibid. 10, 11, 85.

commendable insights today serve the contemporary urban church as it faces continual losses of status, actual buildings, and membership. On the other hand, the urban church, summoned in "servanthood" to be prophetic, is discerning possibilities for involvement at the points of hurt in human right violations, poverty, and increasing inequality. It likely has an unprecedented opportunity for dedicated social justice commitments. There has been an intentional summons from Cox and Winter to the people they influenced. This generation is bound to benefit from all of their writings. Cox is by no means retired as a recent work, *The Future of Faith* dedicated to his grandchildren, illustrates.[15]

Jürgen Moltmann also expressed an avid interest in the "Spirit" resources for ministry in his association with Pentecostal studies. This raises the question of what in once-mainstream Christian denominations has led to indifference even a dismissal of Spirit-grounded and Spirit-driven ministries. Earlier approaches to city ministry were limited to shrewd analyses of urban conditions, according to (mere) rationalist norms, but without honoring a longing for stability or deep rest in the midst of an urban fragmentation. Such a restless instability has come to characterize some of us ministers of outreach and those from whom we seek rest or stability. What one generation of urban theorists or academics were wont to lament in the rise of secularism (from a First Nations' perspective, naming our generation as now a "dead universe"), recent generations affirm as the age of the spirit. This era, according to Cherokee elder and anthropologist, Bob Thomas, and social ethicist, T.R. Anderson, is called a "spiritually alive universe."[16]

The writings of John Vincent of Sheffield, UK, demonstrate a combined church-in-society intentionality through his training modules and once regular publications. Prominent among these are his edited works: *Starting All over Again: Hints of Jesus in the City* (1981) and later *Liberation Theology* (1995).[17] These publications of the Sheffield Urban Theology Unit for the sake of the wider church wrestle with the future of urban ministry.

---

15. See Cox, *The Future of Faith*; also his *Fire from Heaven* with its suggestive subtitle: *The Rise of Pentecostal Spirituality and the Reshaping of Religion in the 21st Century* on the flourishing of spirit-driven ministries, especially in the cities and not merely in Third World countries. This conveys Cox's continued interests in what animates and revitalizes religion in the city time and again—as does his earlier *Religion in the Secular City*.

16. From the late Cherokee elder-anthropologist Bob Thomas via Terry Anderson, personal communication, February 7, 2012; cf. Cox in *The Future of Faith* on the age of the spirit, as Chapter 1: "An Age of the Spirit" and the "The experience of the divine is displacing theories about it," 20.

17. A recent article by Vincent is "The Radical Tradition," 2005, briefly comparing the counter-cultural "radicals" and the more establishment "co-existers."

CHAPTER 2—URBAN MINISTRY AND THEOLOGY'S ENDURING THEMES

Currently, there seem to be no "think tank institutes" similar to this unit in North America. There have been a few urban-ministry or urban-theology designated chairs in seminaries but little sign of these being connected with and available for the practitioner's benefit as in continuing or distant education and training opportunities (although archival insights from previous offerings are available).

The late Kenneth Leech was an East London urban theologian whose lifetime in urban ministry thought and practice bears noting.[18] He affirmed the best of an Anglo-Catholic heritage, heralding before its current popularity, the creative link and tensions of contemplative prayer and parish-focused social justice actions. Leech illustrated the importance of a collaborative theology—contemplation and social action—whereby his parish ministry and his status as an East London residential urban theologian at the time were combined with British urban sociology such as that of Ruth Glass.[19] Leech's theology put theology into practice, concretely and patiently, with the assistance of the tools of other disciplines, including monastic emphases on spirituality.

Such action-reflection and revised-action by an actual residential, parish-based theologian gives to urban ministry an integral model to draw upon. Along with the East Harlem Protestant Parish model, it foreshadows the "new monasticism" discussed below. Leech often emphasizes the role of present "place" and context when engaging urban ministry as he did in *The Eye of the Storm, Care and Conflict,* and in the works anthologized in *Prayer and Prophecy: The Essential Kenneth Leech* (2009). From the latter, Leech asserts that "physical location is a critical element in theological work" and echoes insights about place and human relationships:

> Throughout almost all my writing, there is a dynamic engagement with the question of space and place [. . .]. The idea of place involves emotional bonds, identity and so on. Place is the result of human beings working with and giving character to space. But space is never a neutral background to action. Space in East London is seen through its history as the site of social struggles, and it is in the course of such struggles that it becomes place, contested territory, home. Like the bread of the

---

18. London's East End for Leech is like that of the Italian novelist Ignacio Silone of *Bread and Wine* fame, who reflected out of the one valley of his family and personal life in virtually all of his writings. See Silone's *Emergency Exit,* 63–64.

19. Glass is cited (at least) three times in Leech's "Urbanism and its Discontents," 98, 104, 112.

Eucharistic offertory, place is something 'which earth has given and human hands have made.'²⁰

Again, Leech consistently focused on the contemplative prayer-justice creative tension so much a part of urban ministry and theology writings; *True Prayer: An Introduction to Christian Spirituality* being another of his offerings.²¹

Similarly the Canadian Anglican cleric, Norm Ellis, penned valuable contributions based on his parish ministry in the urban core of Toronto. His notable work is *My Parish Is Revolting* (1974). The writings of Ellis (nicknamed the "sky-pilot") illustrate concrete urban theologizing similar to that Leech and others. Concreteness helps to ground academic theologians, such as the philosophical theologian John Caputo in the writing of his *What Would Jesus Deconstruct?* (2007). Caputo draws on the concrete realism—in the service of hope—of John McNamee's *Diary of a City Priest* (1993). William Stringfellow's witness is equally concrete and theologically instructive. From his *My People is the Enemy* memoir, inspired by his involvement in the East Harlem Protestant Parish, Stringfellow affirmed the role of the poor themselves to be prayerful intercessors for the rich as their oppressors, indirectly or otherwise.

Anthologies, Urban Training, and Action Research

It is one project to cull history of urban ministries from various quarters, (thankfully done in many anthologies).²² It is quite another task to provide actual opportunities for training in the city ministry as have Green, Vincent, and Northcott and these latter two's British colleagues. Green's anthology, *Churches, Cities, and Human Community: Urban Ministry in the United States 1945–1985*, reports and reflects on some of these training opportunities in the United States. For example, at Urban Training Centres (UTC) over several focused decades, church professionals and laity were

---

20. Leech, *Prayer and Prophecy*, 290; cf. his "Agenda for an Urban Spirituality" in *Through Our Long Exile*, Chapter 10.

21. See also the works and website offerings of the Franciscan Richard Rohr, the Jesuit John Dear, the Benedictine Joan Chittister and among Canadians, Ron Dart and Donald Grayston of The Thomas Merton Society (also, Canadian President Ross Labrie) and former United Church of Canada moderator and still a virtual circuit-rider, Bill Phipps.

22. See representatively with their instructive subtitles: *Cities and Churches: Readings of the Urban Church*, ed. Lee; *Urban Theology: A Reader*, ed. Northcott; *Churches, Cities, and Human Community: Urban Ministry in the United States 1945–1985*, ed. Green and *Crossover City: Resources for Urban Mission and Transformation*.

introduced to combinations of theory and practice, and reflection and action disciplines. Located in the heart of major cities such as Chicago in the United States and Toronto in Canada, these UTCs provided, and to an extent recorded, on-the-ground experience with theological reflection arising from intense group encounters. These experiences included discussion with practitioners, access to records of many other case studies, and back-home church follow-ups so as to implement new learning or at least meaningfully reflect upon it in the more ambiguous setting of one's own backyard.

In the Canadian context, Ted Reeve and others provide invaluable insights in *Action Training in Canada: Reflections on Church-based Education for Social Transformation* (1997). With an initially limited circulation and now out of print, this volume contains a record of key urban training centres and processes, networking opportunities, and seasoned experiences unrecorded elsewhere. Such an out-of-print status represents an unfortunate void in urban ministry literature.[23] Nonetheless, the Canadian Urban Training Centre (CUT)—which though inactive marked its 50th anniversary in September, 2015 in Toronto, Ontario—and the Urban Core Support Network (UCSN) are two of the central reflection/action training models (with their indispensable legacies) discussed in this book. Several urban ministry practitioners remain indebted to these networks and genuinely long for a resumption of their activities. While another story remains to be written about why these historical training models ceased, the funding crises in national church bodies remains a factor in the American and Canadian situations. Discouraged leadership staff, most moving on to other pursuits from these training centres, is another. A third factor was perhaps a naïve hope that somehow the social justice training tasks for urban ministers had been done and now it would be up to the next generation to practice the tasks of analysis with the making and keeping of justice. However, these tasks have not been taken up. With the loss of these training centres and networks, there occurred further cuts and losses to social justice and societal ministries' portfolios. Urban ministry literature has not yet reflected sufficiently on the impact of these losses for a meaningful public witness—where the

---

23. There are exceptions of course, especially within Canadian historical, denominational studies. The Presbyterian Church in Canada hosted a 1919 pre-General Assembly with a focus on city ministries, and John Moir draws due attention to the Presbyterian Church's mandate (before splitting to form part of the United Church of Canada in 1925), to encourage an ecumenical cooperation in response especially to returning WW I veterans and immigrants, affirming that the only permanent cure for the evils of our time "requires an application of Christian principles to the whole conduct of life." *Enduring Witness*, 213–14. For this reference, I am indebted to the Vancouver School of Theology's Professor Richard Topping.

biblically-rooted prophetic witness is twinned to that of a public witness. Our predecessors noted a century ago:

> It is not enough to change the environment; it is not enough to transform social life [. . .]. It is essential that the heart be regenerated [. . .] we need a *consecration of the sense of smell*. We will have to get over the feeling that it is an unbearable thing to stand some of the odours that come out of the unsanitary buildings in which, by reason of our economic conditions, they are forced to live.[24]

What Clifford Green concludes in his summary chapter to *Churches, Cities, and Human Community: Urban Ministry in the United States 1945–1985* is instructive. He posed eleven questions to diverse male and female, lay and ministerial, denominational and executive staff and researchers over 3.5 decades. Through his research he discerned four major turning points over five distinct periods. These included WWII as the first turning point when suburban growth emerged as a clarion call for adaptation by the church. The second turning point arose from the crises in the city becoming crises for the church in the city. This was exemplified and exacerbated by the earnest return of the church to the urban core. Returning veterans of the Union Theological Seminary founded the East Harlem Protestant Parish (EHPP). This became a period when "Denominational urban ministry staffs grew to their largest size for any period following World War II, a contributing factor to the bulk of literature generated during the 1960's."[25] A third turning point occurred in the 1970s. Urban ministry activists attempted to integrate otherwise specifically racial—and ethnic—cultures of the church, but basically failed. Instead, funds declined, ethnically homogenous membership persisted (even if in a shared building with the host and other church bodies), and survival strategies were adopted. The fourth turning point was in the 1980s and consisted of dwindling denominational funds, and individual staff rather than denominational bodies pursuing justice concerns. On the other hand, Green notes that there were contributions of research on the nature and meaning of ethnic church life, interest in church-based community organisation "in urban areas where all other social institutions have fled or failed." This period also saw evangelical Protestants reflecting upon and writing about their missionary endeavors, including church growth.[26] Green ends with a similar affirmation to that of Harvey

---

24. Shearer, "The Redemption of the City," 194, cf. 191–96 for "Practical Christianity," (italics added). I am indebted to VST's Professor Richard Topping for this reference.

25. Green, *Churches, Cities, and Human Community*, 361.

26. Ibid., 362.

CHAPTER 2—URBAN MINISTRY AND THEOLOGY'S ENDURING THEMES

Cox: (notwithstanding earlier cautions of *The Secular City* and *Religion in the Secular City*), that "Religious faith is a marvellously persistent thing, and urban change, though modifying it, shows no real sign of destroying it."[27]

The Canadian literature of urban ministry remains incomplete in documenting the rise and fall of past experiments and explorations, though the following provides a start for a useable past. Foreshadowing one of the later urban ministry case studies, there are Stewart Crysdale's research and writings. He was among few at the time in either church or academic circles combining theory and practice by means of participant observation. He combined national church office roles with university sociology teaching and writing, and followed up *The Changing Church in Canada: Beliefs and Attitudes of United Church People* (1965) with his popular account: *Churches Where the Action Is* (1966). This title dovetailed with East Harlem Protestant Parish co-founder Archie Hargraves' metaphor of the urban church as a crapshoot player set free to engage wherever the action could be found. Crysdale's collection of short case studies was the first published account of the newly burgeoning Toronto Christian Resource Centre (CRC). Further noted in this CRC example of intense and enduring urban ministry is Steven Bouma-Prediger's and Brian Walsh's *Beyond Homelessness: Christian Faith in a Culture of Displacement* (2008). This writing was inspired by Walsh's year of being a theologian-in-residence with the CRC—rare in Canadian urban ministry experiences but less so, thankfully, elsewhere.[28] Other accounts in Crysdale's volume include ministries to street kids; coffee houses making creative uses of church basements together with 12-step fellowships; the rising migration of First Nation peoples into the cities (especially from the Canadian north and prairies); interracial projects in Halifax; and urban redevelopment forays into the inner-city poverty zones of Montreal. Noteworthy is the testimony of Peter Katodis who was asked by Crysdale if the clergy were effective in the earlier "war against poverty" strategies in Montreal. He replied, "The clergy are the *avant guard* in taking risks for social development. They can be one of the most virile forces for social change in our society." Foreshadowing later chapter case studies and conclusions of this thesis, Katodis added:

27. Ibid., Green, 363, citing H. Paul Douglas, *The City's Church*. NY: Friendship Press, 1927.

28. This residency via the invitation of the CRC's executive director, Michael Blair; see especially their concluding section "Hope, Home and Imagination" and opening reflections on cultural *displacement* so akin to Alexander's "The *Dislocation* Theory of Addiction," 57–84, (italics added). Elsewhere are the examples of Leech cited above and the experiences of the relationship of theological seminaries and "The Open Door Community," both in Atlanta, Georgia as documented in *A Work of Hospitality* with its instructive subtitle: *The Open Door Reader 1982–2003*.

> As the middle classes have moved out of the inner city, powerless people are left. They haven't the means of getting their hopes implemented [. . .] The question of poverty is closely allied with powerlessness. Most people feel they can't fight city hall [. . .] The clergy can give the people hope [. . .] to gain power and use it in a responsible way just as much as they need money.[29]

Hence, Katodis' Parallel Institutes Project was a timely and bold effort to organize alternatives to what was not working for the poor with whom he identified. Similarly, one could include the unique study of Howard Buchbinder on the then Just Society Movement (a play on then newly elected Prime Minister Pierre Trudeau's campaign slogan, for a "just society"). Buchbinder's resourced Just Society Movement was a 1970s alliance of poor people and single mothers fighting for welfare rights with what was then the Praxis Institute in Toronto.[30] The imperative continues while one looks for urban ministry models and exemplars—as later chapters again attest. To a modest extent more recently, Bill Blaikie has contributed to the experience of being both a United Church of Canada minister and elected politician, focusing on the creative aspects of the social gospel tradition and legacy for both his early urban Winnipeg ministry forays and then his political vocation.[31] Harvey Forster's *The Church in the City Streets* (1942) was a pastorally sensitive precedent, as was Pierre Berton's journalistic *The Comfortable Pew*, and his contribution to *Why the Sea Is Boiling Hot* (1965). Sam Roddan's *Batter My Heart*, an edited history of the United Church of Canada at the fiftieth-year mark, contributed concrete stories on the urban or inner-city scene.[32]

As a precedent, there arose in the 1970s a United Church of Canada study document, *A Dream Not for the Drowsy*. This "Moderator's Consultation on the Church in the Metropolitan Core, 1977," came about as the

---

29. Crysdale, *Churches Where Is*, 110, 111.

30. *Community Work in Canada*, ed. Warf, Chapter 5 case study of "Just Society Movement."

31. Blaikie, *The Blaikie Report* with its agenda subtitle: *An Insider's View of Faith and Politics*, Bill having been was a New Democratic Party MP and United Church minister for 30+ years. See also Deb Cameron Fawkes, *"There is a Power, Not Ourselves, That Makes for Righteousness" Tommy Douglas: Political Life as Religious Vocation* for Douglas' social gospel, influence of Christian realist theology, and his whole political career as a sustained vocation of ministry.

32. Fittingly "dedicated to all those good people who laboured in the vineyard but whose names are not recorded in these pages," *Batter My Heart*. Sam's father, Andrew Roddan, was a towering pastor, 1929–48, during the Depression, in and following the World War II era while with Vancouver's First United Church. In addition to the latter's *The Church in the Modern City*, see also Burrows, *Hope Lives Here* for specifics on Roddan, Chapter 3.

CHAPTER 2—URBAN MINISTRY AND THEOLOGY'S ENDURING THEMES

outcome of an extensive consultation of 130 persons in 18 cities over 3 years. It was revised several times before submission to the national church's highest General Council decision-making body. The final document included this introductory confession:

> We are in deep conflict regarding the nature and identity of the Divine, God's locale and priorities, the city, evangelism, ministry. We have no clear sense of the process of urbanization; we have not yet learned to help each other use contemporary resources for analyzing the dynamics of a community. And we have never learned to use such analysis as a basis for discerning how to be an evangelical and prophetic component in a post-industrial, computerized social system (. . .) There are illusions that need illumination, and grieving that needs catharsis.[33]

Akin to Cox, Winter, and Crysdale's perspectives, the document's authors discerned urbanization as an illumination. "It is an all-embracing social process, with reverberations of tremendous consequence for the most remote of rural communities and the churches there, not less than for those geographically in the metro core." Therein, they further understood the mixed blessings of what urbanisation brings:

> Canada's headlong race into urbanization demands a readiness on our part to perceive the city as a generator of powerful and thus danger-loaded blessing. But also as a source of injustice and despair to those who are oppressed, whether by personal poverty or by the complex systems that treat them as things.[34]

The document noted images of the city that summon the church to be incarnate within and for the city—from the city as a generator of people and power to the church as an animator of community in the midst of otherwise alienation and anomie. Dovetailing with what later "new urbanists" also call the priority of community purpose over mere property rights and values:

> (. . .) *koinonia* is affirmed—an alternative to consumerism. Koinonia means community as partnership [. . .] a sense of being members one of another; together in the bundle of life, so the mechanisms of urban living—economic, political, educational, cultural, religious, scientific, therapeutic, recreational—will

---

33. *A Dream Not for the Drowsy*, an undated, out of print United Church of Canada publication of the Task Group on the Church in the Metropolitan Core to the 1980 Division of Mission in Canada, 3, 5. Moves to re-issue this publication have thus far not succeeded due to alleged "budget cuts."

34. Ibid.

press over onward in the direction of the inter-dependent, as against the paternalistic, the proprietary, the suppressionist.[35]

There has been so little of the Canadian church scene available for historical and interpretive guidance that the longing for this document is more now than ever. As one co-author has since reflected,

> [T]here were urban core ministries in metropolitan cities across Canada fully supported by the church. The study process leading to the writing of the report reinforced the sense of network/community/solidarity among them. The presentation of the report at General Council was a strong affirmation of urban core ministry. CUT (Canadian Urban Training) had been hugely successful.[36]

To a modest degree, the bi-annual "Energy from the Edges" community minister/urban core worker events for United Church of Canada personnel (with relevant national staff present) has followed through; albeit now its funding for actual gathering and mutual support has been eliminated. *A Dream Not for the Drowsy* expresses the hope that the church meaningfully engage rather than retreat from the city's issues and inequalities. Furthermore, in *Coalitions of Justice: The Story of Canada's Interchurch Coalitions*,[37] several more coalitions for justice are explicated; notably a full generation of ecumenically supported PLURA (Presbyterian, Lutheran, United Church of Canada, Roman Catholic, and Anglican Church in Canada), providing regional and national seed funds to the actual poor for addressing and redressing root causes and conditions of poverty. Several church-based urban ministry publications from the 1970s and 1980s have shut down, though their denominational magazine reflections endure.[38] Thus, such secular bodies as the Canadian Centre for Policy Alternatives can be a continuing resource, notably through their regular *The CCPA Monitor* articles on social inequalities. As well, the CCPA has, remarkably, sponsored training sessions and/or leadership schools for young adults on social issues and justice

---

35. Bendroth, and the agenda subtitle "Designing the City: Reflections on the New Urbanism," 15, 19.

36. Jim Houston, e-mail comment to Morris (February 7, 2012) on the hindsight significance of this document to which he had been an original consultant and contributor along with the late Stuart Coles. (used with permission).

37. Edited by Christopher Lind and Joe Mihevc; therein, see lay Catholic Mary Boyd's contributions on PLURA, a once catalytic seed funding source for anti-poverty groups, often associated with and encouraged by urban ministries.

38. For example there were the *Catholic New Times, Practice of Ministry in Canada, The Grail*, and
  smaller publications such as *Wheat & Chaff* and *Unitas*.

practices. These initiatives fill a void where once the church sponsored such youth and young adult sessions. Recently, by way of these graduates, CCPA senior staff has joined burgeoning fresh expressions of the urban church in collaborative efforts to encourage para- or alterative-spiritual communities with social justice intentions (thinking of the three ingredients of a *body of people*, over a *long period*, engaging in *deep conversations*[39]).

Smouldering Embers

City churches engage several options in responding to the challenges of the city. They employ and engage several interesting resources and disciplined practices in the pursuit of their theological objectives or virtues. For example, the spiritually grounding disciplines of Centering Prayer and Christian Meditation—basically simple to learn and challenging to employ regularly—are now more prevalent, as is the confession that while urban ministries talk of justice making and keeping, it is far from simple or quick to maturely practice justice. In the hopeful service of a vital balance, more urban ministers than ever aim to incorporate these spiritual disciplines in the service of advocating and organizing for justice. Notwithstanding the difficulties, several Canadian organizations have taken up the challenge. One greater Vancouver network, *Streams of Justice*, is a welcome example (viewed by some as an exception for its disciplined focus on justice). A representative para-political think tank involved in social justice work is the *Canadian Centre for Policy Alternatives*. A recent model of applying biblically informed social ethics to ground urban community organizing broad-based across neighborhoods and districts is the *Metro Vancouver Alliance*, an associate of the 75-year-old Industrial Areas Foundation.

There are several thrusts that arise from the above and foreshadow the next chapter on the dynamics of urban ministry. They include but are hardly limited to these seven: survive or die, persistent poverty, nuanced inequalities, addictions, globalization, burnout, and the emergence of new monasticism.

Ministries experience death by closure and/or a benign demise of one's historic identity by merger. Norm Ellis' books express the live-or-die forced option. *My Parish Is Revolting* documents the choice to make abundant and mixed use of the *whole* church; this was a 1970s breakthrough, breaking down previously sacred but compartmentalized barriers (sanctuary versus drop-in space likely tucked away in the basement). The author's own urban ministry attests over four decades and five urban ministries. Tim Dickau's

---

39. Carse, "Beyond Atheism."

Plunging into the Kingdom depicts a once ailing Vancouver eastside Baptist Church breathing new life into its building, increasing staff with extra worship services and community houses, and spawning social justice networks such as Streams of Justice. This east side ministry has energized wider ministerial networks and added another Sunday service with a shared husband-and-wife team ministry.

Poverty remains the chief reality that summons urban ministries and their mission statements. The poverty of New York's East Harlem spurred returning WW II veterans, as Union Seminary students, to combine theological studies with real-life concerns and eventually to move into the ghetto to live among its people. Toronto's South St Jamestown poverty sparked affluent United Church of Canada lay-people, aroused by commutes through the district, to organize an on-location ministry to address the stressed situations caused by massive urban development. The downtown eastside poverty of Vancouver is what has contributed for many decades to the steadfast ministry of First United Church. In such cases, the ministries' origins and development—as well as other networks like Streams of Justice (SoJ), A Community Aware (ACA), and the Metro Vancouver Alliance (MVA)—can be accounted for as an aroused and then animated contrast-awareness (a core category that can be induced from an application of grounded theory analysis and to be demonstrated in appendix B.)

There are signs of revival of classical monasticism as a new monasticism refreshes urban ministry. This new monasticism creates ministries to face poverty by moving beyond analysis to organize efforts more favorable to marginalized people. New monastic writers exhibit retrieved if not fresh expressions of the classical vows of the original and continuing monastics. The vows of poverty and obedience, as a listening presence and continuing conversation and/or stability, represent such disciplines.

The book includes an appendix on what the new monasticism needs to critically learn from a Thomas Merton—as well as a Reinhold Niebuhr and a Jürgen Moltmann and their constructive legacies (Appendix A). This also includes references to the three ministry networks of ACA, MVA and SoJ that are discussed in Chapter 7.

Ecumenical social ethicist John C. Bennett spoke of the importance of statistics, but they need to be interpreted compassionately to have relevance. Statistics support Gibson Winter's observation that "we have two urbanizations—one of hope and one of despair." Annual days for noting working people's struggles and issues—May Day and Labor Day being examples—have taken on possibly renewed life due to the impact of the Occupy Movement. With the fragmentation and loss of the prophetic capacity in many Canadian mainline churches, these equalitarian thrusts challenge tendencies to cynicism and status quo passivity, especially as they invite inter-disciplinary alliances for the churches' participation. One Vancouver network attending to this is *A Community Aware* (ACA).

Urban churches have tended to assume that the health professionals and self-help groups like Alcoholics Anonymous (AA) cover the field— ministers being the referral agent or 5th-step "confessor," at best. However, the previous theological generations' attention to alienation and identity crises or diffusion have sparked a renewed interest and inter-disciplinary involvement in addictions in order to understand their causes and the possible complicity of the religious community. "Dislocation" is the heart of Canadian social psychologist Bruce K. Alexander's magnum opus *The Globalisation of Addiction,* with its pertinent sub-title, "A Study in Poverty of the Spirit." [ACA hosts annual seven-week spring sessions on the inter-disciplinary addiction topic, with particular focus on the fragmentation and dislocation roots of addictions, so "it is not about drugs."]

Andrew Harvey's *Urban Christianity and Global Order: Theological Resources for an Urban Future* states that "Globalization is an amalgamation of the most significant forces shaping our urban areas and our world today: a transition far from complete but impacting in unprecedented ways through numerous social, economic, and political projects and practices." The church tends to operates as if issues are local or regional, while the flow of money and business frequently operates beyond such boundaries. Hence, urban ministries experience global realities without being aware of all of the pressures and powers that affect the issues they engage at the local level.

Urban ministry literature illumines the critical and confessional task of addressing what prevents justice from being accomplished. The literature conveys the following: 1) the failure to recognize that steadfast practices of justice are more than a mere issue or project, rally or year-end resolution; 2) weariness and temptations to cynicism; and 3) the collapse of the justice mandate to charity responses. Weariness, if indeed not burnout, has been a reality for generations. Representatively, Barbara Brown Taylor has confessionally noted this in *Envisioning the New City: A Reader on Urban Ministry.*

Critical and New Faithful Responses

The tension of contemplation-action was deemed the purview of monastics. Contemplation was thought to be a deeper, quieter dimension of prayer, accompanied by meditation practices, and action was understood to be the counter-balance in the work within and around the monastery. The "new monastics" proffer a creative complement, a check-and-balance interplay.

Dietrich Bonhoeffer and his life-long interpreter, Eberhard Bethge, affirm the twinning of prayer with justice (as does the Thomas Merton Society). The Franciscan, Richard Rohr, further illustrates this tension. The Canadian Anglican, Ron Dart, has retrieved the life witness of George Grant for his adoption of the contemplative and the active monastic poles.[40] To some extent, this book will illustrate Dart and the others' approach through A Community Aware (ACA) network.

Secondly, the literature indicates a renewal of broad-based community organizing. Active in dozens of American, Canadian, and British cities, (and beyond) the Industrial Areas Foundation model has endured, albeit sensitively revised and more pacefully applied. It offers a crucial mediating link between theological, social, and ethical principles and the immediate and concrete level of pastoral or emergency assistance. This book will illustrate this process by way of the Metro Vancouver Alliance (MVA) network.

Thirdly, one again must note the new monastics for their earnest witness. I could not have conceived of this possibility of these organizations in this role as a theological student of the 1960s and 1970s. To be sure, some of us were heartily encouraged by the quasi-monastic model of the team or corporate ministry of the East Harlem Protestant Parish founders—intentionally naming their four regular disciplines of economical sharing, political involvement, residential living in Harlem, and regularly engaging in Biblical studies and corporate (versus private only) worship. This book will allude to and illustrate this by way of the Streams of Justice (SoJ) network.

Summary Conclusion

What is evident and realistic about this above survey and brief assessment are the pressures and limits of competing interests and conflicting ambitions amid scarcity of resources.[41] What is hopeful are the encouraging resources of urban ministries, including their patterns and processes of interdependence which attest to the presence of that Power that bears down upon them to sustain if not to renew us, to preserve rather than slay.[42] What constitutes a hopeful realism is the steadfastness of ministerial

---

40. See Dart, *The Beatitudes* and further, his web site, http://www.ronsdart.blogspot.ca/. Similarly, see Rohr's web site, https://cac.org/ and a link therein to daily meditations which consistently connect contemplation to action and vice versa.

41. Cf. Anderson, *Walking the Way*, "Budgets: A Test Case for Distributive Justice," 57–61.

42. See Gustafson, *Ethics from a Theocentric Perspective*, Vol. II, "Ethics and Theology," 146, passim.

possibilities affirmed and commended, a legacy into the present era of urban ministry practices. These possibilities are held in balance by the practical requirements related to launching, maintaining, and renewing the limits of what it takes to launch, maintain, revise, renew, and revisit an urban ministry. Sin, ignorance, and finitude persist, but they need not prevail—particularly as attested by Christian or theological realism and hopeful realists in the future.

Chapter 3—Urban Ministry Dynamics and Triad Intimations

> We have for once learnt to see the great events of world history from below, from the perspective of the outcast, the suspects, the maltreated, the powerless, the oppressed, the reviled—in short from the perspective of those who suffer [. . .] neither bitterness nor envy should have gnawed at the heart during this time, that we should have come to look with new eyes at matters great and small, sorrow and joy, strength and weakness, that our perception of generosity, humanity, justice and mercy should have become clearer, freer, less corruptible.[1]

WHEN I PONDER WAYS and levels to depict ministry in the city, these prepositions assist. "In" the city implies being involved where a ministry resides and beyond—beyond the immediate address to the surrounding area, district, and even city-wide region. When an urban ministry engages issues that cannot be addressed and redressed merely within its limited sphere of influence, the wider framework of decision-making comes into play. "With" the city implies an embodied or incarnate sensitivity as to what a ministry can possibly engage by walking and struggling with the city's ministry's people and their concerns. The witness to and fostering of a community within urban environs burdened with dislocation or disconnection is an uppermost aim of most urban ministries. These burdens are more than a mere fragmentation of city life; dislocation and disconnection has political causes and economic and social consequences—widespread implications for addiction, for example.[2] "To" the city implies a pastoral and chaplaincy posture, that of the proverbial summons, sympathetically and supportively to "speak the truth to those in power" on behalf of those for whom the chaplain is advocating. Finally, "against" or being "contra" the city may well arise when a ministry's attention prophetically intuits the presence of the virtu-

---

1. Bonhoeffer, *Letters and Papers from Prison*, 17.
2. Again, see Alexander, *The Globalization of Addiction*, especially 57–84.

ally demonic at work, when pressures and forces bear down upon a ministry and its care of people to the extent that it seems nigh impossible to cooperate lest the ministry starts or continues collaborating in an evil situation. All four of these *modus operandi* express themselves in a ministry's presence, advocacy, prophecy, and prayers for deliverance or exorcism, as attested, by Harvey Cox's *Secular City* and *Religion in the City*, Walter Wink's trilogy on *The Powers* and, among others, Robert Linthicum's *City of God City of Satan*. There is in the midst of the dynamic pressures of city life a relentless drama of good and evil with hope and despair. The challenges of urban ministry stretch and strain its practitioners to wonder what credo, what literary and vocational resources there are for a steadfast, faithful, public, prophetic, and personal witness.

In the Midst of Despair, Hope Intimated

For a concrete sense of urban ministry dynamics, there are a range of themes and responses that one's own ministry undertakes, thinking of a typical day in a composite way. As urban ministry is a fluid and dynamic phenomena, a neat and complete definition is impossible – other than describing it generically as ministry in the city and given gentrification pressures, not merely the inner-city or urban core.[3] However the following contributes particularly in terms of what urban ministries actually endeavour to practise, including the confessions of our sins. There could be more descriptive elaborations of actual urban ministries and, of course, the discipline terms of the triad employed. Here is a composite day in the life of the Longhouse Council of Native Ministry, offered while mindful of many other urban ministries as well.[4] Each day signs the sighs of efforts made but no day exemplifies hopes fulfilled (other than briefly, partially and fragmentarily).

---

3. See Camacho's ironic title and helpful elaborations, *God Loves Gentrification*. He presses: "What does it mean that many have been inspired to seek the welfare of the cities precisely as a growing number of people have been economically displaced from these cities? The theologies that romanticize this shift into the city need to be seriously scrutinized alongside the material realities," 1.

4. There is no one "typical day" in the life of most urban ministries in respect to established or predictable routines and schedules. Many work toward structures that assure elements of stability and trustworthiness while allowing for a measure of flexibility and relevance to a person, situation or issue—a virtual juggling act, reflective of Wells' *Improvisation* and its apt sub-title: *The Drama of Christian Ethics*. See also *The Overnighters* award-winning social documentary by Jesse Moss for both a "typical" yet rare season of one church engaging on its own dire homelessness of the working, migrant poor to the point of sheer exhaustion and virtual burnout for its temporarily heroic pastor, Jay Reinke.

Thus, there is emergency help to persons: from food to transportation, to use of the phone/bathroom, and ad hoc trips to the hospital, to detoxification, to funerals or cemeteries or, if available, "home." There is a response to urgent requests: for a visit to the dying and/or space and help for a funeral or memorial. There is advocacy: for help in saving furniture for future needs when going into detoxification or the hospital. There are visits to a local hospice as well as regional hospitals. There are emails such as to emailaprisoner.com, or for the ministry's seasonal newsletter or for the annual "Advent or Lent Vigils for the Silenced" in the central parts of the city. There are almost endless meetings such as for the monthly Building and Strategy Team of the Metro Vancouver Alliance (of which the Longhouse is a founder). There is the collegial network such as supper with a youth pastor regarding recovery from addictions. There is the hosting of community events such as a regular Tuesday morning "sharing circle" at the Longhouse Church (along with a neighboring school and a recovery-from-addictions First Nations organization). There is a response to a request to cite numbers for a forthcoming ministerial forum on common needs. There is the hosting and conducting of a mid-week Bible Study on the lectionary texts. There is an acceptance of donations of money and food for Thanksgiving, Christmas or Easter dinners through the Longhouse. There is the dealing with volunteers to assist one of the live-in volunteers of the Longhouse. There are family communications with a son's mother regarding her son's well-being. There is the personal as forgoing an evening lecture on harm reduction in order to aim for some rest and recreation. There is study, other than sermon preparations and thesis work, to read for a monthly Karl Barth seminar and attend to relevant news or research reflections, especially on the raw, enduring realities of inequality.[5] There are the endless concerns of

---

5. See <http://www.equalitytrust.org.uk> for "Key Information on Inequality." It reports: "Inequality between the rich and poor in Canada has grown more than in any other OECD country in the last decade except for Germany. Vancouver has the largest and fastest growing income gap between rich and poor of 24 Canadian cities [. . .] In Canada, the average net worth of the poorest 20% of Canadians was minus $2,400 in 2005 (because of debt). The average net worth of the richest fifth was $1,264,200." Also: "In 2009, nearly half of the poor children in BC lived in families with at least one adult working full-time, full-year, pointing to the problem of jobs that pay low wages. The poverty rate for children of lone-parent mothers fell to a record low 24.2% percent, thanks to more mothers with better jobs and fewer families on welfare. The poverty rate for children in 2-parent families, however, rose to 15% percent. Most poor families with children live many thousands of dollars below the poverty line. Poor 2-parent families had incomes $14,200 below the poverty line on average. Inequality remains a serious problem in BC and the rest of Canada. Most poor families with children in BC had less than one-quarter of the personal income of all families with children," *BC Poverty Report Card*, <http://www.firstcallbc.org>. Cf. Hume's "Income Inequality Threatens

follow-ups, such as verifying and communicating regarding a Coroner's Inquest on fire deaths in the neighborhood. There is the invitation to critique, such as for an article by Pieta Woolley in *The United Church of Canada Observer* on debt loads and the First United Church's current state of affairs. There are again, referrals, such as requesting a Victoria, BC, colleague to visit a dying street person from Vancouver. There is the maintenance of the student and volunteer requests for community hours. There is the participation in East-End networks of ministers: two monthly ones, local and regional, both involving prayer and sharing concerns. There is networking: including participation in coalitions, support networks, alliances, and occasionally through regular gatherings. There are fresh calls to visit and/or hold the ailing or anxious in prayerful contemplation, including urban-core, long-term facilities and hospices.

Each of these variables invites elaboration. Those akin to a *hoping justice prayerfully* triad are further discussed in the remainder of this chapter. Suffice to note the range and intensity of what arises from the personal to the political; from the contemplative to social justice advocacy; from on-site or in-house work to that of an outreach ministry; and with interdisciplinary focus—further labours for the sake of long-term organizing. Organizing rarely arises in any natural or automatic way as one might wish for example by organizing an eventual move from charity to advocacy, or to organize for power in the name a faithful public and prophetic witness. Earnest, patient, and perseverant work is required with a realistic anticipation of multiple setbacks and disappointments.

In the Midst of 'Endless' Charity, Justice Intimated

How do these above variables fit on a charity-advocacy-justice-other continuum? For many urban ministries, there is a mixture of these components. Some ministries strive to engage chiefly the justice virtue; others begin with charity and hope to include aspects of justice along the way, while many of us, alas, succumb to a mere charitable response to poverty.[6] A "forced option" comes into play;[7] ministries have little option other than to practice charity responses to poverty, especially in view of the annual funding appeals,

---

Our Society," D5.

6. See Harper's *Urban Churches, Vital Signs* with its instructive subtitle: *Beyond Charity to Justice*, 302–3.; also Dickau's *Plunging into the Kingdom* and Dykstra, "Riff Raff, Bedbugs and Signs," 50–59.

7. Again, Shinn, *Forced Options*, 3.

which dovetail with the irresistible and seemingly irreducible Christmas charity appeals and year-end charitable income tax inducements. Ministries may well be "forced" to practice bread-and-butter charity responses to the inequalities of poverty for the sake of raising funds—by providing statistics and stories to encourage "feel-good" giving (which Streams of Justice and others challenged on the Twenty-Fifth Anniversary of the Vancouver, BC, Food Bank). Later in this thesis, the whole charity/justice tension is explored as it simply will not exit the stage of any urban ministry's life. In a "Charity or Justice?" presentation at a Streams of Justice 2011 forum in Vancouver, Jean Swanson drew from her 2001 *Poor-Bashing: The Politics of Exclusion*. She noted the five factors of charity: fostering unjust power relations; creating illusions that needs are being met; using charity for corporate public relations images; demeaning people who receive charity; and the fact that charity does not really end poverty.

Each of these elements illustrates the responses of urban ministries to what is going on in our cities. Forthwith we ask what should be our fitting response in light of the historic and present responses of others. The Toronto CRC thus drew from the East Harlem Protestant Parish model of the 1950s and 60s, especially a steadfast dedication to the urban core of a city. Urban ministry responses depict city dynamics—the aches and pains and the changes and resistances to what is going on or not going on but which ought to be going on in urban zones. As a Vancouver urban geographer attests:

> The moral frontier so prevalent in inner-city gentrification [. . .] is partly forged through opposing claims and understandings related to the ethics of property [. . .] property surely matters to urban politics [. . .] property can also serve as a site for creative remembering and re-inscription.[8]

Welcome thus are the attestations of other disciplines on the reality of inequality, which is at least as much a geo-economic and political set of forces as it is a moral or social-ethical consideration.

In the Midst of 'Heroic' Weariness, Prayer Intimated

Less obvious in the above comments are the fierce tensions that arise out of the demands of the work, the hours of the work, the temptations to work on and on to attend to the frustrations of incomplete or unfulfilled expectations,

---

8. Blomley, *Unsettling City,* xx, xxi. Cf. Davey's *Urban Christianity*, Chapter 3.

and the frequent outcome of plain weariness or worse: burnout for the actual minister or worker. Veteran practitioners of urban ministry confess weariness and often near fatal burnout.[9] Urban ministers, however, tend to play down these energy-draining pressures and, girding one's loins, somehow soldier on. How such prospective burnout conditions are addressed is another challenge, not usually engaged for those of us in small ministries where workaholic and lone-ranger work styles are tacitly encouraged and/or benignly accepted.

Foreshadowing attending to these creative tensions in later chapters, the following questions are typical. How much charity and how much justice advocacy and organizing is actually possible? When is enough charity offered? How and when are advocacies and organizing efforts for the work of justice thwarted or the work of justice masked by feigned efforts that are called "justice" but really remain charity? How little contemplative prayer time and how much call to action is the order of the day? How much weariness settles in? How often can time and space be found for centering prayer for the purposes of grounding oneself and the ministry? If in a family situation, how often does the work crowd out actual family and/or personal time? This latter query is addressed by people and ministries who currently deem themselves, even if implicitly, as a part of the aptly named "new monasticism"[10]—discussed later and aptly summarized as basically "alternative Christian communities."[11] Suffice it to state that the demands of ministry are constantly in the face of urban ministers as is the desire to render a faithful public and prophetic witness. Often, there seems little relief from these tensions. The hope is that they are more creative than destructive and that parish support for one's ministry is more cooperatively present than competitively draining.

Another tension arises from a denomination's delegation of ministry to the poor to one of their historic urban missions in order that other churches within that city's denomination are relieved from exercising anything more than giving to the designated mission (e.g., food hampers collected at Christmas, Thanksgiving, or White Gift Sunday). This tension is

9. Again, see Taylor, "Looking for God in the City," 18. Cf. Caputo's *What Would Jesus DECONSTRUCT?*, especially Chapter 6 "The Working Church"; it aptly draws on McNamee's *Diary of a City Priest*, itself an urban ministry case study.

10. See Grimley and Wooding, *Living the Hours* with its instructive sub-title *Monastic Spirituality in Everyday Life* and references in Chapters 2 and 3. Aptly, this volume identifies that the very alternative that the desert fathers/mothers sought was in critical response to Christianity's own once-attempted alternative to, but eventual institutionalization within the Roman Empire of the times.

11. See Byassee and the illuminating subtitle "The New Monastics: Alternative Christian Communities," 51–60.

created by the urban mission itself coming to feel used by the wider church by bearing all the burdens of ministering to the poor and not being able to count on the broader church for a prophetic witness. At the same time, the broader church often continues to think of itself as offering valid resources for the mission enterprise and may well refer any crisis calls for help at their door to the mission church "downtown." Other urban ministry chroniclers note additional tensions of a less intense nature.[12]

Search for Theological Containers and Anchorages

Urban theologies arise in the search for what helps make sense of the previously described tensions. Thomas Merton calls this a theological container.[13] Dietrich Bonhoeffer in turn called for a "theological anchorage which holds while the waves dash in vain."[14] There are various ways to conceive of such containers, frameworks, indicative markers, or anchorages. One way to depict a search is in "the search for the lost chord"[15] which could be an over-arching image or integral concept that summarizes as it depicts the dynamics and tensions of urban ministry endeavours (akin to Baderstcher's "iconic analysis of the city", below). Such contenders include "peace" or "shalom," as described in *Seek the Peace of the City* by Marc Gornik. For others, there arises "covenant-making" as with covenant partners and, above all, one's covenant with God; "hospitality," as at the First United Church or Grandview Calvary Baptist in Vancouver; "integration," as in the Montreal City Mission Society; "justice

---

12. See Bakke's tensions such as creation/redemption; individual/community; power/powerlessness; certainty/mystery; past/future, *A Theology as Big as the City*, 204.

13. Merton expresses the "container" need thus: "What we need is a theology that *supports* prayer, that *goes with* prayer and *gives it structure* because otherwise, if you have nothing but prayer and no theology, it is like having water and no pail to put it in. Prayer doesn't escape you, but if you do have a theology that can contain it, put outer limits around it, then you know where you are. You can stay with it, but it is the water, nor the bucket, that counts. If you pay too much attention to the bucket, you forget about the water and you get into difficulties again [. . .] *Biblical theology gives you a container for prayer*," Merton, "Prayer, Tradition, and Experience," 115–16; (italics added).

14. When Bonhoeffer called for a theological basis for world alliance via a 1932 paper at a youth peace conference in Czechoslovakia, cited in Clements, "Ecumenical Witness for Peace," 160.

15. The Moody Blues' lyrics express: "I struck one chord of music/Like the sound of a great Amen [. . .] It seemed the harmonious echo/From our discordant life [. . .] It linked all perplexed meanings/Into one perfect peace" from *The Search for the Lost Chord*, http://themoodybluesalbum.tripod.com/id7.html. Cf. the original 1877 poem of Adelaide Anne Procter, http://www.events-in-music.com/the-lost-chord.html.

making and keeping," as in the Streams of Justice movement; the bold affirmation that "Hope Lives Here," as described in Bob Burrows' *Hope Lives Here: A History of Vancouver's First United Church* and Victoria, BC's Dandelion Society or a former "Hope Mission" or a former "Partners-in-Hope" ministry. There are small yet steadfast offerings by way of theme titles of ministries: "Jacob's Well," "Potter's Mission"; "animation" as a Spirit-grounded-and-driven move to organize to engage or redress inequality for the long haul—be this as in involvement with the Metro Vancouver Alliance's community organizing aims, Toronto's Christian Resource Centre, or one's own research through a steady perusal of headlines and feature stories as basic urban realities are portrayed.[16]

Each of these images seeks to capture and depict aspects of urban ministry marks of mission. "Peace" or "shalom" captures the biblical invitation to attend to God's presence in the city for the sake of reconciliation. "Shalom" brings to mind the prophetic affirmation that, even in exile and cut off from the hope of one's welcome homeland, one must seek the welfare or shalom of that place because, therein, as Jeremiah confesses, is our peaceful well-being too (Jeremiah 29:7).

"Covenant-making," the stuff of steadfastness, captures that which names humans as God's covenant partners, such that in life, in death, and in the hope of life beyond death, *we are not alone*. "We are not alone" is part of the creed of the United Church of Canada, and this creed honors this relationship as in an active partnering relationship. "Covenant" remains as a basic notion for theological ethics.[17] "Hospitality" conveys the recent offerings of buildings, staff, or volunteers to assist the homeless and the hard-to-house (by virtue of too many strikes and burdens against them). "Hospitality" is also a basic concept of social ethics, inviting a response by ministries to go deeper in asking what should be our fitting response to what is going on.[18] The "search for the beloved community" (a term used

---

16. See McInnes, "Human Development Index Reinforces Occupy's Mantra," B1. To wit: "Although Canadians have among the highest life expectancies in the world, we lose some marks on the equality scale [. . .] because the life expectancy for aboriginal Canadians is so much lower than for the rest of us [. . .] the gap continues to be shameful. They earn less, they go to jail more, they aren't doing well in school, they get sick more and they die on average five years earlier than other Canadians [. . .] (Thus) with echoes of Occupy Vancouver, Canada's ranking in this year's United Nations Human Development Index was knocked down by this statistical portrait of an unjust society."

17. See the instructive employment of covenant (see sub-titles) in Allen's *Love and Conflict: A Covenantal Model of Christian Ethics* and Anderson, *Walking the Way: A Christian Guide to Ethics*.

18. See Ogletree, *Hospitality to the Stranger* especially Chapter 4's "The Activity of Interpreting in Moral Judgment." See also above cited *A Work of Hospitality*, ed. Gathje.

by Martin Luther King, Jr.) arises earnestly as ministries strain and stretch to offer some semblance of acceptance to the dispossessed and in helping to provide them with a home away from home (if such a thing as "home" ever existed for them!). Though often felt to be near at hand, "community" is elusive.[19] "Integration" might be in itself a mission statement—to be present and welcoming—to welcome into the safe centre of one's place and supportive presence those who exist at the margins of society and feel split off and unwelcome. Put otherwise, it means "to enable the journey from exclusion to community." This urban ministry requests in a 2011 newsletter:

> Dear friend, we ask for you to assist us in this vital work of integration and community building. The people we serve are among some of the most vulnerable in our midst. They also have strength, an important story to tell, and a unique contribution to make when given half the chance. Your donation will afford them that chance—a chance to belong.[20]

Questionable is whether such e-mail appeals make a difference. Nonetheless, urban missions tend to use first-person "success" stories and/or the price of a served meal to cajole real money responses.

Intimated above, justice advocacy-and-making is central to the entire biblical and social-ethical mandate. Even if in eclipse, it is certainly basic in the "Occupy" movement and, in Canada, the "Idle No More" movement with their equality mantras. Justice is the heart and soul of the Streams of Justice network included later in this thesis. Once the dominant thrust of social gospel ministries, justice has become now more an evangelical mission focus—for example, with East Vancouver's charismatic Vineyard Ministry's study of the oft-cited Micah 6:8 passage. Justice increasingly receives due attention from urban planners applying social ethics and philosophy perspectives, while many churches are more inclined to limit their attention to mere pastoral and emergency-aid levels of response to city inequalities and indignities. Justice has the capacity to incorporate and integrate many of these themes in urban ministry, especially hospitality, covenant, integration, and the call for a new paradigm. However, a ministry does not move easily or naturally from charity measures of relief to measures of actually strategizing for how to redress indignities and inequalities toward their positive and constructive opposites (dignity and equality).

---

19. "According to Wikipedia, '(t)here were ninety-four discrete definitions of the term (community) by the mid-1950s," Bergman, "Taking Care of Each Other."

20. See Montreal City Mission Society website, http://www.montrealcitymission.org.

The virtue discipline of "hope," intimated above, is illustrated in recent and continuing urban ministries, many by the actual ministry name itself. Hope depicts theological reflections on the nature of the very call to be present and, in the United States, to take collaborative advantage of government funding as "restorers of hope" with the poor—since churches or community ministries could impart and bring with them actual financial interests.[21] Hope has been the rallying theme for issue-centred advocacy efforts, such as the Coalition of Hope movement facilitated by the Longhouse Ministry and animated by now retired alcohol and drug counselor Jim Leyden. This movement was founded by disillusioned alcohol and drug counsellors at a time when harm reduction strategies were threatened. Thus, the Coalition of Hope fought for drastically improved facilities while pushing hard for the then-fragile "Four Pillars" approach to set in place 1) education; 2) detoxification and treatment resources; 3) harm-reduction measures, rather than all or nothing; and, as a final step, 4) legal action against people once deemed to be plain outlaws!

"Animation", inspired by more than just an awareness of raw inequalities, is a call to engage in and do justice for the long haul. It may well be a Canadian form of mass or broad-based community development and/or organizing. This qualifies as another urban ministry response. It is not the presence of mass media headlines that may grab our temporary sound-byte attention as much as it is a genuinely conscious-arousing and social-conscience-gripping phenomenon. To offer oneself willingly and at a level of focused attentiveness, the presence of prayer comes into play. Animation incorporates one's prayerful "awareness" and helps to sustain a long-term "animation" for the sake of "alternatives" (to poverty's inequalities and indignities), albeit oft with "anguish" in the frequently painful labours involved in the service of the prayed-for Reign of God.[22] Indeed, the Toronto CRC's origins illustrate just this in a later case study chapter in this thesis.

Sometimes the search for the lost chord may be a reflective call for a new way of being the church—a "new paradigm" as Valerie J. Stubbs described it in the 1990s:

> In searching for a sense of our role as church in urban ministries, we must recognize that we represent only a part of those who are seeking wholeness and justice community. We are not complete as ministries until we coalesce with others who are

---

21. See Sherman, *Restorers of Hope* and its illumining subtitle: *Reaching the Poor with Church-based Ministries that Work*, 226.

22. See Morris, *Engaging Urban Ministry* for the 4-a's of *availability, animating alternatives*, with *anguish*.

> seeking similar goals [...] This model of partnership includes a value assumption that we are learners as well as teachers, receivers as well as givers.[23]

Such a paradigm is being honored as urban ministries strive for a consistent integrity of purpose in their missions. Such is neither an easy, quick, nor sure accomplishment; an insecure, competitive territorialism prevails.

As an integrating concept to give a compelling and comprehensive urban ministry perspective, further conceptions of the "lost chord" have been issued. There are occasional manifestos or clarion calls for attention. I think of my own denomination's 1980s *A Dream Not the Drowsy* that encouraged thoughtful reflection on life in the city and our churches' responses or lack of responses to serious inequalities and indignities. And, from a United Church of Canada Energy from the Edges biennial event—sadly now on hold due to, again, alleged budget cuts—the following is a description of those who are trapped and desperate in their urban poverty situations:

> They are the people who received meagre social assistance, only to see that cut by 22 percent recently by the government, so that others more well off could get tax cuts. They are the people who went off welfare to go to school and then found themselves still unemployed and back on welfare with a huge student loan to pay. They are the people on welfare, who, if they do not declare other income, such as a student loan, face the risk of criminal charges and a lifetime ban from welfare. They are the people who, under house arrest and no income, decide that the only way out is suicide. They are the people who work for a minimum wage that is far below the poverty line. They are the people who sometimes need two or three jobs in order to make ends meet and then are criticized for not being there for their kids [...] Yes, these are the people we hold in our hearts as we work, on behalf of the church, to bring about justice.[24]

People caught in such enduring situations ache for due attention even as they long for human dignity: from cradle to grave, and all along the way of struggle. Such a catalogue of life conditions indicates the ground for the credo of urban or community ministries lest both the agents of ministry and their population base be neglected. Indeed, they are the people of and

---

23. Stubbs, "Toward a New Paradigm for Specialized Urban Ministry," no page.

24. Citing Hurtig, *Pay the Rent or Feed the Kids* with its subtitle purpose: *The Tragedy and Disgrace of Poverty*. Their quote is further credited to *People We Hold in Our Hearts*, November 2008, The United Church of Canada. no pages cited.

from the struggle, as alas, those urban ministries attending to these people struggle themselves to endure.²⁵

Venture of Crossovers and Hybrids

Sometimes the search for the master theme of the mission—the "lost chord"—extends to partnering situations once thought suspect if not impossible. They were suspect due to the secularization temptation, surviving at the risk and the price of losing the soul of one's ministry mission, especially when pursuing, accepting, and rationalizing public funding in order to survive. There have been, however, creative exceptions. Public schools' responses to poverty and crisis concerns provide partnering possibilities for neighboring churches. This was the case for the Longhouse Church when, fourteen years ago, a liaison worker for the Hastings Community School First Nations initiated a shared response by involving church and another First Nations' agency to offer local parents a chance to discuss their personal and family issues. Since then, a simple but profound sharing circle has developed that meets regularly, year-round—and has been extended to include formerly active parents and old and young singles.²⁶

The notion of "hybrid" or "crossover" expresses the need for enriched, long-term collaboration. Crossover is the title theme in *Crossover City: Resources for Urban Mission and Transformation*, an anthology from a British urban mission and theology group, helpfully edited by Andrew Harvey. One of them writes:

> How can we break open our silos? Who will help us? [. . .] When we have status, power and authority to lose, we hang on for dear life to our silos and our ring-fenced pastures, but when our lives are lived in total vulnerability, we graze where we can [. . .] there in the cross of Christ the ingredient that will enable us to come from our theological silos and enter into foreign territory [. . .]

---

25. See The Women's Collective of St. Columba House, *Hope is the Struggle*, 1–4.

26. A school principal in the city of Burnaby has shepherded his Edmonds Community School to respond to one-third of the school being refugee students and another half learning English as a second language. David Starr writes of the experience over the past four years: "'In some ways I came to Edmonds with almost as much to learn as my students' he says in *From Bombs to Books*. 'The level of commitment demanded of the staff is high; here emotional burnout is an occupational hazard. But for those who come, stay, and learn to love the students and the neighborhood, the rewards are extraordinary,'" Steffenhagen, " 'From Bombs to Books' indomitable spirit of ESL students inspired the principal to the write book," *Vancouver Sun*, November 19, 2011: A2. One wonders about the response of churches in the area of the Edmonds school.

the cross is what stands out at the very center of this endeavour to break out and live.²⁷

It is, indeed, such a willing and adventuresome spirit towards the vulnerable—one sure indicator of the meaning of the cross of Christ for institutions as well as leaders—that arouses traditional urban ministries to want to sustain a willing and adventuresome ministry and, when necessary, revised, if not hybrid, models of engaging ministry. In Vancouver, this includes First United Church; in Toronto, it includes the Christian Resource Centre; in Victoria, it includes Our Place Society; and in several other Canadian cities, it may soon come to include most of the once traditional, often historic, urban missions. Such endeavours are risky because a mission may lose its once solid identity and even funding base. These enterprises are adventuresome because, in the face of the institution's almost certain continuing decline and eventual death, what, pray tell, is there to lose, other than one's former secure identity in the service of a city or wider community aching for respect and a shared way of responding to raw needs?

"Hybridization" or a yoking of one's ministry with others is an extension or application of the meaning of crossover. It may mean the consistent move by what were once mainly church-supported urban missions to more of a shared funding with governments, foundations, public solicitations, and contract grants for particular pieces of work (as the *Restorers of Hope* book attests).²⁸ It may mean consistent moves to integrate boards of directors to include numerous non-church persons, and especially people from the corporate and financial world who can offer prestige or clout. It may mean the hiring of executive directors—sometimes called "superintendents of mission"—with lots of non-profit, large agency work, and with particular skill sets in fund-raising, public relation campaigns, leadership development, and perhaps some actual quasi-prophetic social justice and issue analysis experience. It may mean fewer church-appointed authorities at a mission—if even called that any longer—and more elected boards or governors from registered public societies (along the lines of community centres or registered charitable urban ministry organisations, such as Victoria's Our Place Society and Toronto's Christian Resource Centre).

There are risks to hybridization. What are the potential losses in the venture? Will an historic urban mission become only a social agency, hosting emergency shelters for the homeless—earnest disclaimers aside?²⁹ Will

---

27. Green, "'I Can't Go There,'" 11.

28. See Sherman, *Restorers of Hope*, 226.

29. First United Church states that it is a church *not a social agency* and it is *not running a shelter, but a refuge with an open-door policy*, Newsletter, November 18, 2011.

a faithful public-prophetic witness sustain an urban ministry through the thick and thin of constant funding struggles, and, hence, a struggle for basic survival? Can survival be achieved only by way of mergers, as so many once-mainstream churches have been doing in order to keep a semblance of a once-mainstream church presence? Might there be corollary insights for once mainstream missions from the evangelical stream of Christianity in its urban missions?

A single term or cluster of terms names a theological marker; it seeks to convey what an urban ministry aspires to and practices. Of all the concepts or images cited, this book commends the discipline virtues of hope and justice to be basic. The virtue of prayer is a third element which provides a check and balance grounding (as all three terms provide). Prayer is grounding since it provides the depth and inner discipline of preparation and readiness that the work of justice entails. Without such a prayerful—and indeed triadic—grounding, one could not likely be available at all or, when available, one could be prone to project one's current batch of frustrations or pent-up angers.[30] Herein then the search for the lost chord is manifest, even if short of perfection. Commonly, a chord has three notes, and in this aimed-for harmony, it images the core thrust of the triad for this book (even when a chord has two notes but the third is implied to complete its triad nature).

Inspiring, Sustaining and Renewing Themes

In the search for a compelling and defining urban ministry perspective, there arise indispensable concepts. These are thematic concepts that contend to be the dominant concern to express a hoped-for thrust of the urban ministry's practices. "Shalom," as described earlier, is one such offering. A prophet such as Jeremiah employs a biblically prophetic theme. With his own hindsight insights and with an empathy to those cut off from their very homeland of Israel, he expresses that in the health or welfare of the cities in which the addressed captives-in-exile find themselves, is also their own shalom (Jeremiah 29:7). Shalom is a mission statement goal of the Longhouse ministry in Vancouver and many other ministries.[31] Shalom stretches

---

http://www.firstunited.ca/; (italics added).

30. See Merton, "Contemplation in a World of Action," 172–79.

31. Thus, see the Longhouse Ministry, which Villafane and Gornik's volumes of urban ministry reflections and sub-titles illustrate, respectively: *Seek the Peace of the City: Reflections on Urban Ministry* and *To Live in Peace: Biblical Faith and the Changing*

to cover many urban ministry variables from emergency care to social service programs, advocacy, co-operation or collaboration with others, within faith communities and across disciplines. It also again attests to the social justice summons. This is again an inherent part of Jeremiah's prophetic passions, especially the affirming: "(. . .) for in these things I take delight [. . .] I act with steadfast love, justice, and righteousness in the earth [. . .]" (9:23–24). Yet for all the dense power that the theme of shalom conveys, can any one theme provide the critical check-and-balance perspective necessary to sustain a steadfastly faithful and prophetic urban ministry? Shalom could correct a charity-based and benevolence-orientated ministry with the self-critical depth of its prophetic roots while acknowledging the immediate need for charity responses to poverty. Nonetheless, a deep and comprehensive perspective is sorely needed as poverty persists and worsens, and with it, a pervasive cynicism. Generations of sociologists and anthropologists have spoken of what it takes for poverty to be honestly redressed. Charles Valentine's *Culture and Poverty: Critique and Counter Proposals* (1968) stated that, above all, that the poor have a need and right to be consulted in advance of political/economic decisions on the very concerns that affect their lives and living conditions. As well, they have a need and right to be present when such life-condition decisions are being made as well a need and right to be present when the decisions are being implemented. This remains a far-reaching order as these proposals tax the patience of seasonally benevolent bureaucrats whose tolerance, once challenged, tends to be short-lived.

One thinks of the University of Winnipeg social ethics professor emeritus, John Badertscher, who proffers an iconic analysis to stimulate a more creative engagement with city issues and images of a more dramatic form than what he termed an otherwise "banal" interpretation through the once dominant Chicago schools of urban sociology depiction that had influenced him. Badertscher's remarks include:

> I came to the conclusion that we live in a post-civil (post-city in the true sense) era by studying what cities have been, and by taking Aristotle's *Politics* seriously [. . .] criteria for an iconic analysis of the city include: sustainability, along with a presence of genuine community/hospitality; justice or common good; beauty or environmental harmony; and, faith/hope contending death's power to want the last word. I also propose a series of questions: who holds power? What happens to the poor? How is waste disposed of? What kind of art is encouraged? And, last

---

Inner City.

CHAPTER 3—URBAN MINISTRY DYNAMICS AND TRIAD INTIMATIONS   49

but not least, which "gods" are worshipped and what sacrifices are required? [32]

One wonders if there exists any level or part of the church attending to such an iconic analysis—given the discipline or skill set needed to probe and to endure. Vancouver's First United Church's 2010 Winter Olympics' "share the gold" image strategy expressed a small aspect of an iconic approach to urban life's dramatic aches. It was a call for social housing supporters to pledge funds to the church's emergency shelter by identifying the donations as a win-win endeavour. However, this was an effort to practice public relations rather than challenge the Olympics' inequitable repercussions—including false promises to the district's poor.

In understanding the "desire" to search for the lost or new chord, one could draw respectively from John Caputo and Wendy Farley. They conjure this root theme of desire; that which both beckons and nourishes. Caputo rhetorically affirms:

> Suppose we imagine God [. . .] as the heart of a heartless world? Suppose we think of God not so much in terms of everything we desire, which seems a little acquisitive, but in terms of everything that desires us, everything that draws us out of ourselves and calls upon us, calling from below being to what is beyond, that summons up what is best in us that asks us to go out from our creaturely way of being and live generously, to live and love, to live and let live, to love and let love, to live by loving, unconditionally? [33]

There is also again, Farley's emphasis on desire as a supplementary resource (and her closing insight for discerning the reality of an animating contrast-awareness).

---

32. Badertscher, in Morris, *Engaging Urban Ministry*, Appendix C-3. Speaking of "the gods" being worshipped, see Linda McQuaig's "Restraint for everything but sports: Canada spends $6 billion for Olympics but budget holds line on health and education." Cf. Marsha Lederman's "This Vancouver Isn't in the Brochures," R4 citing Artist Isabelle Hayeur: "I've been shocked by what I could see in the downtown eastside—like most of the people who see it, I guess. I wondered how this was possible in a rich country" adding, "(*Fire with Fire*; a four storey building video installation which simulates a building on fire) expresses something of the Downtown Eastside that was before the games. [. . .] Nevertheless, since the Olympics tend to increase gentrification, social inequalities and censure, there is currently a special need for critical views." Finally, see Trothen, *Winning the Race?* And its illumining subtitle *Religion, Hope, and Reshaping the Sport Enhancement Debate*.

33. Caputo, *The Weakness of God*, 36.

> Far from leading us away from the pain (desire) leads us through the demon-haunted wilderness that blocks us from the courage to love the world, to feel compassion for its aches, and to delight in its beauty [. . .] We are not reconciled to life as it is given to us: [. . .] Our actual experience and our capacities for understanding or satisfaction remain achingly incommensurate. *Desire resides in this gap.*[34]

The importance of desire lies in naming what it means to prayerfully access the animating presence of God—akin to Micah's question: what does the Lord require of us? Desire helps to name that which arouses an urban ministry's faithful, just response to the gaps related to social inequalities and indignities. Later, we will depict what has led urban ministries and their arising networks to engage city challenges and to adopt and adapt justice-based community organizing models that attend to an energy-aroused desire that fuels the move from the "world as it is," to the "world as it ought to be."

Triad, Critical Responses and Hopeful Realism

To re-emphasize, the professed triad pursues the following questions in the hope of being faithful to and in a public and prophetic witness. When the pursuit of justice in urban ministry is thwarted, blocked, wearied of, and/or supplanted by charity alone, for what should and can we hope? How does praying for justice affirm and animate a faithful urban ministry? What is the theological grounding for the conjunctive interplay of this triad?

To recall, justice has taken a back burner in many urban ministries. Along with the reality of "compassion fatigue," there are secondly the complexities of what justice analysis and advocacy means and what a steadfast, faithful, public, and prophetic witnessing entails. A third related consideration is the long-haul discipline that the work of justice summons and requires and possible resistance to this discipline—akin to an "opposition defiance disorder"—which could be a reaction. In the face of mere token nods to the need for justice advocacy and organizing,[35] a fourth factor is

---

34. Farley, The *Wounding and Healing of Desire*, xviii, 2; (italics added).

35. E.g. see McCourt's "Homelessness: System Does Not Prepare Youth in Care for Eventualities of Adult Life on Their Own"C5, where a recent survey the Vancouver Foundation conducted across the Province of BC notes a "reluctance within the community to provide appropriate resources and support for young people aging out of care (only 29% listed support funding safe, affordable housing as a way to prevent homelessness)."

CHAPTER 3—URBAN MINISTRY DYNAMICS AND TRIAD INTIMATIONS

the willingness to risk changes and the dedicated courage to do so because changes can be exceedingly unpopular and are often unsupported by even one's own sources of ministry legitimacy (even in the short-term). Union Seminary's current Reinhold Niebuhr Professor of Social Ethics, Gary Dorrien, cites the virtual father of the American social gospel, Walter Rauschenbusch:

> (. . .) because changes can be fiercely unpopular all of us working in and through religious organizations on behalf of social justice causes, this is necessarily a time of retrenchment and rearguard battles. But it is also a time of bold faith and hope. Unlike the social gospelers, we have no illusions of being carried along by a tide of cultural progress. For us history must be about struggle, not progressing in and through religious 'approximation' of a just social order: 'The Kingdom of God is always but coming. But every approximation to it is worthwhile.'[36]

While no set of triad terms, however much qualified, attains perfection, we again point to these Dorrien-like notes of encouragement "to do justice, love kindness and walk humbly with thy God" (Micah 6:8) nevertheless for the long haul. Herein, the theological triad of *hoping justice prayerfully* illumines urban ministry dynamics by providing a marking framework or container. Justice is basic as the apex to the triad; it is a rendering of what it means to be faithful to God's reign (again, Micah 6:8, with Amos 5:24 and Jeremiah 9:23). Justice thus provides an interpretive and imperative marker in the call to covenant partners—God and humans—to practice a faithful public witness in urban ministries. The longing for and witness to hope is basic, as long as it means not a quick-fix or expedient shortcut, but an attentive, active waiting with help from the helpmates required for the witness and work of hope for these tasks. Hope thus provides an interpretive and sustaining marker in the inclusive vision that restlessly aches from anguish at the sheer inequalities of the present in the practice of an urban ministry's faithful, public witness.

As the usually shared Lord's Prayer is earnestly prayed, it is a "Thy Kingdom Come" prayer together with accompanying petitions. These petitions resource the New(er) Testament's classic tension of the "already" presence of the Kingdom and the "not-yet" of its absence though hoped-for arrival and realisation—similar to later elaborations of Niebuhr's grace-based serenity prayer. The public and personal nature of the Jesus prayer provides a marker and anchorage for what a being faithful public witness

---

36. Dorrien, "Society as the Subject of Redemption." Cf. similarly titled essay and approximate content in Dorrien, *Economy, Difference, Empire*, 3–28, especially p. 19.

in urban ministry means. There is a volunteered willingness to be present to begin again or anew in the awesome engagement of urban ministry endeavours in all of its ever-present forces and dynamics. All three triad terms assist. They prayerfully empower urban ministry practitioners to "stand their ground."[37] The triad terms assist to the significant extent that prayer is a resistance to the powers that otherwise bear down upon, stifle, and grind if not destroy the life of the poor and sinned against in the cities. The triad assists to the extent that hope, like peace, "stabs inexorably in the flesh of every unfulfilled present"[38] and to the extent that, by way of the triad's horizon, justice longs to kiss peace (the imagery of Psalm 85) and God's home is with humans everlastingly (Revelations 21). With illumination, the triad of prayer, hope, and justice nurtures a faithful, public, and prophetic witness in urban ministry. This book argues that a sound theology of the integral, interactive, or conjunctive relationship of prayer, justice, and hope illumines and addresses the challenges facing urban ministries.

Summary

A hopeful realism affirms the need for an honest admission of limits so as to curtail or minimize a naïve optimism which assumes that prayer—especially apart from the hard work of analysis and trial and error—might suffice for any and all situations. Realism does not dismiss prayer as a hopeful mode and level of attending to the situations of ministry in the city. However, such situations invite and require due research, exploration, risk or adventure, and holding the tensions of life in general and the ministry in particular in a creative, vital balance. Such a balance is not one of convenience or one that justifies one's ministry as in a balanced set of accounts and keeping it right with the Federal Government in terms of annual income tax reporting and, in Canada's case, keeping within the very narrow bounds of only being allowed to engage in advocacy to a limit of 10% of one's time and, to boot, only to alleviate conditions of inequality and indignity but not "allowed" to prevent such, lest the ministry's eligibility be jeopardized.[39] A hopeful realism provides a vital balance that is rooted in such prayers as time-tested and

---

37. Cf. "Chief Stands Her Ground" was the front page headline when Chief Marilyn Baptiste challenged the New Prosperity Mine proposal with the Tsilhquot government regarding First Nation territory at Fish Lake, BC, the same day that several urban core groups, including Streams of Justice, stood their ground in Vancouver against the demolition of buildings for condo construction instead of social housing, *Vancouver Sun*, November 29, 2011, p. A1.

38. See Moltmann, *Theology of Hope*, 21–22.

39. See Vandergrift, "CRA Audits," 10.

CHAPTER 3—URBAN MINISTRY DYNAMICS AND TRIAD INTIMATIONS   53

diversely exercised as this book's oft-evoked grace-based serenity prayer. Such prayers are vital and hence resourceful so that indeed a ministry can accept, at least temporarily, what cannot be changed; so that there is the exercise of courage to change the things or conditions that ought to be changed (as well as adventured so they can be); and so that, all along the way, there be a willingness and wisdom to discern—and ask for and practice the humility—for the wisdom to distinguish the one from the other.

We now move to ground the virtue terms of the above triad. We will thus explore further urban ministry/theology literature on hoping justice prayerfully, examining three key theologians' convictions, and devoting a following chapter to the chief actors in some social justice and urban ministry networks complementary to Vancouver's Longhouse Ministry. This book proposes that praying justice hopefully is what animates, nourishes, and critiques a faithful, public, and prophetic witness in urban ministry. All together, this conjunctive provides the framework and content for how hopeful realism, in turn, provides steadfastness. Haikus expressed:

> *Immersed forwards/Ministry anguishes backwards/Pray hopeful justice [. . .]* And, on the other hand: *Hope surfaces horizons / Justice currents animate/ Prayer dives deeply.*

Chapter 4—Hope via Moltmann and Urban Ministry Intimations

The depressing truth is that despite all of our achievements, the twentieth century was possibly the bloodiest in human history so any notion we are getting better is not entirely tuned into reality. Maybe God has to tell us where to go so often because we repeatedly head in the wrong direction. If we truly want to participate in the movement of God in the world, we have to start by acknowledging the world as it is, broken as well as beautiful [. . .] Finding God's horizon and walking toward it is a spiritual practice that requires willing and persevering feet.[1]

Introduction

THERE IS A WELCOME abundance of writers, not only theologians or urban ministers, who reflect on the virtue and discipline of hope. However, the contemporary theologian who I believe has researched and reflected the most deeply on hope is Jürgen Moltmann. Like the voluminous writing and legacy of Niebuhr and Merton, Moltmann provides compelling testimony to resource the long haul of ministry in the city. He does this by way of the autobiographical writings and related anniversary reflections, sermons, several inter-disciplinary and inter-faith endeavors, and prayers. This is further assisted by helpful biographical reflections.[2] One noted student and colleague of Moltmann, offers this perspective:

---

1. Shroyer, *The Boundary-Breaking God* and its illumining subtitle *An Unfolding Story of Hope and Promise*, 11–12.

2. Cf., Meeks, *Origins of the Theology of Hope*; Bauckham, *God will Be All in All* with its instructive subtitle: *The Eschatology of Jürgen Moltmann*, and Althouse, "In Appreciation of Jürgen Moltmann," 21–32.

CHAPTER 4—HOPE VIA MOLTMANN AND URBAN MINISTRY INTIMATIONS   55

As a result of the theology of hope all theologies may be able to find a new locus of praxis. It will be between the mission to which all Christians are called and the churches, which despite their patent lack of 'orthopraxis,' have their identity alone through their faithful witness to their commissioning to this mission. For some time modern theology has known that it had to live with one foot in the church and one foot in modern society. With the 'dialectic of reconciliation' this delicate balancing feat is historically possible.³

To be sure, Moltmann has his critics. A representative critic is Flora Keshgegian who questions Moltmann's emphasis on eschatology as if there is an actual "end" to it all. She calls instead for a combination of spiritual and cultural practices—ranging from Buddhist to First Nations to one's own autobiographical reflections—to revise or at least complement a futuristic focus of hope. She emphasizes the remembrance of one another's sufferings in and through shared struggles thus: "Faith and hope together engender solidarity and enable ongoing struggle. To speak of God's power as mighty is to proclaim that the divine is on the side of life, but not to talk of victories or final triumphs, or of goodness being realized fully."⁴ Pressed for clarifications, she elaborates: "Moltmann and I would differ especially on the notion of resolution at the end—that is, everything is resolved at the end of time, in eternity. I think there is suffering that is never resolved and that the need for resolution makes it more difficult for us to live with the ambiguities and contradictions in life. My definition of hope is life ongoing."⁵ The following summary narration of Moltmann's theology implicitly acknowledges Keshgegian's critique.

Moltmann's Theology toward Hope

To summarize the challenge of hope in Moltmann's several volumes of essays, sermons, prayers and memoirs, it could be expressed that hope is a beckoning and energizing horizon of inclusive concern. Hope is a given of God's grace, an indicative grounded in God's ever-present and widening impact—where, as philosophers profess, God is that Being or Circle whose "center is everywhere and whose circumference is nowhere."⁶ As an impera-

3. Meeks, *Origins of the Theology of Hope*, 163.
4. Keshgegian, *Redeeming Memories*, 235; cf. her *Time for Hope*, 164–66: "Non/Sense of an Ending" for implicit criticisms of Moltmann.
5. Personal e-mail communication of June 9th, 2009 ((used with permission)).
6. See Voltaire citing Timaeus of Locris, via http://blog.onbeing.org/

tive, hope is the goad of a promised future that both stabs inexorably into the unfulfilled present and interferes with what otherwise would happen predictably or fatefully—and all this in the service of redeeming and fulfilling the longings of creation: that God be all, in all. Put otherwise, and fueled with justice longings, God is all, to all, in all (I Cor. 15:28). The perspective and virtue, discipline of hope, as it accompanies the traditional theological virtues of faith and love, evokes and provokes or animates life out of death and liberation out of oppression. This animation occurs by ever born-anew covenanters. As with Thomas Merton, we are willingly opened and rendered available to begin again in prayer, and indeed, a prayer informed or for prepared justice. Elaborating on the associations of hope with the Christ event, Moltmann shares why it was that *The Crucified God*, the second of a trilogy, came to follow the *Theology of Hope*:

> It was during an international Theology of Hope conference of 500 theologians at Duke University at the beginning of April 1968 that Martin Luther King was shot in Memphis (on 6 April); and it was then I that I came to arrive at the idea that my next book should be on the theology of the cross [. . .] Without the *memoria passionis Christi*—the memory of Christ's passion— there is no Christian *meditatio vitae futurae*—no meditation on a future life; and conversely, without hope for the coming of Christ, the remembrance of Christ loses it power.[7]

Such an affirmation typically expresses Moltmann's grounding in biblical theology and his vocational dedication to extending this theology's cardinal confessions and applications to politics, economics, ecology and a theological integration of them all. It is what rouses one to desire integration—it is that which accompanies and, even if only temporarily, satisfies urban ministry agents who hunger for the sustenance of a faithful public and prophetic witness. What is integrated is all that Moltmann draws from and reflects on—as well as what animating networks he associates with to draw from and reflect on. Such networks included his life partner, his local and ecumenical church communities, and a talented assemblage of mentors, allies, and constructive critics who make up the nodes of any significant and enduring network. This contribution of networking—as connecting nodes—is what we have noted so far and continue to look for in this book.

---

post/29501612837/god-is-a-circle-whose-center-is-everywhere- and sometimes attributed to Augustine, because similarly expressed by him in his *Confessions*.

7. Moltmann, *A Broad Place*, 103.

What Brought Moltmann to Hope

Moltmann exemplifies how people are drawn to embrace and reflect on hope. As a young captured WW II German soldier, he was taken to two camps, the first in Scotland and the second in England. Full of despair and tinged with a gnawing guilt over his country's role in the war and especially the concentration/extermination camps, Moltmann felt overwhelmed by the hospitality of visiting neighbors whose respectful treatment of him conveyed a plain, graceful neighborliness. Moltmann attests:

> In Feb. 1945, I was taken prisoner by the British, and had more than three years to think about the horrors of war I had gone through, and the German crimes against humanity in Auschwitz [. . .] I needed what the Heidelberg Catechism calls 'comfort in life and death', and through the chance reading of the Bible and the undeserved kindness of Scottish and English Christians, I *found the comfort in the Christ who in his passion became my brother in need, and through his resurrection from the dead, awakened in me too to a living hope.* [8]

In subsequent decades, Moltmann felt moved to embrace and reflect upon the whole multi-dimensional theme of hope—thereby illustrating that more than a fad or footnote, hope is a disciplined effort over a life-time. Such themes haunted Moltmann. However he experienced a paradoxical gift in imprisonment for there he felt free (freed up) to contemplate and make changes in his life—choosing resources and companions who would challenge him for the rest of his life. He continues:

> (. . .) Christian faith began with a despairing search for God and a personal struggle with the dark sides of 'hidden face' of God. At the end of July 1943, as an air force auxiliary, I experienced the destruction of my home town Hamburg through the RAF's 'Operation Gomorrah', and barely survived the fire storm in which 40,000 people burnt to death [. . .] that night I cried out to God for the first time 'My God, where are you?'. And the question 'Why am I alive and not dead like the rest?' has haunted me ever since . . . . [9]

Not surprisingly, Moltmann refers to this core body of experience often, a virtual paradigm for him.[10] However, Moltmann's story is not so linear.

---

8. Moltmann, *Experiences in Theology*, 4. (italics added).

9. Ibid, 3–4.

10. These irresistible autobiographical reflections recur notably in *Source of Life*; *Experiences of God*; and, *In the End—the Beginning* with its illuminative subtitle *The*

In his earliest prisoner-of-war experience, while in Belgium, an American chaplain happened to give him a Bible and he began to read—initially out of boredom—the drama therein. The Scriptures appealed to his imagination, resonating deeply with his emotional need. Summarized by Michaud, a theological interpreter and early biographer of Moltmann:

> They (words of Scripture) opened his eyes to the God who is with the broken-hearted. Moltmann found the God who was present even behind the barbed wire. But whenever he tried to profess or grasp this experience of the presence of God, the experience evaded him. 'All that was left was an inward drive, a longing which provided the impetus to hope' (*Experiences of God*, 7). His inexpressible experiences led Moltmann to become interested in theology.

Michaud continues: "Fortunately he was allowed to study theology in a Protestant theologian's camp, Norton Camp—an educational camp run by the YMCA and supervised by the British army—near Nottingham in England. Since then, the experiences of the life of a prisoner have left a lasting mark on him: the suffering and the hope which reinforce each other."[11] With the war over—but its legacy existentially abiding, so that life could be lived differently—Moltmann's deeper studies, along with wider ecumenical travels and forums, combined science with theology and philosophy. He also enjoyed and sought to convey aspects of the seminal work of *the* philosopher of hope, Ernest Bloch.[12] Bloch's writings, bordering on esoteric or neo-Marxism, stressed biblical themes of imagination, the future and principles of hope as borne by its virtually messianic human burden bearers in and out of suffering. It was Bloch who, as also a neighbor, especially helped Moltmann to articulate the perspective and discipline of hope.

Long-Haul Resources via Moltmann's Theology of Hope

Moltmann's studious embrace of the dialectic of the cross and the resurrection of Jesus as the Christ pervades his writings about hope. While his

---

Life of Hope; also in reminiscences with contemporaries, see Moltmann in *How I Have Changed* with its apt subtitle: *Reflections on Thirty Years of Theology*; and, again *A Broad Place.*.

11. Michaud with Hyung-Kon Kim, "Jürgen Moltmann", 1–2, (italics added).

12. With Moltmann's *A Broad Place* and its Bloch references and acknowledgments, see Cox, "The Pull of the Future" as representative of Bloch's leavening influence, 191–203.

1965 *Theology of Hope* drew on the social and eschatological meaning of the resurrection, his subsequent *The Crucified God* named the Cross as the very content of what was raised in the resurrection. Moltmann's retrieval of what led him to the Cross, in *The Crucified God*, is an important profession of faith.

> I had long been preoccupied with a theology of the cross, before the theology of hope. I had come to the Christian faith in God through fellowship with the assailed Jesus [. . .] the traditional interpretation of sin, sacrifice, and grace did not reach into the depths of my experiences of death. I was still unliberated [. . .] When I was 17, I experienced not just suffering but also annihilation [. . .] and without any apparent reason [. . .] the eclipse of God descended on my world, and the dark night of the soul took hold of my heart and destroyed my spirit [. . .] When I began to take the history of Jesus' crucifixion seriously in a personal sense, I had to read of Golgotha, the darkness of Good Friday, and Jesus' dark night of the soul together with my own annihilating experience [. . .] that took me to the theology of the cross.[13]

The crucifixion-resurrection tension takes on poignancy in this light-amid-the-darkness discernment, akin to novelist and theologian Chaim Potok's credo, from the holocaust-influenced *The Condition of Jewish Belief* that "I would rather discover light in the darkness, than to extend darkness to where there is now light."[14] Helpfully, for any student of his thought, Moltmann continued to press by way of his autobiography the origins, development, revision, and—pertinent to this urban ministry book's focus—applications of his understanding hope.[15]

As with Niebuhr and Merton, Moltmann draws on many resources for his theological reflections. These include: biblical sources and studies; Jewish sources, studies and concepts (as Shekinah and Sabbath); ecology which is itself inter-disciplinary and social-ethical; theological doctrines

---

13 Moltmann, *A Broad Place*, 189–90.

14. In *The Condition of Jewish Belief; A Symposium*, compiled by the Editors of Commentary Magazine.

15. See Moltmann further: "Preliminary work for *The Crucified God* can already be found in the *Theology of Hope* of 1964 [. . .] In 1989 I presented the book . . . before the theological faculty in Basel under the title [. . .] (God in the Cross of Jesus). In these years my theological interest shifted from the resurrection of the crucified Christ, and the horizon of hope which that throws open, to the cross of the risen Christ and the spaces of remembrance of the experience of absolute death. *The Crucified God* was intended to be the other side of "the God of hope," *A Broad Place*, 192.

(especially the Trinity); his own and others' historical and current experiences (from Bonhoeffer to his contemporaries[16], particularly as related to their steadfast sense of injustices and indignities); and not least, polemical and dialogical engagements with many thinkers. The latter makes a read of his footnotes a worthy endeavor. Moltmann is as much a biblically ecumenical and inter-faith theologian as he is a systematic and constructive thinker. Throughout his sources and networks, Moltmann continues to engage the virtue and discipline of hope. He conveys a biblical witness to hope and draws on the biblical parables as a witness to and experiment in hope, all in anticipation of "the pull" within and from God's future.

Hoping Justice Prayerfully Intimations and Urban Ministry Implications

Hoping (for) *justice prayerfully* attempts, conjunctively, to postulates that there cannot be any contentment unless there is peace, with justice for all and, and there cannot be rest until peace with justice is complete or fulfilled.[17] To change the order emphasis of the triad, *praying (for) justice hopefully* stresses the necessary persistence of a faithful witness, that the long-haul bearing of witness to God's reign be real and respectfully peaceful, and that reconciliation comes to include victims *and* persecutors. Re-ordering the triad terms yet again, *just prayer hopefully* acknowledges the temptations of self-righteousness and cynicism. There are the realities of judging others unduly and out of one's own harshly projected insecurities, and on the other hand, being humbly present in ministry work, and through the work of prayer, clearing space for one's own and others' contributions. One must also include the work of reconciliation, which is never a small, short-cut, or once-and-for-all feat. As a check-and-balance relationship, prayer needs the analytical and vigilant work of justice just as justice needs the patient and multi-layered perspective of prayer. One of Moltmann's significant influences, Dietrich Bonhoeffer, (with the indispensable help of his life-long friend, Eberhard Bethge) dialectically expresses it thus:

> Righteous action (aka: 'doing of the just') among people saves prayer from becoming an escape into self-satisfied piety. Prayer saves righteous action among people from self-righteousness.

---

16. There are eighteen references to Bonhoeffer in Moltmann's *A Broad Place* and several in *On Human Dignity* with its instructive subtitle *Political Theology and Ethics*.

17. Cf. again, Hammarskjöld, *Markings,* 35 and: "Forward! Whatever distance I have covered, it does not give me the right to halt. Forward! It is the attention given to the last steps before the summit which decides the value of all that went before," 145.

> Righteous action saves prayer from the hypocrisy among the pious which the children of the world will never fail to spot. Prayer saves righteous action from the fanatical ideologizing through which those are who are committed to change become bad representatives of their own commitment. Righteous action saves prayer from pessimism. Prayer saves righteous action from resignation. Action keeps prayer in the realm of reality; prayer keeps action within the realm of truth.[18]

Moltmann is also indebted to the helpmate of fellowships, with their mentoring, sustaining, renewing, cajoling, and check-and-balance reference groups' contributions. In *Hope for the Church: Moltmann in dialogue with Practical Theology*, the whole sacrament of baptism is evoked, with the emphasis of baptism being an enlistment for life-long discipling—akin to Doug John Hall's understanding of the disciple as a life-long-learner term in his trilogy. M. Douglas Meeks' introduction to this volume thus summarizes:

> If the church is to be an advance guard of the kingdom for which Jesus called, baptism will have to be a sign of enlistment rather than automatically being associated with birth, family and tradition. It should be a matter of conscious commitment to a life of discipleship in a community under the lordship of Christ. This can be symbolized and expressed, claims Moltmann, only by a 'baptism into Christian calling' [. . .] a baptism that celebrates the faith and discipline both of the community and of the one baptized.[19]

Finally, it is crucial to read and grasp Moltmann on the whole justice theme, which can never be divorced, if comprehensive, from the content of hope:

> All that grows on the foundation of injustice is organized peacelessness. So unjust systems have feet of clay. They have no lasting development. The hidden presence in world history of the divine justice in God's spirit 'destabilizes' [. . .] human systems of injustice, and sees to it that they cannot last [. . .] the fellowship of the Holy Spirit is also the antitype of the human communities which are built up on injustice and violence . . . .[20]

---

18. See Wartenberg-Potter, *We Will not Hang our Harps on the Willows*, citing Bethge, 31; original in Bethge's *Prayer and Righteous Action*, 26–27.

19. Meeks' introduction to *Hope for the Church*, 19.

20. Moltmann, *The Spirit of Life*, 143.

Mindful of this tension of peacelessness and injustice, the discipline of hope looks for ways by justice may be engaged and practiced—rather than slipping into and remaining trapped in isolating despair. Hope needs the work of justice. Prayer is one of the animating helpmates—perhaps, the key helpmate—for this earnest search; all along the way, and including for emphasis, alluded before: "Thy Kingdom come, Thy will be done."

There are further Moltmann-inspired urban ministry implications. Urban ministries struggle, in hope, to practice a faithful public witness rooted in love and aspiring steadfastly for justice. One imagines some of the early Christian gatherings and movements, as attested in Luke and Paul's writings, thinking similarly to contemporary people and engaged in mass-based community organizing. Eventually, they would be likely to proclaim that "we are people of—and from—the struggle."[21] Prayer assists this endeavor by being present in the struggle in and out of season, with thankfulness for the seasons of the church year. Indeed, the penitential seasons of both Advent and Lent arouse the shared feelings of anticipation and, again, animate movements toward the incoming reign of God, even though we humans impede if not resist these arrivals of God's reign. Moltmann's consistently honed check-and-balance interplay of the cross and resurrection grounds urban ministry struggles in a hope for justice, with the peaceful presence of prayer as an advocating helpmate—enabling us, time and again, to 'begin again'.

Moltmann offers deep biblical teachings for urban ministry practitioners, professional and lay, from out of the koinonia community of shared experiences, rooted in the hoping-justice-prayerfully triad. Characteristically biblical, these teachings are rooted in the two significant core events or paradigms of the Exodus and Christ event. Therein the promises of the past, like throbbing emotions, hurl themselves forward into a new transcendent act.[22] Moltmann thus reflects:

> Just as the Exodus event opens Israel's history with God, so the event of Christ's death and resurrection opens up the history with God of the fellowship of Christians among the nations. There (Exodus) God's power is liberation from a historical

---

21. Though likely a common expression in social justice struggles, I retrieved it from a Public Broadcastings Video on the work of Saul Alinsky and community organizing in East Brooklyn, N.Y. "The Democratic Promise: Saul Alinsky and His Legacy" by Hercules and Orenstein.

22. See Whitehead's *Adventures of Ideas*, 177, and on transcendence as overshooting the confines of established discourse, see Marcuse's *One-Dimensional Man*, xi, n. 1 and his concluding affirmation, citing Walter Benjamin: "'It is only for the sake of those without hope that hope is given to us,'" 257.

tyrant; here (Christ event) it is liberation from the tyranny of the power of death in history. There the Exodus leads into the promised land of liberty . . . Here the event which opens history and throws open the future [. . .] is made present in Christ's feasts, so that believers can live 'in' the Christ who has died 'for them' and has risen ahead of them.[23]

As with Merton, so with Moltmann arises the desire to combine justice with the prayer theme in his life, teachings, writings, and legacy. In a recent reflection, *In the End—The Beginning: The Life of Hope,* Moltmann prophetically cautions while pastorally encouraging urban ministries who are in for the long haul. "All despair presupposed hope. The pain of despair lies in the fact that hope exists, but that there appears no way for the hope to be fulfilled. Where hope for life is frustrated in every respect, the hope turns against the hoper and eats into him." In this same passage, such insight may well touch communities of faith—certainly as urban ministries feel commissioned to practice a ministry of both empathy and sympathy and to manifest an accompanying patience with the sinned against and thus despairing. Completing the above, Moltmann attests to the prophetic task that accompanies the pastoral and priestly roles:

> There are conditions in history which are in obvious contradiction to the kingdom of God and his righteousness and these we have to fight against. But there are also conditions which are in accord with the kingdom of God, and these we have to promote [. . .] We shall then have parables of the coming kingdom now, in the present, and shall already anticipate today which will come about on the day of God [. . .] We can call this an action in creative expectation, just as during Advent we prepare for Christmas and, with the children, live in expectation of the feast . . . .[24]

This theological credo heralds and carries comforting and challenging words of hope. But little comfort that comes easily or quickly. One thinks of the testimony of Rev. Al who has reflected on a frequent discouragement during early morning street patrols and other errands of mercy during his ministry with Victoria, B.C.'s Our Place Society (and now with the Victoria's Dandelion Society):

> The gospel for me has helped me discern that prayer is my spiritual muscle, and the more I engage in it, the braver I become in

---

23. Moltmann, *Experiences in Theology,* 36.
24. Moltmann, *In the End—the Beginning of Hope,* 94, 92.

asking the age-old question: where in the hell are you, God, in all of this? And as I ask the question, I bury another of his children, the night before holding them in my arms in the hospital as they took their last breath. The encounter profoundly placed me in the middle of my prayer. Prayer for me is not easy. It's not result-oriented. Rather, prayer for me engages me in that which I fear the most, facing God with empty hands.[25]

One also thinks of the *Vigils for the Silenced*, and what that motley ecumenical group of us in greater Vancouver musters the will to offer during the Advent and Lent (church seasons of the year). Contemplatively, these penitential seasons readily lend themselves to public as well as personal meditation and reflection. These vigils began out of a shared despair. Despair with the political authorities in power and with the fact that many people were indeed experiencing being shut out, shut down, and plainly, "shut up"! Previous recourse to appeals—via meaningful tribunals capable of actually hearing one's cry for help—were cut back and cut down. Legal Aid was similarly cut back and cut down.[26] Our representative church bodies or denominations, alas, had also slowly cut back and cut down. To boot, our otherwise specialized, designated ministries to engage the various issues stemming from inequalities and indignities on multiple levels, had also been cut back or cut down. Now, for the most part, they have been limited to mere charity levels of response—though thankfully, in some cases, serious advocacy help is still available. All of us desperately need divine patience.

Advent is a penitential season of both judgment and grace, dependent as we intuit ourselves to be—and consent to be—on God's in-breaking Grace. I think of the depth of grace that a Moltmann draws attention to, particularly in his sermons and prayers. In one of Moltmann's accounts, we read:

> Where the rebirth of the whole of life is as Advently near as Jesus proclaimed it to be, then the chains begin to hurt. We can no longer come to terms with them. We begin to rub ourselves raw on them until they break. 'The crime on the streets is not the worst of it,' said a friend in New York. 'What is far worse is that one gradually gets used to it.' If redemption is close at hand, we

---

25. E-mail communication, June 10, 2008, (used with permission).

26. Legal Aid cuts remain and duly vigiled/challenged for their negative impact on accessing and asserting one's rights; as M.G. Cohen & D. Martinson's "Who's the Judge: Reform is needed to the Supreme Court appointment process to ensure minorities and women are represented," *Vancouver Sun*, Oct. 22, 2012, A9.

stop being accustomed to evil; the habit of mind that accepts it is broken.[27]

Summary

We may induce from Moltmann (at least) the following for urban ministries: 1) he gives grounding content to the ingredients of hope, including intimations about those who engage in the exercise of hope;[28] 2) he seeks to arouse conscientiousness by alerting us to those contradictions in life that impact the poor or the oppressed and creation itself (and the inter-relational dimensions of those not poor, not oppressed, remaining aloof from creation's cries);[29] 3) he retrieves for fresh consideration and application significant biblical and other core, paradigmatic events that can inspire and guide urban ministry practices (and as with Merton, be ever renewed);[30] and, 4) he evokes a synergy with others in parables of hope rooted in and roused by political and liberation theologies. This synergy extends to Marxist humanists and bold secular thinkers and muckrakers, Pentecostal kindred colleagues, and ecologists straining for a hopeful future; all of these

---

27. Moltmann, *The Source of Life*, 73–74; Moltmann also evokes by means of the dialectic of the cross and resurrection tensions, the presence of Golgotha in the Manger. In "The Liberation of the Future", he expresses that "Life and action in anticipation of God's future is like life and action in the Advent that leads up to Christmas. It is a life in the community of Christ following the guidelines of his Sermon on the Mount. As in the peace movement of 1979–1981, this means that 'peace is possible' in the midst of a time when missiles are being stationed in a mutual threat of universal annihilation. It also means: righteousness that redeems, puts to rights, creates justice . . . . " 286.

28. See also Anderson, *Walking the Way,* 130–33. Cf. McCarroll's *The End of Hope—The Beginning*, which is Moltmann-influenced and devotes important space for grounding hope and discerning its agencies, 28–33 and helpful literature review on hope, 17–50.

29. For Moltmann's creation/ecology writings, see *God in Creation* and on the point of creation's contradictions and cries for liberation, 12, 16, 34, 39–40, 59, 103, passim; cf. the role of suffering with hope in *The Source of Life*, 119–20.

30. Insufficient attention has been drawn to Moltmann's closing guidelines and recommendations to the church and urban ministries in his foundational works in theology; therefore, see the closing sections of *Theology of Hope*, op. cit, the "kindling of live hopes" thrust prefacing "The Calling of Christians in Society," 328–38; *The Crucified God*, "Vicious Circles of Death" and "Ways toward Liberation," 329–38; and *The Church in the Power of the Spirit*, "Double Strategies and the Community Principle," 326–36, and "The Marks of the Church," 337–61; especially: "Unity in freedom, holiness in poverty, catholicity in partisan support for the weak, and apostolate in suffering are the marks by which (the church) is known in the world," 361.

partnerships—as with his life-partner Elisabeth—demonstrate a faithful public and prophetic witness for the long haul.[31]

It is said that hope is less an absolute than it is relative. Hope is relative to what it needs for its fulfillment and all along the way, what it needs to accompany its journey. Among many, Tinder and Lynch profess thus that the discipline of hope needs and welcomes what these helpmates offer. As a preface and link to what follows in Niebuhr on justice and Merton on contemplative prayer, we concur thus: that hope needs helpers to "hop" or adventure from restlessness, aroused and animated by contrast-awareness experiences, to draw on all that which grounds hope and pulls its goals.[32]

Finally, given all of the raw and empathetic experiences of Moltmann's life, hope is twinned with realism. Recall that Moltmann embraced hope and stayed with it out of a life of personal suffering, guilt, and encounters with evil (what Frankl depicts as logotherapy's "tragic triad" [33]) as well as subsequent ministry, teaching, writing, and copious networking. From the outset, he has reflected on hope needing to be realistic lest it lapse into wishful thinking or thinking of hope apart from its necessary spiritual helpmates. From *Theology of Hope* Moltmann thus attests:

> Hope alone is to be called 'realistic', because it alone takes seriously the possibilities with which all reality is fraught. It does not take things as they happen to stand or to lie, but as progressing, moving things with possibilities of change [. . .] the despair which imagines it has reached the end of its tether proves to be illusory, as long as nothing has come to an end but everything is still full of possibilities [. . .] the world is not a fixed body of facts but a network of paths and processes [. . .] it is a realm in which necessity means the possible, but not the unalterable.[34]

Hope seasoned with realism—realism grounded in and energized by hope—need the grounding complement of justice which we will now explore.

---

31. Among their other writings, see Moltmann and Moltmann-Wendel's *Passion for God* with its apt subtitle: *Theology in Two Voices*.

32. For the insight of hope being a relative term needing helpmates thus, again see Tinder, *The Fabric of Hope* and Lynch, *Images of Hope*, and for the "hop" in hope, see Norris, *Acedia and Me*.

33. Frankl, *Man's Search for Meaning*, 161.

34. Moltmann, *Jürgen Moltmann Collected Readings*, 16.

Chapter 5—Justice via Niebuhr and Urban Ministry Intimations

... (T)he successes of the modern state now pose challenges to its authority, as businesses, cultural movements, and scientific inquiries cross borders in ways that render laws governing employment and wages, education, intellectual property, and biomedical experimentation largely ineffective [. . .] And Christians, as always, will not settle for realism without hope. Without a dialectic between love and justice [. . .] realism might become an apology for order. Without a dialectic between the diversity of human goods and the unit of the human person, realism might accept general prosperity as a reasonable substitute for the common good. These are mistakes that modern societies have made locally in the past. It may now be possible to repeat them on a global scale [. . .] (P)rudent realists will [. . .] keep a sharp eye out for the return of old problems that have been consigned to oblivion. (Meanwhile) people on the margins of society often [. . .] claim a justice that is closer to divine love [. . .] they sustain hope by an appeal to God, precisely because no power within the framework of justice in their society can deliver the justice they seek.[1]

Introduction

JUSTICE IS AT THE heart of urban ministry endeavors; it grounds, informs, and critiques a faithful, public, *and* prophetic witness. Justice is thus the *apex* of the triad of praying justice hopefully disciplines.[2] Accordingly,

---

1. Lovin, *Christian Realism and the New Realities*, 82–83, 68–69.
2. I thank (Professor) Bruce Alexander for this apt way of naming the significant location of justice as the *apex* in the triangular nature of the triad. Personal

Reinhold Niebuhr and his theology of justice merit the most detailed elaboration in this chapter. The life and work of Thomas Merton will then be introduced to exemplify the discipline of prayer, and the life as has work of Jürgen Moltmann will be introduced to express what hope could mean in the context of urban ministry as has the life and work of Moltmann in the last chapter.

Each theologian grounds and offers a focused reflection on one of the triad's terms. Each discipline requires practice so as to be available when needed and yet is not discussed in definite detail. Merton underscores this lack of detail as he affirms that discipline is less about finding and making maps than it is "to sharpen our own sense of direction so that when we really get going we can travel without maps."[3]

There is much literature available that one could consult on the virtues and discipline of justice, prayer and hope. Such literature is noted in other chapters and in several of the annotated footnotes of this chapter. However, it is upon the life-long witness and reflections of Niebuhr, Merton and, Moltmann that this writing seeks to draw. To be sure, each theologian offers insights into all three themes: Niebuhr relates to prayer and hope; Merton relates to hope and justice; and Moltmann relates to justice and prayer. While studying the triad components in these three theologians' lives and thought, we will also be searching for an operative perspective for urban ministry that includes a mission purpose, strategies for pursuing this, and a presence of evaluative, self-critical checks and balances. Our analyses will afford guidelines for creative living amid the tensions of charity and justice, and despair and hope, in a life of vitally balanced prayer and social action. Also, we will note the indispensable networks that each theologian—especially in their public and prophetic witnessing—used to animate their ideas and enable the depth used in their teaching and pastoral roles.

Niebuhr's work in relation to justice has had critics. Among them have been the very Professorships endowed in his Union Seminary name, including Larry Rasmussen who has creatively moved beyond Niebuhr to give due attention to an inclusive justice or ecology and a sense of earth ethics; the current Union Niebuhr professor who writes prolifically of the history of social ethics and a need for renewing economic thrusts, Gary Dorrien; and the late Beverly Wildung Harrison.[4] A generation ago she wrote of the

---

communication, Sept. 18, 2013.

3. Merton, *Contemplation in a World of Action*, 126–27. He adds that while spiritual life is not complicated it is difficult; see *Through the Year with Thomas Merton*, Oct. 8th entry, cited from *The Sign of Jonah*, no page.

4. See Rasmussen, *Earth Community Earth Ethics*; Dorrien, *Economy, Difference, Empire*; and, Harrison, *Making the Connection*, "The Antiradical Legacy of Social

need to critique Niebuhr on his time-bound lack of feminism[5] and the need to challenge a perceived hard-line realism of Niebuhr and his "school" by retrieving the socialist impulse of the early Niebuhr (and adding feminist tones). In addition to one of the earlier liberation theologians, Rubem Alves and a Canadian social gospel veteran, Brewster Kneen, caution that realism could become an entrenched ideology of the establishment[6] (though when realism is twinned with "virtue ethics" such as justice and compassion, it indeed nourishes and sustains justice seekers).[7] Finally, the criticism by Nicolas Wolsterstorff should be noted.[8] He maintains that Niebuhr was too harsh in grounding his theology of justice chiefly in sin so that justice is thought of as conflict rather than caring. These criticisms of Niebuhr are implicitly acknowledged and incorporated in what follows.

Niebuhr's Understanding and Implications of Justice

Justice, for Niebuhr, is rooted in love and regulated by the strategic principles of freedom, equality and order. His autobiographical reflections and the witness of his students and critics attest to a consistent interplay of love and justice. Love commands and informs the meaning and content of justice. Sometimes love negates the outcomes of justice, especially if the means used are less than loving (as when the poor or prisoners of war are unrepresented

---

Theory Used in Social Ethics: Reinhold Niebuhr," 58–63 and later, *Justice in the Making*, "Working with Protestant Traditions: Liberalism and Beyond" 79–84, and "Critiquing Christian Realism," 178–82. Canadian social ethicist Marilyn Legge's contributions to the latter volume are germane to urban ministry theology needs and the thesis triad. In her "Ongoing Vision for Justice in the Making" she posits: "Hope is grown in the soils of struggle for non-violent relations [. . .] Movements of hope persist because they tend the roots of healing and justice," 223. Kuile's *The Virtues of a Christian Realist* further redresses the feminist critique of Niebuhr's realism; see her Chapter 3.5 "Critiques of Niebuhr's Framework of Theological Anthropology" as well as Chapter 4 "From Niebuhr's Realism to Christian Realist Virtue Ethics."

5. This has been gently critiqued if not refuted by another feminist, Aurelia Takacs Fule. See her "Being Human before God: Reinhold Niebuhr in Feminist Mirrors" in *The Reinhold Niebuhr Centenary Symposium*, McGill University, Sept. 27, 1992 published in *Reinhold Niebuhr [1892–1971]: A Centenary Appraisal*, 55–78..

6. Alves, "Christian Realism: Ideology of the Establishment,"173–76 and Kneen's *Journey of an Unrepentant Socialist*, 55–59.

7. See Kuile's important work where there is a timely combination of virtue ethics with realism in the service of social justice ministries and, for the long haul; *The Virtues of a Christian Realist*, especially her conclusion, 269–80.

8. See Wolsterstorff, "Love & Justice" Lang Lectures. Also his "Niebuhr's Non-classical Agapism" in *Justice in Love*, 71–72.

before the Courts, even if and when they do get to Court!). Niebuhr writes that through the medium of grace, which engages and redeems sin, love perseveringly moves to assuage the relentless longings of justice. Justice consists of and is balanced with order such that the chaos of anarchy and the tyranny of arbitrariness are minimized if not prevented. Justice is creatively and dynamically regulated by the principles of equality and liberty. It is also held and practiced in tension for the sake of a socially just order. A "loyalty to covenants"—core commitments that may be both secular and spiritual—is also discussed by Niebuhr in the service of these principles.[9] The pursuit and practice of justice is assisted by the helpmates of forbearance, humility and compassionate concern. Concreteness is another helpmate, which sharpens the focus of injustices and evokes the cry for justice.

The work of justice is renewed by prayer and sustained by hope. As earlier noted, all three elements of *hoping justice prayerfully* form a conjunctive triad. As later noted, any two ingredients without the third ingredient are inadequate to faithfully and steadfastly bear a public and prophetic witness in an urban (or any) ministry. Niebuhr's life illustrates all of the above. His theology for justice is as much an account of his thought in all of its dense richness as it is a compelling witness of his actual pastoral-prophetic ministry and public and intellectual life. This also includes a deep accompaniment of his life-partner's tireless support and understanding, Ursula Niebuhr; she was his advisor, family caretaker and resource for ideas and book themes.[10] With his due emphasis on justice, Niebuhr and his legacy fuel and resource the working triad of this book. Such a legacy is possible also because of the rich nodes of Niebuhr's circle of friendships and social justice fellowships and their accompanying journals that illustrate the animating energy and steadfastness that those networking friendships provide. These friendships and fellowships fueled networks and provided forums to Niebuhr to help him to reflect and write, publish and engage in social and political activities—all the while teaching, preaching and organizing (or lending a hand if not finances for organizing).

---

9. Niebuhr affirms "loyalty to covenants" along with equality, liberty, and order, all rooted in and operative by virtually the same spirit of love and spirit of justice in at least "Augustine's Political Realism," *Christian Realism and Political Problems*, 135.

10. Niebuhr belatedly acknowledges Ursula's intimate role in his life and thoughts, especially in his last memoir, *Man's Nature and His Communities* (see dedication and opening reflections and note below).

Love Is Not Enough: What Brought Niebuhr to Justice

Leaves from the Notebook of a Tamed Cynic[11] describes how, through Niebuhr's life and relationships as a pastor in Detroit, he came to undertake a lasting mandate for justice. *Leaves* grounded virtually all his lifetime of preaching, speaking, lecturing publishing, organizing, as well as his tireless support of issues and people of renown in difficult situations. These people include Paul Tillich and Dietrich Bonhoeffer, for whom he spearheaded sponsorships to come to the Union Seminary in New York during the German Nazi era. *Leaves* bristles with realism, yet always with hope.

A prime influence on theology, Niebuhr's major contribution was the theological realization that, given the awesome power of collective sin, love on its own was not sufficient for serious and sustaining justice work— though justice needs love as love needs justice. Love may well be enough for pastoral care, inter-personal relations, and—as it is a core theological virtue—for mature living. But given the presence of sin, love is not, on its own, enough to analyze and address such injustices as those related to racial, labor, gender, class, climate, inter-faith, domestic, and international political issues.[12] This realistic awareness was a forerunner to the later "Christian realism" perspective of engaging a social justice mandate. It avoided the extremes of an easy optimism and a bitter cynicism; it was rooted in the biblical prophetic witness. It was mediated and accompanied by Niebuhr's mentors, among whom was the Jewish social justice activist, lawyer, and philanthropist, Fred Butzel. Niebuhr later reflected that he "was in many ways the most remarkable man I have ever encountered, either before or since."[13] Complementing his *Leaves* references, Niebuhr shares further that Butzel was the "uncrowned king of the Jewish community", and "from him I learned . . . co-operation across a religious line . . . the very great resources that the Jewish community has in their passion for practical justice." Indeed,

---

11. *Leaves from the Notebook of a Tamed Cynic*, passim.

12. See Niebuhr's classical statement of "The Kingdom of God and the Struggle for Justice" in *Human Destiny*, Ch. IX, Vol. II; also Davis and Good, *Reinhold Niebuhr on Politics*, passim.

13. Cited in Fox, *Reinhold Niebuhr*, 92. Fox adds: "Butzel was the first Jew Niebuhr knew intimately; from that time on Niebuhr constantly celebrated 'the very great resources that the Jewish community has in their passion for practical justice.' He rarely came across a Protestant equivalent of Butzel: unsentimental, unpretentious, benevolently tough-minded, gifted with practical wisdom" ibid, p. 93; cf. *Leaves from the Notebook of a Tamed Cynic*, 187–88.

Butzel was "a rather curiously cynical man—that is, realistic to the point of cynicism—and yet with a great heart and compassion."[14]

An event which deeply affected Niebuhr was the loss of a dear friend, Episcopalian Bishop, Charles Williams. In *Leaves*, Niebuhr grieves while illumining this mentor's enduring personal and analytical influence:

> Nowhere have I seen a personality more luminous with the Christ spirit than in this bishop who was also a prophet [. . .] His fearless protagonism of the cause of democracy in industry won him the respect and love of the workers of the city as no other churchman possessed it [. . .] But society resists every effort to bring its processes under ethical restraint so stubbornly that one must finally be satisfied with preserving one's moral integrity in a necessary and yet futile struggle [. . .] The bishop did not change Detroit industry, but if the church ever becomes a real agency of the kingdom of God in an industrial civilization, his voice, though he is dead, will be in its counsels.[15]

Such mentors are clues as to how Niebuhr found the wisdom to discern and the courage to advocate and stay with the practice of such principles for justice as equality, liberty and order. Equality was the first such operative norm, and this Niebuhr perceived to be basic to address—and once unionized, to redress—the working aspirations of Ford Motor Plant workers. Union organizers came to Detroit and made use of Niebuhr's Bethel Evangelical Church on Sunday evenings although not without ecclesiastical tensions and criticism. According to Niebuhr, these meetings explored "the fundamental themes and problems of life," a process "worth more than many sermons."[16] Equality was also the clear goal of inter-racial relations in Detroit. Niebuhr became involved in committees and commissions to try to engage and redress racial tensions. Indeed, along with the Emergency Committee for Strikers Relief of 1926, he chaired both the Detroit Pastor's Union and the Industrial Committee of the Detroit Council of Churches. He was also appointed the vice-chair of the Mayor's Interracial Committee in 1925. Perhaps, such efforts were realistically felt to be too little, and in any case, too weak to be genuinely effective. But Niebuhr affirmed that justice requires a lot of hard, prolonged effort, and organizing power. It takes more than mere committee work and pronouncements. Valuably, Niebuhr's biographer Fox reports:

---

14. Niebuhr, *The Reminiscences of Reinhold Niebuhr*, 23.
15. *Leaves*, 72, 73.
16. Ibid, 145, 111.

(The Mayor's Interracial Committee) report, 'The Negro in Detroit', came out in March, 1927—Niebuhr summarizes the problems faced: "'Black Detroiters faced: overcrowded housing, usurious rents, refusal of white neighborhoods or the banks to countenance moves beyond the Negro district, police 'severity', not to say brutality', exclusion of black women from factory work and of all blacks from certain professions such as high school teaching, failure of white churches to assist black congregations even of their own denominations.' Reading the report filled (Niebuhr) 'with a feeling of despair.'[17]

Long Haul Resources for What Kept Niebuhr Committed to Justice

To grasp Niebuhr's steadfastness in social justice endeavors, it is vital to consider the following characteristics and ingredients of his work. These show how any ministry committed to justice work over the long haul must establish several critical-constructive resources to sustain its efforts. They include: 1) resisting the temptation to use charity or benevolence to mask (if not avoid all together) the need for justice; 2) recognizing in community organizing, the need for a balance of power in justice-making and justice-keeping; 3) recognizing the place and role of mentors; 4) discerning the place and role of solid, self-critical fellowships or reference groups; and, 5) living with the tensions of ministry and social justice struggles through the tenure of one's ministry vocation.

If only a single element of Niebuhr's theology could be highlighted, the basic distinction of charity from justice would qualify. Love is a basic command and it is a critical leaven to understanding and applying justice; however, love can deteriorate into a mere sentimental, occasional gesture of charity. Here, Niebuhr was consistent from the earliest *Leaves* to his last theological book-length publication: *Man's Nature and His Communities*. This mid-career selection from *Self and Dramas of History* captures the distinction:

> (L)ove in its purest form may not be as immediately relevant as either equality or liberty to the issue of establishing justice within the structures and traditions of community [. . .] Love may easily be corrupted, so that a powerful man will use benevolence in personal relations as a substitute of granting justice

17. Fox, op cit, 93–94; cf. Niebuhr, *Leaves,* 143–44 and Bingham, *Courage to Change,* 157–160.

in the basic organization of life [. . .] he displays his power with his goodness while justice challenges his power as incompatible with goodness. These facts are withheld from the wise but they are known by the 'simple', particularly if they should be the victims of the 'benevolence' of the powerful.[18]

A second central factor sustaining Niebuhr's biblically-grounded social justice struggles arises from his early development of a social ethic. The realism of more than loving kindness was needed—more was needed than the mere application of the instruments of reason and good will. A mature or true love requires the instruments of justice making. This concept is akin to St. Augustine's dictum that "charity is no substitute for justice withheld."[19] To attain actual structures of justice, effective strategies are needed. Thus, for justice to have even a modest chance, steadfastly serious planning and organizing is necessary, lest charity remain the substitute, default position.

The organization of power from below to match entrenched power from on high requires the painstaking, adventuresome, and fearless details of organizing. Years after Niebuhr's writings, Saul David Alinsky would take the indispensable witness of Niebuhr's writings—along with the trial and errors of John Lewis, the key organizer for the United Mineworkers about whom Alinsky wrote—to extend union-organizing goals, principles, strategies, and tactics into mass or broad-based community organizing efforts. As Niebuhr learned from his Detroit mentors and the then-failed efforts of the American Federation of Labor to organize the semi-skilled auto workers, so we learn from our mentors. For both, John F. Kennedy's insight that "experience is that name which we give to our mistakes" was crucial. Niebuhr's and Alinsky's legacies of resources have thrust themselves upon the willing and eager seeker. The need for mass-based community organizing endures (see Chapter 7).

Thirdly, Niebuhr drew not only on individual mentors but also on the fellowships of like-minded activists to sustain long-haul commitments to social justice advocacy and organizing. This strategy remained crucial from the beginning of his Detroit ministry. These various fellowships (or networks) have been duly noted in the literature on Niebuhr, especially by his historians and on-going biographers. Representatively, John Hutchinson's

---

18. Niebuhr, *Self & Dramas of History*, 186; cf. *Moral Man & Immoral Society*, 80–81 and *Beyond Tragedy*, 186–87.

19. See Niebuhr's "double love commandment" sermon wherein the need for strategies and structures of justice is implied and certainly affirmed. See No. 3 of the *Reinhold Niebuhr Audio Tape Collection*. Augustine's dictum is cited in Sidney J. Harris' *A Majority of One* (Boston: Houghton Mifflin, 1957), 283.

edited anthology of *Christian Faith and Social Action*[20] states that it is difficult to grasp the import of Niebuhr's influence and indispensable support apart from these fellowships. Niebuhr's biographers and commentators have described the following historical periods of fellowship development and transition: the origins and roles of the 1930s Fellowship of Socialist Christians and its later 1940s Frontier Fellowship (and their networking journal *Radical Religion*); and the 1950s Christian Action group (and its networking organ, *Christianity and Society*). There was also the instrumental role that the *Christianity and Crisis* (C & C) Niebuhr-and-circle journal came to play, as a challenge to the established *Christian Century*, from the 1940s to its unfortunate closure in the 1990s.[21] It was through these fellowships and publications that a socialist revisionism took place. Such revisionism was expressed in self-critical moves from a Marxist-grounded socialist optimism (or, utopianism) to a more cautious and refined democratic socialism—or, with more modesty, social democracy—and currently the enduring perspective of Christian realism.[22]

Some Niebuhr interpreters may be inclined to downplay the role of these mentors and their fellowships, instead choosing to emphasize the more individual nature and even the "heroic" stature of Niebuhr, especially in his academic and political roles and activities. This assessment would, however, be a mistake. He complemented academic affairs and general political actions with organizing networks of support out of Union Seminary to the likes of the East Harlem Protestant Parish which, in turn, inspired the founding of the Toronto Christian Resource Centre. Throughout, Niebuhr was able to attain his public reputation and stay the course of his public career due to the support of peers, colleagues, dedicated students, and many others. An important source of support included his mother in his Detroit pastorate who helped enable much of Niebuhr's extra-curricular and extra-parish involvements and again, his wife and virtual collaborator, Ursula Niebuhr.[23] We note Ursula's steadfast and creative influences from

20. Hutchinson, ed. *Christian Faith & Social Action*, passim.

21. See Hulsether's *Building a Protestant Left: Christianity & Crisis Magazine, 1941–1993*. See especially his narration of Christian realism motifs, 11–23, 263–71. See Fox, *Reinhold Niebuhr*, 196 on C & C's challenge to the *Christian Century*. Finally, Hutchison, "Two Decades of Social Christianity," 1–22.

22. In addition to chapter 1's references on realism, see Niebuhr's reflections in *On Man's Nature & His Communities*; Lovin, *Reinhold Niebuhr and Christian Realism* and as a more general overview, Ottati, *Hopeful Realism*. Also see Fawkes' *"There is a Power not Ourselves, That makes for Righteousness" Tommy Douglas*, 34–36 on Christian realism.

23. See Ursula Niebuhr's edited collection of life letters in *Remembering Reinhold Niebuhr* and former students' recollections, representatively Stone's *Professor Reinhold*

references to her in any of a number of acknowledgements and prefaces to Niebuhr's books, essays and prayers.[24] One biographer wrote of Niebuhr's steadfast support from his mother for actual parish and household duties as exemplifying a "new kind of monasticism" since he was freed for a dedicated ministry unencumbered by family obligations or demands.[25]

There is finally, Niebuhr's living with the tensions. Hope-and-realism's tensions are uppermost in this book's theme. Niebuhr's thought deepened, to continue the practice of prayer in his vocational offerings and, with the perspective of hope, to sustain a steadfast public and prophetic witness, all the while dealing with fierce and unresolved tensions. Out of the likely stresses and strains of an often frenetic life, there followed a serious stroke in the early 1950s, and he was basically sidelined for the rest of his life. Nonetheless, he soon wrote *The Self & the Drama of History*.[26] Niebuhr provided encouraging resources by living with and through such tensions—attested in yet another reflection near to the end of his life.[27] It is his life example that demonstrates how the justice-hope-prayer triad is so basic and sustaining for a steadfast urban ministry—if one component is absent little of a vital balance occurs. Thus, if justice were without prayer, then a critical imbalance would occur opening the doors to self-righteousness. If justice exists in an urban ministry without hope, would there be a mature trust that this life has an ultimate meaning? As Niebuhr professed: "No possible historic justice is sufferable without the Christian hope."[28] Even if prayer and justice are present but hope is absent—to the extent humanly possible—could there be a trustworthy framework of meaning for us to endure, short of the right to expect fulfillment in our lifetime for our efforts? Without hope, and " . . . without the 'grace' of love (the leavening ground and aim of justice), justice always degenerates into something less than justice."[29]

Niebuhr and Hall's *Remembered Voices,* especially chapter 3, "Reinhold Niebuhr: An American Theology of the Tragic and Beyond" and his organized Centenary event on Niebuhr at McGill in 1992. Along with the Niebuhr Society's occasional and annual American Academy of Religion meetings' presentations/ publications, see Rice, *Reinhold Niebuhr and His Circle of Influence* which focuses on higher profile intellectual "friends."

24. In addition to *Justice & Mercy*'s selected, edited sermons and prayers by Ursula Niebuhr, there is Reinhold's due "Dedication" and "Autobiographical Introduction" in *Man's Nature & His Communities,* 25–27.

25. See Fox, *Reinhold Niebuhr,* 87.

26. Niebuhr, *The Self & Dramas of History.*.

27. See Niebuhr, "View from the Sidelines."

28. Niebuhr, *Love & Justice,* 29.

29. *Ibid,* 28.

Again, what brought Niebuhr to his dedication to justice and kept him there? Surely, his early pastoral experience did, with all the trials, errors, and consequent insights. He was moved to intensely engage the issues, and, with sustaining breadth, to relate to what it takes to practice the biblically prophetic mandate of doing justice. He reflected:

> (T)hat you might have to force a powerful factor in the community by a counter-weighing power did not occur to me. The element of power was not considered at all, because the persistence of individual and collective self-interest was simply not considered. As I saw this sprawling industry, the moral pretensions in it, and the rather feeble little moralistic sermons that I preached, I was quite overwhelmed by the erroneousness of the whole show.[30]

That Niebuhr was willing to partake of the witness of his mentors[31] was a sustaining encouragement and vital part of his legacy to students and practitioners in the social ethics and urban ministry fields. Niebuhr sought to link the biblical drama to the dramas of history and his time. He had a keen sense that a faithful, public, and prophetic witness required a combined discipline of worshipping faith communities and particular fellowships to serve the role of mutual support but also, a self-critiquing—even repentant—reference group. Niebuhr's presentation of the Gifford lectures amid WW II bombings in the United Kingdom provided a mature and thoughtful justice perspective. Mature, in that Niebuhr emphasized that justice draws on prayerful hope for its nourishment as much as justice draws on hope for its resurrection content. Niebuhr drew on St. Paul to profess "that God may be all in all"—and like a Dag Hammarskjöld, to affirm that peace needs justice (if it is to last), and there cannot be peace with justice unless it is for all with "no rest until all has been fulfilled."[32]

---

30. Niebuhr, *The Reminiscences of Reinhold Niebuhr*, 27; cf. Anderson, "The Thought of Reinhold Niebuhr the Twilight of Modernity in Canada" in *Reinhold Niebuhr [1892-1971]*, 14: "'Niebuhr's criticism of inequalities—racial and economic—never ceased.'" For Niebuhr's astute and classic distinctions of the individual and collective levels of reality and forced options on the latter's less, and even lack of, morality, see *Moral Man and Immoral Society*, xxxi and Gilkey's sharp introduction in the Westminster John Knox 2001 edition.

31. Niebuhr's biographers note the influence of mentors as do anthologies of letters and his circle of friends. Also his "Intellectual Autobiography," 3-7. Finally, see again Rice, *Reinhold Niebuhr and His Circle of Influence*.

32. I Cor. 15:28; cf. Romans 8:22-26 and Hammarskjöld, *Markings*, 35.

Praying Justice Hopefully, Intimations, and Urban Ministry Implications

Niebuhr's theology of justice assists urban ministry reflection and practice. His theology has contributed to the love-justice relationship and dialectic; the reality of sin and what this means for collective, social life; the notion of "realism" and the tendency of charity measures to mask the need for justice as a redistribution of power; and the importance of fellowship or support groups for sustaining one's long-haul involvement. Niebuhr's theology is also important in its intimations for the full triad of hope, justice and, prayer, and summarily, the grace-based Serenity Prayer because of its engaging in action when the issues are still muddy.

The love-justice relationship assists urban ministries to extend biblical love commandments, from personal and interpersonal concerns to concerns for society and the Earth. Noted earlier, love is the motivating ground, force, and the norm that urban ministry strategies may employ to engage and redress conditions of inequality and indignity and accompanying class conflicts where there is fairness neither in process nor in outcome. Countering sentimentality, a mature love employs the virtue of justice and its strategies in contests of power. Niebuhr's regulative principles of liberty, equality and order as well as people's covenants of loyalty could be utilized in the organization of power among the poor or less powerful so as to match the already entrenched power of the most powerful. Otherwise, justice, as a balance of power, might well be ignored, suppressed, or naively rejected (on the assumption that love or charity is enough). These perspectives provide a long-haul maturity for a faithful, public, and prophetic witness not only by the organized church and/or its urban ministries but also by the government of the people at large. This affirmation merits elaboration as Niebuhr himself aptly provides. He discerns that mutual love informs and challenges the practice of justice to:

> (. . .) extend the sense of obligation towards the other a) from an immediately felt obligation, prompted by an obvious need, to a continued obligation in fixed principles of mutual support; b) from a simple relation between a self and one 'other' to the complex relations of the self and the 'others'; and, c) finally from the obligations, discerned by the individual self, to the wider obligations which the community defines from its more impartial perspective. [33]

---

33. *The Nature & Destiny of Man*, Vol. II, 248.

CHAPTER 5—JUSTICE VIA NIEBUHR AND URBAN MINISTRY INTIMATIONS   79

The pervasiveness of sin illumines a second urban ministry implication of Niebuhr's theology of justice. Justice is needed because love on its own—unless one understands justice as part of, as extension of a "true" or "mature" praxis of love[34]—is necessary but not sufficient in the collective and because a balance of power needs to be achieved. For justice to be approximated, relatively powerless people and institutions need to be organized to challenge and negotiate with an already well organized power on high. This is where Niebuhr's grasp of mutual love (or, brotherhood/sisterhood), distinct from love as mere charity, is compatible with the advocacy for justice. Community organizing takes the self-interests of already organized bodies—harnessing the self-interests of its members to join, and remain in place—uniting them across and into cross-class, multi-cultural, inter-faith, and organized labor alliances. My experience with the Longhouse Church's ministry illustrates this reality over twenty-plus years of merely attending to charity responses. To adopt the strategies of justice-making, so that justice is not withheld, our ministry decided to support (having been a founding contributor to) the Industrial Areas Foundation model of community organizing by way of the recently formed Metro Vancouver Alliance (MVA). This task and process has not been accomplished easily, quickly, or cheaply; such organizing entails an organization or institution's persistence, patience, and forbearance of ambiguities. It requires leadership training workshops, listening campaigns to discern common good issues with the wider alliance of organizations, and annual dues to provide and protect the relative autonomy of MVA. All this relates to Niebuhr's consistent notion of realism: that self-interests are stubbornly inherent in human behaviors especially in the collective spheres.[35] A serious manifestation of sin identified by Niebuhr, as above, is the use of charity to serve as a substitute for challenging power imbalances. It is easy for unjust practices, rooted in sin, and for inordinate power to conveniently hide behind the splash of generosity or an announced "good will" at Christmas charity time.

A third implication of Niebuhr's theology of justice is that there are fellowship groups that serve as reference groups or more than mere membership entities; they provide a check-and-balance support for the long haul of social justice involvements. Niebuhr's biographers and students speak of his "fellowships" as being key resources for aspects of Niebuhr's life,

---

34. I am indebted to Terry Anderson for insisting on this view of "true" love, that when/as mature or "true," inherently, intensively, and extensively love includes the discipline work of justice (via personal communications).

35. See Niebuhr's "Augustine's Political Realism" essay in *Christian Realism and Political Problems*, 119–46 as well as Lovin's recent writings, *Christian Realism and the New Realities*.

complementary to his pastoral and academia contributions. Mindful of the benefits of such groups, I have sought to organize or participate in the support of several similar fellowships and networks to help critically sustain the long-haul witness of justice and, sometimes, action campaigns.[36] Otherwise, short of actually suffering burnout, I would have been reduced, at best, to simply maintaining the status quo, though I had begun with earnest and prophetic intentions.

Fourthly, there are Niebuhr's theological contributions on justice—contributions that draw sustenance from the disciplines of prayer and hope. Otherwise, there may occur a despair that arises from undue isolation. Otherwise, efforts to be consistently realistic may well fall short of a just hope and deteriorate into a raw cynicism. To be nudged and encouraged to pray is to practice hope; that is hope as the future aspect of faith. Prayer is a response to the question of "why bother"—as new monasticism attests and proffers.[37] Hope encourages us to engage in and remain with a prayerful attending, with patience thus, for one's ministry and for our work towards God's justice. Niebuhr's lengthy Detroit pastorate affirmed his commitment to justice—encouraged by the support of his widowed mother and his mentors which enabled increased speaking, writing, and organizing activities. Of the ministers and ministerials that I network with, those who intentionally include intercessory prayer for one another and our wider spheres of involvement tend to go the deepest and widest in terms of discussion and support (one thinks further of Dietrich Bonhoeffer's *Life Together* chronicle[38]). Later urban network reflections will comment further on the resourcefulness of prayer for long-haul justice advocacy. Prayer—and particularly again Niebuhr's original and revised popular grace-based serenity

---

36. E.g., I have initiated and helped sustain until recently (due to moves, deaths and incapacities) an elders consultation group to elicit the shared wisdom of hindsight trials and errors in ministry; a founding member of the *Streams of Justice* network, elaborated in Ch. 7; co-founding the *Coalition for Migrant Workers Justice*; contributing to the steering committee of *A Community Aware* which sponsors quarterly forums on community issues; spearheading and maintaining the annual Advent and Lent *Vigils for the Silenced*; and again, co-founding the *Metro Vancouver Alliance* to bring to bear and try to apply the time-tested Industrial Areas model of broad-based community organizing.

37. Claiborne and Wilson-Hartgrove, *Becoming the Answer to Our Prayers*, passim.

38. See Bonhoeffer, *Life Together*, 85–87 on "intercession" and ministries of listening, helpfulness, and bearing, 97–103. A Vancouver East-End Ministerial meets monthly and opens its sessions with a triads grouping to name over the month both an encouraging and discouraging incident or memory and incorporates this for intercessory prayer, one to another.

CHAPTER 5—JUSTICE VIA NIEBUHR AND URBAN MINISTRY INTIMATIONS   81

prayer—is inextricably linked to justice, with both prayer and justice linked in the far-reaching horizon of hope's inclusiveness.[39]

Fifthly, then the "Serenity Prayer"[40] is a summary expression of Niebuhr's life and thought—a point stressed by many of his students.[41] His daughter, Elisabeth Sifton, called attention to the grace element and foundation in the origins of this prayer. She clarified, corrected, and completed the popular form of the prayer. It notably includes the first person "we" (not merely "me"), the "ought" imperative (not merely "can"), and crucially, "grace" as an indispensable grounding ingredient (along with serenity, courage, and wisdom).[42] This inclusion of grace comes as no surprise for Niebuhr students; justification by grace through faith was indispensable to his whole life and thought. This cannot be overemphasized. Thus:

> Justification by faith in the realm of justice means that we will not regard the pressures and counter pressures, the tensions, the overt and covert conflicts by which justice is achieved and maintained, as normative in the absolute sense; but neither will we ease our conscience by seeking to escape from involvement in them.[43]

The influence of the Serenity Prayer extends to twelve-step fellowships (of all varieties) for recovery from addictions, sharing and healing circles, opening and closing prayers for *Kairos* gatherings, and often overlooked, the prayer's pertinence and frequent use for social action events and processes. Along with other prayers of Niebuhr and those like them,[44] this grace-based serenity prayer includes and typifies a vital balance of ingredients that corrects tendencies to practice ministry in manners that are too shallow or too

---

39. See Pat McSherry's testimony on this critical relationship, arising in her intense involvement in her parish and the work of MVA, Chapter 7.

40. Again, the popular form (with the original in brackets via Sifton) is: "God, grant me (us) the (grace to accept with) serenity to accept the things I (we) cannot change; the courage to change the things I (we) can (ought to); and, the wisdom to know the difference (to distinguish the one from the other)." Sifton, *The Serenity Prayer*, 292–93.

41. See Hall, *The Future of the Church*, 79, with a due emphasis on grace as well, and Clarke, *Serenity, Courage, & Wisdom*.

42. Sifton, *The Serenity Prayer*, especially chapter VII.

43. Niebuhr, *Human Nature & Destiny*, II, 284.

44. Besides other Niebuhr prayers, as in *Justice & Mercy*, complementary and illustrative are the popular Prayer of St. Francis, "make me a channel of your peace"; Rob Johns' hymn prayer "In Suffering Love" with the line "Lord, to our hearts your joy commit, into our hands your pain" in *Songs of a Gospel People*, #53; and Rev. Juanita Austin's First United Church internship prayer within the "Hastings Street" hymn—to wit, "God take the anguish that we feel, transform it to a love that is real" [. . .] as well, the closing "heal us once again . . . ." in Morris et al., *The Word on the Street*, 121.

naïve. Nonetheless, the prayer mandates courage to participate in change processes.

Summary

Love without justice is too sentimental, and justice without love can be too legalistic or impersonal. Both love and justice, apart from hopeful realism, may be too limited in scope. The horizon of the reign of God's kingdom is never "just ours"! As imperfect as all the above influences and contributions of a Niebuhr and his theology really are, his influence in supportive fellowships and their practices of ministry or social witness networks in the city form working, nourishing, check-and-balance bonds. Such bonds are indispensable for the depth and range of ministries that seek to be a public *and* prophetic witness—that seeks to endure. And that endurance is the "rhythm of faith."[45]

---

45. See thus the sub-title of McNamee's *Endurance,* the author also of *Diary of a City Priest.*

Chapter 6—Prayer via Merton and Urban Ministry Intimations

> Ironically, until people have had some level of inner God experience, there is no point in asking them to follow the ethical ideals of Jesus. It is largely a waste of time. Indeed, they will not be able to even understand their meaning and purpose. Religious requirements become the source of deeper anxiety. Humans quite simply don't have the power to obey any spiritual law, especially issues like forgiveness of enemies, nonviolence, self-emptying, humble use of power, and so on, except in and through union with God. The Spirit in me awakens the only power that can obey the law or know its true purpose.[1]
> —Fr. Richard Rohr, Center for Action and Contemplation

OF THE MANY ONE could consult for a theology of prayer, I deem Thomas Merton to be fitting. He is fitting because of his dedicated life as a monastic, influencing connections to the "new monastics" noted in prior chapters and evidenced in networks like Vancouver's Streams of Justice. Merton offers abundant and various modes of writings (especially journals and letters); earnest and ruthless honesty; and not least, the urban ministry implications of his life, thought, and prayers. All this contributes to the previously noted *praying justice hopefully* triad in the service of compelling content for what it means to practice a hopeful realism.

To be sure, Merton is not without his critics. Chief among them is Ron Dart, a University of the Fraser Valley, B.C. political philosopher, scientist, and religious studies professor. Dart, a long-time member of the Thomas Merton Society, constructively criticizes the absence of a realism in Merton's social criticisms. There is an underestimation of the role of institutions or mediating structures between the plain individual and her or his critical, constructive participation in society. It takes more than mere pronouncements, even when prophetic and learned, to make deep, lasting reforms and

---

1. Rohr, *Things Hidden; Scripture as Spirituality*, 82, cited via cac.org.

curtail the dangers of militarism, racism, classism, sexism, ethnocentrism, climate crises, urban inequalities, genocide, and ecocide. He clarifies and elaborates further:

> It was difficult for Merton as a monk to move beyond prophetic protest—Ken Leech, for example, suggests that prophetic activism is as important as verbal protest. Merton could, obviously, not do street activism, although he inspired others to do so. The even more difficult task of being involved in the process of political parties as a political activist [. . .] (or) the actual engaged work of the prophet via political parties was not something that Merton could do—Merton did see the problems of institutions and their numbing of conscience and unjust activities (whether it was a corporation, military or the state—power elite), but he was limited in how he could challenge such goliaths as a monk.[2]

The following incorporates such a critique since Merton is employed not alone for his offering to what the triad of this thesis affirms as necessary—his resourcing the subject of prayer as a personal and corporate discipline in the service of a steadfast, faithful, public-prophetic witness in North American and other urban ministries.

Merton's Theology of Prayer

What is Merton's theology of prayer? It is at least a call for and means of compassion in the service of ministry at whatever levels of realism and struggle there are. "What we can gain from a theology of prayer is the capacity to experience contradictions and struggles and sufferings as sharing in the cross [. . .] as Christ suffering in us. This cannot be done without passion. A theology of prayer is going to have to be a passionate theology. . . ."[3] It is a constant invitation to pursue and live in vital balance. The vows of stability and conversion of manners of life—as well the traditionally named ones of poverty, chastity, and, obedience—provide a foundation for the kind of "container" Merton calls for in and out of a theology of prayer. He journals on the stability imperative:

---

2. E-mail communication to author, May 18 2013, Vancouver, B.C., (used with permission).

3. Merton's "Toward a Theology of Prayer," 192–93. From a personal and psychological viewpoint, Bruce Alexander characterizes "sharing in the cross" as a "chronic pain of the soul"; personal communication with author of Sept. 18 2013, Vancouver, B.C.

CHAPTER 6—PRAYER VIA MERTON AND URBAN MINISTRY INTIMATIONS 85

> Saint Benedict, like the Desert Fathers on whom he based his Rule, had a very realistic sense of human values. He introduced this vow into his Rule precisely because he knew that the limitations of the monk, and the limitations of the community he lived in, formed a part of God's plan for the sanctification of both individuals and of communities. By making a 'vow of stability' the monk renounces the vain hope of wandering off to find a 'perfect monastery'. This implies a deep act of faith. . .[4]

To read Merton on prayer and its contributing streams—anticipating its urban ministry implications—is to be reminded of those steadfast ministers or lay persons who persisted life-long and often in one place or with one ministry.[5] Currently, urban ministers tend to endure in their postings even though some are in considerable isolation and vulnerability, thus often marginalized. They come to feel less an actual fellowship-sharing or *koinonia* part of the faith community they represent and faithfully seek to serve (including the wider parish community beyond merely the church building and in-house programs). Merton's theology of prayer conveys an encouragement to live in the creative tensions of contemplation and action, which may well collapse or tempt one to short-cuts, a crucial weakness for urban ministries. There is a need for a framing container that a theology for prayer provides. This theology summons the urban minister to be a humble beginner in the art of both life and prayer, peace with justice and, a hope for all—ever again. Such a container seeks to integrate how prayer is often understood and interpreted in the various disciplines of theology and urban ministry practices. This yearning for an integration of prayer with the other vital disciplines of justice and hope will lead into the subsequent thesis chapter's interrogation and analysis of actual urban ministries.

With his own prayers, Merton's frequent reflections and correspondence on prayer elaborates on and complements Niebuhr's grace-grounded serenity prayer.

> All life tends to grow. . . in mystery inscaped with paradox and contradiction, yet centered, in its very heart, on the divine mercy [. . .] Without this gift (of the Holy Spirit) we would have no philosophy, for we could never experience such simplicity in the

---

4. Merton, *The Sign of Jonas*, 9–10.

5. One recalls Keith Whitney whose commitment, to the untimely end of his life (aneurysm), with Toronto, Ontario's Fred Victor Mission was marked by his willingness to stay the course, uncharacteristically at the time, to commit for the rest of one's working life. Such a practical "vow of stability," along with an accompanying "vow of conversation"—to commit to an on-going dialogue and soul searching—has inspired some of us in urban ministry to think of and commit to similar long-term involvements.

midst of contradiction. Without the grace of God there could be no unity, no simplicity in our lives: only contradiction. We can overlay the contradiction with statements and explanations, we can produce an illusory coherence, we can impose on life our intellectual systems and we can enforce upon our minds a certain strained and artificial peace. But this is not peace [...] The evil is in us all. It is the blindness from which we must pray with tears and anguish that we may be delivered. [...] Those who give up the struggle are themselves in turmoil and impose their turmoil on the human race. Those who continue to struggle are at peace. If God wills, they can pacify the world.[6]

Along with courage and wisdom, hopeful justice—or, a just hope—is affirmed. Such a container also realistically incorporates the recognition of sin. In his "Towards a Theology of Prayer" address, Merton observes that sin can move and even seduce us to want to hide from God, and hence from all of the obligations flowing out of that primal, covenantal relationship.[7]

Merton's work has affinities with Moltmann's theology for hope, and in particular the dialectic of the cross and resurrection, despair and hope, and how each shed light on the other. These creative tensions go a long way to resource a long-haul commitment to and in urban ministry where evidence of the Cross and its accompanying despair are regular, verifiable realities in the people being served, attended to, thought of, prayed for and of course, evident in us urban ministers. The eleven years of practicing Advent and Lent Vigils for the Silenced in urban core Vancouver attest to the necessity of honestly acknowledging despair and the hope, via Merton, that both are alike since both lead to a dependency on God.[8] Merton's theology for prayer is the gentle yet firm reminder that we are centered beings via prayer, and, when de-centered, we "pray to pray."[9] We pray as much out of gratitude as because we are asked or as we are commanded or obliged.[10]

6. Merton, "First and Last Thoughts" In *A Thomas Merton Reader revised edition*, ed. McDonnell, 17–18.

7. Merton, "Toward a Theology of Prayer," 198; he adds: "Job is someone who is in trouble, suffering, who dares to come close to God and challenge him on the issue rather than doing what we all do—as soon as we experience trouble and suffering we go and hide from God. This is the sign of original sin, this is what Adam did. As soon as he got into trouble he didn't pray—he hid."

8. See Merton, "A Letter on the Contemplative Life," ed. Hart, 221.

9. Merton, "One prays to pray," December 7th, entry in *A Year with Thomas Merton*, 357.

10. Both senses are combined in the Portuguese *obrigada/o Obrigado* for masculine, *obrigada* for feminine; both conveying feeling gratefully obliged for an act of unselfishness.

CHAPTER 6—PRAYER VIA MERTON AND URBAN MINISTRY INTIMATIONS 87

Prayer assists to open and present us to the occasion of the moment; it also renews us time and again, for the long haul. Time and again, Merton notes the basic importance of being "beginners"—for we are always but beginners.[11] Paraphrasing aspects of his reflections and relating them to both Moltmann and Niebuhr, prayer cautions us about frenzied activities that could issue in self-righteousness and/or burnout. Prayer critiques our penchant for taking short-cuts such as the quick fix of achieving justice without a patient, discerning, and, detailed analysis and courageous risk of doing or supporting the work of justice. Prayer can move, offer, and extend us into a wider vision—that horizon vision that Moltmann's theology of hope affirms and that Proverbs (29:18) speaks of, where without a vision, the people perish. When coupled with the wisdom of hindsight, prayer assists us to be cautious of some people's power vision, since from such a vision some people indeed have perished.[12] Prayer assists in questioning the temptation to continue practicing merely a Christmas and end-of-the-year charity or society-rewarding benevolence—understandably lured by the self-interest incentives of tax deductions—instead of a basic justice that beckons us into a vital balance with ourselves, with others, and in God (the triple love commandment).

Sometimes, prayer summons us to resist—to resist short-cuts or convenient means and measures that only serve to "save our skins" and avoid the kind and level of risks incurred in the service of the Kingdom. Rather, prayer serves to resist "the powers" that seduce us into thinking and acting as if they are really in charge or more subtly, that we are in charge![13] Not

---

11. See *Contemplative Prayer*, 37; cf., *New Seeds of Contemplation*, 237, and, *Contemplation in a World of Action*, 172–79. Also, a *Conjectures of a Guilty Bystander* entry: "Our destiny is to go on beyond everything, to leave everything, to press forward to the End and find in the End our Beginning, the very ever-new Beginning that has no End," *Through the Year with Thomas Merton*, August 29th

12. Cf. Proverbs 29:18, where there is no guidance (*if* trustworthy, as a caveat) a people falls. I pitched this notion of a wide rather than a tunnel vision to a Dec. 13, 2010, City Council Vision Vancouver-led special meeting, as #78 of the speakers, challenging the proposed budget cuts in the name of a greater "public or common good"— with a singular lack of "success"!

13. Particularly see Wink's trilogy on "The Powers," summarized in *The Powers That Be*, 1–36, 180–200; Stringfellow's *An Ethic for Christians and other Aliens in a Strange Land*, dedicated to Thomas Merton; and, a Progressive Christianity contribution via McAfee"s "The Strength to Resist: the life of Prayer" in *Resistance: the new role of progressive Christians*, ed. Cobb, Jr., 32–54, which, Merton-like, writes of contemplative prayer arising in and out of our own inward, voluntary displacement and which draws from Soelle's *The Silent Cry*, Wink again, and Suchocki's *In God's Presence* and the concept, though easily dismissed for its sometimes connotation of a compartmentalized piety, of "prayer warriors."

so incidentally, Niebuhr's principles of justice and accompanying markers both invite and need the help of prayer. This is so because the regulative principles of equality, liberty, and order, along with the markers of forbearance, concreteness, and compassion, must be held in contemplative prayer so that courage be asked, received, and modestly engaged for steadfast commitments. In Haiku form—any line capable of being in any order: *Centering pilgrims / hoping justice prayerfully/ Being beginners*

Long Haul Resources for Merton's Theology of Prayer

The first key source that brought Merton to prayer and his earnest reflections on it was his mentors. These mentors were resourced by way of his disciplined monastic life and, while he was there, ten years of regular teaching to the Gethsemane novices, retrieving and proffering the originating sources for both their Trappist (Cistercians) Order and the Monastic life in general.

Secondly, there are correspondents with Merton as well as commentators and students of his life and thought that accompanied him and continue to press on. Merton's correspondence illustrates the import of his contemplative life and work; indeed, Merton's letters incorporate and are affirmed as the very work and presence of prayer.

> Each of his letters is a prayer. Merton is trying to call forth the saving presence of God in each of his cold war correspondents, and implicitly in everyone on earth. Writing in what he perceived as total darkness, the monk is praying his way through these individual letters in pursuit of the global miracle needed to save us from our own violence [. . .] enabling us to see how a necessary but impossible collective change could happen, through a miraculous process beyond any power but prayer [. . .] this monk was praying very consciously at the edge of the abyss.[14]

Thus, numerous anthologies focusing on prayer or contemplation—and combining them as contemplative prayer—convey their importance for Merton. Representatively, there is Patrick O'Connell's current series transcribing Merton's ten years of "conferences" of novice teaching. There are Jonathan Montaldo's anthologies on Merton, with a prayer focus. There

---

14. James Douglass, introduction to the *Cold War Letters*, ed. Bochen, xii–iii. See also the introduction and emphasis noted therein of the selected anthology and its indispensable subtitle of *Thomas Merton: A Life in Letters: The Essential Collection*, xi–xiii.

CHAPTER 6—PRAYER VIA MERTON AND URBAN MINISTRY INTIMATIONS

are compact yet comprehensive meditation readers which any Merton student could hardly exhaust in even a year's reading; and among many other resources, there are fresh perspectives on Merton that in relating his body of thought to that of a Simone Weil, pressing the thesis that prayer is an "unmixed attention." There is much to mine with and out of Merton.[15]

There are, thirdly, Merton's experiences of prayers as from his first major work, *The Seven Storey Mountain* public journal. For example:

> It was night. The light was on. Suddenly it seemed to me that Father, who had been dead more than a year, was there with me . . . I was overwhelmed with a sudden and profound insight into the misery and corruption of my own soul, and I was pierced deeply with a light that made me realize something of the condition I was in [. . .] an urgency unlike anything I had ever known before [. . .] for the first time [. . .] I really began to pray [. . .] *praying out of the very roots of my life and my being, and praying to the God that I had never known, to reach down towards me out of His darkness* and to help me to get free of the thousand terrible things that held my will in their slavery.[16]

Early in Merton's spiritual reflections he attests that the experience of prayer is rooted in one's being, and autobiographically, like Augustine, he observes how prayer arises redemptively to engage one's revealed restlessness or instability or plain lack of peace to be rendered open to the gift of rest, stability or peace.[17] There are many other examples of Merton's prayers to express the point that therein are traces and clues of his theology of prayer—prayers that nourished and sustained him, frustrated and challenged him, and moved

---

15. In addition to Appendix B, see O'Connell's selected and edited series of Merton's Conferences with the Monastery's Novices for ten years, entitled "Monastic Wisdom Series" such as *Cassian and the Fathers* and *An Introduction to Christian Mysticism: Initiation into the Monastic Tradition*; McDonnell's *A Thomas Merton reader*; Bochen's *Thomas Merton: Essential Writings*; McDonnell's *Through the Year with Thomas Merton*, with similarly, Montaldo's *A Year with Thomas Merton* as well as Montaldo's introductory comments in *The Intimate Merton*; also Waldron's *Thomas Merton: Master of Attention*, 20, 60 and some interpretations linking Merton to writers like Simone Weil. Each of these volumes draws due attention to prayer as a mode of attentiveness. See also social justice rooted evangelical scholarship on Merton in Ringma, *Seek the Silences with Thomas Merton*.

16. Merton, *The Seven Storey Mountain*, 140, (italics added).

17. See Wills, *Saint Augustine's Childhood*, Confessiones Book One, 87 rendering of *inquietum . . . donec requiescat*—"instability" instead of mere "restlessness." One may discern an early embrace of this enduring Merton prayer theme, as the *New Seeds of Contemplation* Chapter 6 title expresses, "Pray for Your Own Discovery."

him far afield of merely the monastic grounds and walls of Gethsemane (while confirming such "grounds" to his end).[18]

Fourthly, what kept Merton in and with prayer is a basic contemplation-and-action dialectic. In creative tension, one without the other jettisons the most essential ingredients to an enduring social justice witnessing and advocacy. Contemplation and action summarize other tensions, while going deeper. In my own Seminary years and decades since, love remains in critical tension with justice (via Niebuhr, Tillich and Soelle as well as social justice organizers like Cesar Chavez and Dolores Huerta) and justice in tension with faith, with all three virtue disciplines contributing to the practice of a hopefully faithful public-prophetic witness.[19] Merton's students cannot but help to note and emphasize these tensions. Among many, Charles Ringma's *Seek the Silence with Thomas Merton* affirms that: "A holistic approach to life and ministry" is rooted in and nourished out of action and contemplation. He cites Merton: ". . . action is charity looking out to other men, and contemplation is charity drawn inward to its own divine source. Action is the stream and contemplation is the spring."[20]

Action on its own has tended, in recent decades, to be given prior billing. It is claimed to be the key, praxis priority—an "ortho-praxis"—for social justice endeavours. As a corrective strategy towards more of a balance of thought and action, it has been psychologically proven that it is easier to act yourself into a new way of thinking than it is to think yourself into a new way of acting.[21] Biblical warrants include: prophetically, the writings of Amos 5:24; Jeremiah 23; or Hosea 6:6; eschatologically, the writings of Matthew's gospel, as the parable of the last judgment, "inasmuch as you have done it to the least of these my brothers or sisters. . ." ; or pastorally, from the Epistles the writings of James' caveat that pure religion is just action, or

---

18. In addition to Merton's interfaith prayers, especially attested in *The Asian Journal of Merton,* eds. Burton, Hart and Loughlin, especially the Appendices', there is Merton's oft-cited epiphany on the corner of Fourth & Walnut in Louisville, Kentucky, which expresses his street-level mystical/universal sense of being connected to a world of inter-connected beings, *inter alia* see McDonnell, ed., A *Thomas Merton Reader,* 345–47 ("a member of the human race"). On the concreteness and comprehensiveness of this epiphany as a "new and energizing liberation," see Higgins, *The Unquiet Monk,* 69.

19. See Paul Tillich's *Love, Power and Justice* and Dorothee Soelle's last work, *The Silent Cry,* with its sub-title thrust: *Mysticism and Resistance.* Later for me came Henri Nouwen's own early summary of Merton's thought, *Thomas Merton,* in its sub-title: *Contemplative Critic;* the original title being, "Pray to Live," yet a further tension thus: praying and living.

20. Ringma, *Seek the Silence with Thomas Merton,* 163, citing Merton, *No Man is an Island,* 70.

21. See Mowrer's *New Group Therapy,* 68 who credits missionary writer E. Stanley Jones for this dictum.

contrawise, "faith without works is as dead as a body without a soul" (2:26). Liberation theology re-enforces this action priority in its emphasis on "the one thing needed"—to draw from Jesus' invitation to Martha on Mary's focused action of attentiveness when needed and as possible (Luke 10: 38–42) to be in solidarity with the poor or oppressed.[22]

Contemplation or meditative prayer or "Christian meditation" or "centering prayer" disciplines have emerged thus as corrective balances. Indeed, if Ringma had cited Merton further (above), we would read, thus: "The spring (of contemplation) remains more important than the stream (of action), for the only thing that really matters is for love to spring up inexhaustibly from the infinite abyss of Christ and of God."[23] This last added emphasis, again, affirms the creative tension at work lest the vital balance be lost— lest burnout, compassion fatigue, or cynicism come to dominate justice advocacy possibilities and the inevitable risks therein, including of course an insidious self-righteousness.

In *Contemplation in a World of Action*, Merton again presses the relation of contemplation to action, emphasizing the grounding priority of the former and professes summarily:

> He who attempts to act and do things for others or for the world without deepening his own self-understanding, freedom, integrity and capacity to love will not have anything to give others. He will communicate to them nothing, but the contagion of his own obsessions, his aggressiveness, his ego-centered ambitions, his delusions about ends and means, his doctrinaire prejudices and ideas [. . .] A certain depth of disciplined experience is a necessary ground for fruitful action. Without a more profound human understanding derived from exploration of the inner ground of human existence, love will tend to be superficial and deceptive.[24]

---

22. Where an act of solidarity is worth all the theologies, political theories, and sociologies in books; see Gutierrez's *A Theology of Liberation*, 171–74, especially the last two sentences of the "Solidarity and Protest" section.

23. Merton, *No Man is an Island*, 70, see further 221–22: "When I am not present to myself, then I am only aware of that half of me, that mode of my being which turns outward to created things [. . .] to lose myself among them [. . .] (Recollection) brings the outward self into line with the inward spirit, and makes my whole being answer the deep pull of love that reaches down into the mystery of God [. . .] *In order to be recollected in action, I must not lose myself in action. And in order to keep acting, I must not lose myself in recollection.*" (italics added).

24. Merton, *Contemplation in a World of Action*, 160–61, 154.

This is crucial to urban ministry practices. Thus, it is instructive to hear Merton on the various ways by which contemplative prayer, contrary to previous generations' tendencies to relegate it to a withdrawing passivity, relates contemplation to a rousing capacity to animate other activities of the church—as well as to being animated by the Church's lively heritage. He extrapolates for his monastic readers and beyond, for fellow travelers— implied, if not named, in his public and personal journals, and volumes of collected letters. Hence:

> Contemplation does not feed the hungry; it does not clothe the naked; it does not teach the ignorant; and it does not return the sinner to peace, truth and union with God. [. . .] (However) without contemplation we cannot understand the significance of the world in which we must act. Without contemplation we must remain, small, limited, divided, partial: we adhere to the insufficient, permanently united to our narrow group and its interests, losing sight of justice and charity, seized by the passions of the moment; and, finally, we betray Christ [. . .] we betray Him by not seeing Him in those whom we harm unconsciously while we 'innocently' pray for them.[25]

Herein is a tall order which requires a lifetime of study and practice; no wonder a new monasticism has arisen to carry and support the trials and errors encountered in virtually any ministry in the city if it is to render a faithful public-prophetic witness in the service of justice beyond charity, hope out of despair, and prayer rather than resignation.

Fifth and last, there are several renderings of prayer that are tantamount to ideal "definitions" of prayer. Thus from one of the Merton meditation readers:

> Prayer is freedom and affirmation growing out of nothingness into love. Prayer is the flowering of our inmost freedom, in response to the Word of God. Prayer is not only dialogue with God: it is the communication of our freedom with his ultimate freedom, his infinite spirit. It is the elevation of our limited freedom into the infinite freedom of the divine spirit and of the divine love. Prayer is the encounter of our freedom with the all-embracing charity which knows no limit and knows no obstacle. Prayer is an emergence into this area of infinite freedom.

---

25. Preface to the Argentine edition of *The Complete Works of Thomas Merton* April 1958, printed in *"Honorable Reader" Reflections on My Work*, ed. Daggy, 42–43.

Prayer, then, is not an abject procedure, though sometimes it may spring from our abjection.[26]

There is much here that conveys and expresses Merton's theology of prayer, especially the mutual indwelling of Divine and human spirits. How it is that prayer and/or contemplation are so utterly basic—historically, personally, vocationally, ecclesiastically, politically, and of course, eschatologically (the beyond in our midst and ever renewing). Petitionary prayer becomes intercessory prayer—and other prayer forms as praise or thanksgiving and confession—when there is a centered listening so as to be simply still and open, a focused engaging so as to be available, and out of disciplined solitude, a shared communing with the rest of creation.[27]

Just Prayer Hopefully, Triad Intimations and Urban Ministry Implications

Biblically affirmed for Christians if not all persons of faith, prayer is life's very breath and vice-versa: life is breathed in and out prayer.[28] We pray as even we are breathed into—breath, energy and spirit being interchangeable translations of the biblical *ruach* and the greek *pneuma*.[29] Urban ministry students could helpfully think of William Stringfellow's *My People is the Enemy* confession, reflecting ironically on his seven years as a storefront lawyer when he was a part of the East Harlem Protestant Parish group ministry:

---

26. Merton, Jan. 15th entry "Definitions of Prayer," in McDonnell, *A Thomas Merton Reader*, 9–10.

27. See John Higgins, whose volume on Merton's theology of prayer I have not here done justice to, on the role of silence in "awakening one's inner self," through an "inner awareness of God's direct presence," the fruit of yearning for God's presence, understanding of the Word, and a willing capacity to hear and thus obey, *Merton's Theology of Prayer*, 49, 50, and 52. Cf. Hammarskjöld, again: "There can be no peace, unless it is for all; no rest until all has been fulfilled," *Markings*, 35.

28. E.g., Genesis 1:27 and 2:7; Psalm 104:29–30.; Romans 8: 22–27; and John 20:22 as well as classical or contemporary hymns as "Breathe on me, Breath Of God" and "Spirit of Gentleness/ Spirit of Restlessness" respectively in The Hymn and Worship Book of the United Church of Canada, *Voices United*, # 382 and 375. Also see Thomas Keating and John Main's writings on the breathing/mantra disciplines of/in centering prayer and Christian Meditation; respectively, *Intimacy with God* and Dart, *The Spirituality of John Cassian* out of which Dart conveys Main's reflections.

29. And breath-as-prayer, prayer-as-breath, intimate and integral to Jesus' commissioning of the disciples, post-resurrection as in John 20: 21–23; practiced in church circles when a priest being commissioned by way of the preservation and transmission of a Patriarch or Bishop's very breath ("insufflation") for an eventual, far off ordination; see Raymond E. Brown, S.J., *The Gospel According to John XIII–XXI*, 1023.

"The travail of the poor is *intercessory* for the rich—for them, on their behalf, in their place, it substitutes for their own suffering."[30] His subsequent writings continued to reflect the East Harlem experiences, including the interlocking prayer and justice themes. *A Simplicity of Faith: My Experience in Mourning* conveys especially "a need to pray" in the Conversion chapter and, "a lawyer's work" in the Joy chapter.[31]

Merton wrote of hope in earnest. Sometimes he reflected on hope in the midst of despair and how much they, alas, were alike. This is strongly present in his thoughtful, though likely hurried and abridged 1967 "A Letter on the Contemplative Life."[32] Sometimes he conceived of Niebuhr-like fashioned dictums or pithy proverbs such as *New Seeds of Contemplation*'s "Sentences"— chapter 15's opening dictum: "To hope is to risk frustration. Therefore, make up your mind to risk frustration."[33]

Paralleling prayer reflections of urban ministry practitioners in the service of a tough city ministry, here is one sampling of prayer's indispensable presence in and with the thesis triad:

> Prayer for me is a dynamic presence but also a groaning, a pleading, a sweeping up, an offering of God's good creations in people and wonderful sentient companions (that rejoice but also suffer) and the awesome structures that populate Earth and space [. . .] I do pray by traditional formulas and have to work hard to enter their spirit: often I do not succeed. However, that kind of prayer creates a certain spiritual environment which I believe is also very nurturing and upbuilding. It represents an open spirit and wholesome, desirous stance [. . .] something akin to the physical intimate immediacy of the universe (posited in quantum physics.).[34]

Elsewhere Carmel Hili shares that Merton's Jesuit-like discernment tradition of contemplative prayer—assisted by the Ignatian spiritual exercises of steadfast silence with the help of a spiritual director for as long as forty days and nights—has sustained Hili over the long haul of urban core Toronto ministries with both the United Church of Canada and an on-going

---

30. Stringfellow, *My People Is the Enemy*, 29. (italics added).

31 Stringfellow, *A Simplicity of Faith*, 125–30.

32. Merton, in *The Monastic Journey*, ed. Br. Patrick Hart , 218–23.

33. Merton, *New Seeds of Contemplation*, 104.

34. Carmel Hili to Barry Morris, July 20, 2006 e-mail communication (used with permission). Hili, a former Jesuit-educated and Jesuit-trained brother, recently retired from thirty-plus years with the Toronto Christian Resource Centre while continuing avid volunteering with parish and community concerns.

CHAPTER 6—PRAYER VIA MERTON AND URBAN MINISTRY INTIMATIONS 95

commitment with his Catholic Church.[35] As Hili and other urban ministry practitioners attest, a spirit of competition pervades their urban ministries and those of others competing for scarce resources in the city—as perhaps in circles and spheres of academia. Perhaps the practice or discipline of prayer contributes to enable urban ministry practitioners and administrators to resist that which otherwise thwarts or shuts down their ministry's openness to and need for co-operation and capacity-building alliances.

Participants in recent Truth and Reconciliation Commission processes[36] and recovering addicts could intuit Merton's insight that we are, time and again, but beginners and that we are in need of grasping and practicing a life of contemplation and/or prayer that stresses a beginner's simplicity (and the simplicity of beginning). The simplicity of the notion that justice is a balance or creative tension to all this is at the heart of making amends and restoring justice to people harmed along the hurtful way. It also helps the self-aching for reconciliation. For recovery to have a realistically hopeful chance "to work," it needs a stable, supportive context. I have officiated at too many funerals of those who have died prematurely or untimely—witnessing only temporary resolve and hope to choose life among the grieving, shocked survivors (especially if a death by violence and its many forms, such as from an overdose or being sinned against over a lifetime). Tangible, immediate opportunities—and invitations—are needed, to be a part of an alternative power base. Such is needed in order to be an integral part of a mutually supportive group who are more than "virtual reality" and who will participate with one through the tough work of recovery, to counter the principalities and powers, so seductively and bafflingly present in those addictive, toxic spirits, *spiritum*, which is contra to *spiritus*. It is apt to draw from Carl Jung here. He expresses in a key letter to AA co-founder Bill Wilson:

35. See Hili's remarks in *The Word on the Street*, 141–42 and my own Th.M. thesis' Appendix C, passim. Hili has also shared: "For me, I stress the importance of the rhythm of the interface between personal /communal spiritual-prayer life and action. Onesidedly, prayer can become a personal devotion; activity, an ideology or addiction. I found out that we can be so obsessed with work that sometimes we become worldly, end up competing with each other, showing off and playing politics and blunt the simplicity and power of the spirit within us. We have to guard against getting lured into a savior mind-set and acting as the lone cowboy coming in and saving the town. Rather than unstintingly praying and working communally and taking on whatever lead or humble roles coming to us in our long haul in the building of spirit-suffused world community," e-mail communication of Oct. 26, 2009 Hili to Morris, (cited with permission).

36. I refer to the recent Truth and Reconciliation Hearings in Vancouver, B.C., the fourth of five that occurred, as well to Desmond Tutu's *No Future without Forgiveness*, especially Chapter Two's "Nuremberg or National Amnesia? A Third Way."

> (Roland's) craving for alcohol was the equivalent, on a low level, of a spiritual thirst of our being for wholeness expressed in medieval language: the union with God [. . .] You see, 'alcohol' in Latin is 'spiritus' and you use the same word for the highest religious experience as well as for the most depraving poison. The helpful formula therefore is: spiritus contra spiritum.'[37]

Thus the above "vow of stability" is again evoked and affirmed. Such stability is based upon and nurtured, in turn, by the life of persevering prayer—praying to be open, present to, and willing to be available, to attend to cultivating the habits of the heart. Helped by Merton's insights, then, ". . . a monk commits himself to continuous conversion of life which involves a life of poverty and chastity."[38] Merton added elsewhere:

> It is the vow to respond totally and integrally to the word of Christ, 'Come, follow Me' by renouncing all that might impede one in following Him untrammelled, all that might obscure one's clarity of intent and confuse one's resolve [. . .] the persevering determination to bear with patience and courage all the trials one may meet [. . .] carrying one's cross and following Christ.[39]

Recovering addicts come to know this "vow of conversation" and as beginners, to renew time and again. "With all the earnestness at our command" is one of the implicit vows needed to initiate and sustain the awesome recovery process. "A day at a time" and "let go (so to) let God" are two further 12-step fellowship mantras.[40] They serve the perennial Mertonian beginning again, and indeed, steadfastly thus once again for the long haul of shared life possibilities as fellow strugglers in community. Merton and 12-step fellowships grasp this significant note of realism, in hope.

> . . . (W)e really do experience in ourselves at the same time as the power of Christ, the power of the cross to create community. We find in ourselves everything that goes against community,

---

37. Cited in *The Spirituality of Imperfection*, eds. Kurtz and Ketchum, 113. Also, see both Alexander and Mate's 2008 published works and their instructive subtitles, respectively, *The Globalization of Addiction: A Study in Poverty of the Spirit* and *In the Realm of the Hungry Ghosts: Close Encounters with Addiction*, both with spiritually struggling title/sub-title themes, akin to the point in Jung's letter.

38. Cited in Bochen, ed., *Thomas Merton*, 25.

39. "Conversion of Life," 149; and Merton's crisp affirmation, again, of a "thorough and ruthless determination" required of would-be learners/disciples of the desert fathers and mothers; introduction to *The Wisdom of the Desert*, 24.

40. See *Alcoholics Anonymous*, 3rd edition, 58–59; also *Hope & Recovery* and its instructive subtitle: *A Twelve-step Guide for Healing from Sex Additions*, 99–108.

and we have to be completely aware of this fact. We are and we are not communal people. It is taken for granted that we are all sociable. But we are and we aren't. We are also weak and selfish, and there is in us this struggle between trust and mistrust, where we all believe and don't believe. We trust other people and we distrust other people. We are [. . .] full of ambivalence, and we must take this into account.[41]

A Summary Triad: Grounding Reflection

Each theologian has been chosen for their particular theme discipline that supports this thesis and helps to ground the triad of praying justice hopefully. All the cumulative life witness and life writings of Niebuhr on justice, Merton on prayer and Moltmann on hope combine to help to integrate a theological grounding for the triad as a whole. Their lives serve as compelling, faithful, public, and prophetic witnesses. They illustrate what the late James Wm. McClendon, Jr. calls "Biography as Theology" with the sub-title "how life stories can remake today's theology." Indeed much of this book could be aptly depicted as a sustained exercise in biography—with autobiography, too—as theology. The following chapters' urban ministry networks are herein thickened and complemented by these three theologians' life contributions and now, legacies. As with the contention of the thesis triad, ". . .they intertwine, balance and enhance one another."[42]

All three theologians offer insights for justice, Niebuhr more than Moltmann and Merton. However, Moltmann's emphasis on the theme discipline of hope serves as the catalyst to move his readers from indifference to a familiarity with inequalities and toward a more inclusive horizon. Merton's emphasis on contemplative prayer, in turn, asserts the necessity of finding one's inner ground as foundation in order that advocacy has sufficient depth and width to withstand the "slings and arrows of outrageous fortune" (Shakespeare's *Hamlet*). This foundation must also minimize projections of one's inner frustrations, unresolved guilt and/or self-righteous judgments. All three theologies exercise caution about the kind of activism that could be merely temporary bursts of frenzy or obsessions with "results"

---

41. Merton, "Building Community on God's Love," 100–1.

42. See Jones, "Review of (David Kelsey's) *Eccentric Existence: A Theological Anthropology*," stating the need of the conjunctive triad of praying justice hopefully, but given sin, "We pray without loving our neighbors, drifting toward mean isolation; we love without praying, lapsed into arrogance, conformism, and do-nothingness. We live in bondage to a past from which we have been released," 793.

at the price of burnout or cynicism.⁴³ All three theologians offer insights for hope, Moltmann more than Niebuhr and Merton. However, Niebuhr kept the virtue of hope close to his hindsight reflections right to the end of his life by way of elderly, sober, sermonic, or essay offerings. Merton, like Moltmann, discerned how similar despair was to hope in that both were rooted in a basic dependency on God. But despair on its own could become unduly isolating and overwhelming. Finally, all three theologians offer insights on prayer with Merton expressing more of a due emphasis than Niebuhr or Moltmann. However, Niebuhr's prayers, especially his bequeathed, grace-based serenity prayer, and Moltmann's carefully crafted Trinitarian-based prayer behold the mystery beneath, above and penetrating all of life. This is similar to Rabbi Joshua Abraham Heschel who professes prayer as the human response to the inconceivable surprise of being alive at all,⁴⁴ and being alive, summoning others in order to share with his or her community and beyond.

To summarize: justice is at the apex of the triad and is thus the discipline term prepared, enriched and complemented by prayer and hope. Prayer is what assists one's willingness to be attentive to people and situations and aids a ministry's empathic presence and, when necessary, resistance to that which dehumanizes⁴⁵—the very work of the justice command. As one patiently endeavors to practice the praying for justice mandate, he or she is drawn into the whole accompanying and energizing ethos of hope, contra the temptations of cynicism.⁴⁶ In terms of the triad, the horizon of

43. See Merton's letters to James Forest counselling a patient attentiveness to the concern and process of a cause and not succumbing to the temptation to obsess with "results" while prayerfully intuiting, trusting in God's presence, in *Cold War Letters Thomas Merton*, eds. Bochen and Shannon, 58–60, 69–70, 121–23, and 132–34.

44. Heschel's prayer is cited in *Answers in the Heart*, July 7th, and Moltmann's Trinitarian-based prayer is found in *The Source*, 145: " . . . Unite with yourself your torn and divided world/ and let us all be one in you/ one with your whole creation." Cf. Moltmann's the "God of Hope" sermon which concludes: "Father, we know that we cannot come to you without our brother [. . .] We pray to you for grace for the indifferent and the tired, for the small of faith and the hopeless [. . .] for patience for the godless, for the heathen, for the atheistic [. . .] for the coming of your righteousness for the degraded and the offended [. . .] for the arrival of your freedom for the oppressed. Let nothing which serves your freedom be brought to defeat. Let us find patience with our neighbors, and give us the courage to practice daily of hoping in patience. Lord let your kingdom come . . . ." in *The Gospel of Liberation*, 32–33.

45. See Moltmann, *Ethics of Hope*, 8.

46. Moltmann, *Ethics of Hope*, "Hope is always a tense expectation and *rouses the attentiveness of all our senses,* so that we can grasp the chances for the things we hope for wherever and whenever they present themselves," 3, (italics added). Cf. Terence Anderson: "The combined virtues of hope and patience are the only true antidotes to cynicism and despair," *Walking the Way*, 134. Singer Danny Fabello expresses it thus

CHAPTER 6—PRAYER VIA MERTON AND URBAN MINISTRY INTIMATIONS

hope is ever before us (Moltmann), aching to accompany the praying justice community even as hope is grounded in prayer ("thy kingdom come"). While mindful of commitment for the long haul, the practices of hope, with prayer, goad us to begin again or anew (Merton). Ministers are often aroused and stirred to fresh conscientious endeavors when they encounter contradictions in their midst, assuming a patient and paced attentiveness. With the helpmate of hopeful prayer, urban ministries are summoned and sustained to engage justice. For the sake of bearing a covenantal steadfast and faithful public-prophetic witness for North American urban ministry, these three theologians bequeath a grounded and comprehensive perspective. An exploration and explanation of how such perspectives illumine and illustrate actual urban ministries—and indeed how, in turn, the triad is illumined by the meaning and staying power of at least Canadian urban ministries and networks in the service of a faithful public *and* prophetic witness—is our next task.

---

from "Always, There is Hope": "As long as we live/ hope greets/ at yearning's end/ the dreams/ that we cherish/ shall never fail/ . . . if only we dare to struggle" from *War & Roses,* 39.

Chapter 7—Longhouse Ministry and Networking

'The only guarantees are the people on the right and the left of you.' But acting with those people is itself what manifests hope. 'You bind intensely with people around you who are like-minded in the belief that the other world that is possible is the one we are creating right now in this space. There's the possibility, or hope, that it will catch on. But here's the point—we don't have any other alternative. The current alternative is so deathlike. You have no power, no personal agency, no discretion. So connecting and bonding with like-minded others to claim a new world is the only way to proceed.[1]

Introduction

THE LITERATURE ON URBAN ministry and theologies tends to emphasize established missions of the mainstream or once-established churches. They are institutionalized ministries that have less difficulty with successorship and/or awesome challenges with the routinization of charisma, when magnetic leaders' visions and possibly, policies are sought to be succeeded and sustained. Smaller ministries might sink or swim depending on the success of whom there is—or alas, is not—to succeed the departing founder or long established anchor person. Also, small ministries tend to depend a lot on networking—some kind and level of looking for outreach and supportive opportunities to deepen and widen the mission of the ministry by way of persons, places, other ministries or organizations. The initial and sustaining funding for urban ministries—or the decline and feared demise of a ministry—as well as a ministry's continued legitimacy so that sustainable funding remains intact and possible are all not guaranteed. In any case, networking for a lot of urban ministries is crucial lest they suffocate in isola-

1. (Bishop) George Packard in Oyer, *Pursuing the Spiritual Roots of Protest*, 226.

tion from the oxygen of deep and wider breathing. In *Action Training in Canada*, Roger Hutchinson writes of "linking with", "consultation on" and "partnership(s) between" groups or ministries that contribute to making a network and keeping it alive.[2]

An animator of the United Church of Canada with networking responsibilities regarding the recent Truth and Reconciliation Commission hearings and outcomes further comments that this is a process whereby "people are the nodes of the net; we are all connected."[3] Almost literally then, the nodes and links of a network are crucial to networking. Actual nodes of clustered persons—and the reverse, individual and groups of persons for the nodes—make it possible for a network to occur, develop, engage in constructive criticism for renewal, and thus remain vibrantly active. Animators speak of a network as "a fishing net—with the knots, and the spaces." There are networks by and between persons and networks by and between organizations, no matter the size. The Longhouse Ministry's *modus operandi* depends upon networks, immediate and near at hand, and extensive and city-wide (even provincial in scope or influence). Without such networking, the ministry would be severely limited in the nature and scope of its efforts to bear a faithful public witness. Without the networks, there would be little opportunity to exercise a faithful *and prophetic, public* ministry. The depth and width of such nodes are vital to develop. One presses to ponder: are such nodes thick enough to bear the weight, to persevere under and with the strain and stress of hanging in with each other?[4]

Indispensable Networks

One of the several of the Longhouse Ministry's important networks is the Metro Vancouver Alliance (MVA). It is an alliance by the very nature of its formation and maintenance and is formed by the careful and patient process of relating to an organization by way of its leaders or key supporters and, in turn, the organization's decision to join with others to form an alliance. This resembles a coalition which for our practical purposes is the same as an alliance. A coalition may differ in the length of time of the commitment of two or more organizations to associate—perhaps briefly for addressing a single

---

2. Hutchinson, "Education for Social Transformation," 7.
3. Cecile Fausak, Email Feb. 5, 2015. (used with permission).
4. See Bonhoeffer on perseverance as "bearing under the weight" while caring, "The Secret of Suffering," *A Testament of Freedom*, 291. Cf. Whitehead's summary affirmation that creativity arises from that creative tension of intensity (vs. triviality) and harmony (vs. discord), *Adventures of Ideas*, 259–68, 279–85.

issue and then disbanding; perhaps engaging a few issues over a long even undetermined time period; perhaps forming with the intent to complete the actions required. The MVA is rooted in the long legacy of the Industrial Areas Foundation (IAF) where, not so coincidentally, its founder, Saul Alinsky, drew from Reinhold Niebuhr's reflections and life experiences in especially social, economic and political justice. He drew particularly from Niebuhr's work in the making and keeping of justice by way of organizing power from below to try to match and thereby meaningfully negotiate with power already entrenched on high. Alinsky's successor, Ed Chambers, contributed to the virtual trilogy of IAF reflections—*Reveille for Radicals* and *Rules for Radicals* followed by a well-waited-for and much needed volume, *Roots for Radicals*. The book's *organizing power for action and justice* sub-title depicts the *raison d'etre* of the IAF and its offshoots, including the MVA. Without the MVA, the Longhouse would be without a meaningful forum, a vehicle and a sound strategy for patiently engaging justice on a larger urban scale, more than its limited sphere of a neighborhood influence. Without or apart from the Longhouse, it is possible that the MVA would not exist, at least not yet and not in its present form. The Longhouse, via its minister, spearheaded the moves to research and, by way of many trials and errors, engage steadfast though often teetering ways to introduce the very IAF model into the difficult city of Vancouver for serious and long-term community organizing possibilities. This has been no small, quick feat since Vancouver has been notorious for entertaining single-issues for only brief periods, chiefly by way of short-lived coalitions but with those ending as soon as the issue is aired or given perhaps mass-media attention.

Some persons entered the formation of MVA from the trade union sectors, others from the community agency and/or non-profit sectors, some even from the small business sector, and many of us from the religious or faith-based community sector. Some have parleyed their healing or recovery from addiction experiences—felt to be life-long for many of us—into connecting with the philosophy and strategies of broad-based community organizing. The present and only fulltime staff person of MVA, Deborah Littman, has adapted her prior union activities, a long acquaintanceship with the common or public-good understanding of society, and intense years of campaigning for a "living wage" in London, England (and Canada) into her current organizing of the MVA. Her move back to Canada heralded her eventual hiring with MVA and continued field training, mostly via the USA's IAF. It has been an especially sensitive process to take the entire project slowly and carefully—with a disciplined focus on relationship building among and between organizations' members and key leaders. An important revision of early IAF models of organizing, with their emphasis on beginning with issues and building on them for the sake of the larger whole, even if such issues were lost, consists of beginning instead with the "relational meeting", so that mutual trust has a meaningful chance to occur and be sustained.[5] One lay person in the Anglican Church in Canada, for example, commented on a teach-in training event in this vein:

> What I found to be most useful was learning how to tell my story in a public context. Engaging people through our shared interests and values is the difference in the IAF model organizing. The pressures on families caused by alcoholism are universal. Sharing my experience, strength, and hope in a public context can help me move forward through the public/private tension towards accomplishing mutual interests. I also found useful the identification of the elements of the 'Organizing Cycle', the 'Power Analysis', and planning an 'Action Organizing Cycle.'[6]

A second network is A Community Aware (ACA). By way of some older adults who had benefited from social justice and educational workshops leaving with the challenge to go and do likewise in their communities, ACA was created. It provided educational forums and hosted annual working sessions of several weeks' duration on the nature and duration of addiction and its mammoth scale to the point of being global. However, it did not arise in consistent calmness and apart from the challenged stresses and strains of thwarted hopes for change. Co-founder Terry Patten (with Bruce Alexander) expressed a working *raison d'etre* on ACA to a University of British Columbia First Nations Studies Program research student, Andrea Reid:

> One day I went through the exercise of listing all the things that have happened in the 21st century. The list is amazing; I stopped after one typed page, one-liners. There's just so much going on. Who am I to say things aren't going to change? That's a ridiculous stance. But it's so easy to get discouraged. So my stance is to concentrate on what is ethical, to not expect outcomes, to not invest in outcomes that would disappoint me but just to keep my eye on the ball and to keep going on with Community Aware as I long as I have the strength and hope fully we

---

5. See Chambers, *The Roots of Radicals*, 44–54 on the emergence of the relational meeting, as a distinct revision of earlier IAF training philosophy and methodology,

6. E-*mail communication*, December 2, 2009, Pat McSherry later added in a Christian Meditation group that prayer grounds and connects her to justice-making and -keeping activities. (used with permission).

can pass that along and it will survive and people will have a place to go and talk.[7]

When the Longhouse Ministry via its sole minister linked hands with ACA a few years ago, ACA was somewhat refreshed and invigorated to press further and probe deeper. Monthly and even weekly gatherings have occurred addressing the various layers of meaning of a "poverty of the Spirit." As well, the nature of a *spiritual community* has been engaged drawing on the CBC-radio series on "beyond atheism", its marks characterized as when a *body of people* meets over a *long period of time* to *engage deeply*. Such engagement topics include dying and death, the origins and legacies of the social gospel in North America, and the creative revival of existentialism (its philosophy, therapy and literature). It includes book studies on e.g. William James' *Varieties of Religious Experience*, Ernest Becker's *The Denial of Death* or *Escape from Evil*, Victor Frankl's *Man's Search for Meaning*, Gerald May's *Addiction and Grace*, Naomi Klein's *This Changes Everything: Capitalism versus the Climate*, and others. The annual addiction sessions have sparked a follow-up series on the meanings and practice of meditation, exploring the 11th step of Twelve Step fellowships ("sought through prayer and meditation to improve our conscious contact with God"). Without ACA, the Longhouse would miss a wider sphere of inter-disciplinary connections which seek to probe and redress alternatives to the contributing conditions for global addiction of fragmentation and dislocation. On its own, the Longhouse could not possibly extend itself to such a diversity of people on the range of concerns and issues that ACA has come to explore and engage. And, on its own, ACA would lack a home base or a natural, actual place to host regular sessions with a warm atmosphere of hospitality and now regular, shared sessions on the art and methodology of mindfulness (of 8 to 9 weeks duration with monthly check-ins).

A third meaningful network for the Longhouse Ministry is Streams of Justice (SoJ). As with another looser, less often meeting but Longhouse-hosted Coalition for Migrant Workers Justice (C4MWJ), the Longhouse is a founding member of SoJ. Complementing remarks in Appendix B, it was essentially founded by a couple, Dave and Teresa Diewert, long involved in Vancouver's east end who, with and out of their home church, availed themselves for extensive volunteer work. This consisted of labor- intensive hosting of drop-ins, providing a live-in group home for street people, serving weekly, hot meals and hosting over-night shelter space and befriending

---

7. Terry Patten, a recorded and unpublished interview by Andrea Reid, Feb. 2, 2013. (used with permission). See also Appendix B's *Viva Voce* where more is included on MVA.

CHAPTER 7—LONGHOUSE MINISTRY AND NETWORKING

many community persons, often loners in and out of hospitals or prisons or detox/treatment facilities. It meets often and energetically supports larger bodies of social justice concerns, ranging from advocacy for those conveniently labeled "illegal immigrants" to the urban need for affordable housing and, with this, a stalwart opposition to forms of gentrification that lead to eviction (gentra-viction). SoJ communicates with and deepens its own membership base by employing methods of study or hosting educational events; actively supporting other social justice organizations or networks; and, extending opportunities for reflection. It earnestly reaches out to other Christian faith communities to share biblical understandings of justice, including the challenge that any notion of justice can be reduced to mere charity (and vice-versa). Indeed, SoJ seeks to de-construct charity as a cheap substitute for justice (recalling an endeavor profoundly akin to the views of both Augustine and Niebuhr). SoJ has moved in its regular studies of and support to aboriginal or indigenous peoples' history and their ongoing struggles. SoJ now practices an opening, conscious-raising acknowledgment. It states: "We acknowledge the unceded Coast Salish territory of the Musqueam, Squamish and Tsliel Waututh peoples, on whose traditional territory and we live and work." And in its current statement of purpose, SoJ adds: "As settlers on the path of justice, we stand against the ongoing colonization of indigenous lives, communities, lands, and traditional life-ways, and support the indigenous struggle for sovereignty and self-determination."[8]

Without an involvement in SoJ the Longhouse would be missing a vital check and balance—a virtual reality check—on and for an enduring prophetic grasp and enactment of a public ministry that seeks to be hopeful as well as engaged in actual witnessing to concerns of justice. On its own, the Longhouse could not possibly extend and deepen its grasp of the range of meanings of justice, and especially the constant art of moving on from the necessity of providing charitable responses to poverty and inequalities, and not remaining stuck with such an otherwise forced option. SoJ is not independent or fully autonomous—unique among the networks. It is embedded in the host or home of Grandview Calvary Baptist Church (GCBC, as its co-founders were and, for the most part, with other core participants are still remaining). The Longhouse, nonetheless, helps to provide another actual church to the SoJ's membership base, a membership which professes the biblical mandate to do justice and love kindness (including charity), confessing to being caught in the dynamic tension which yearns to be and

---

8. See SoJ web site: www./streamsofjustice.wordpress.com. Also Appendix B *Viva Voce* for more SoJ testimony.

remain creative. To complete the Micah 6:8 triad, the Longhouse, like that of GCBC, practices the discipline of prayerfulness or walking humbly with thy Lord. That is something that biblical commentators are understandably apt to confess and profess[9] and what SoJ used to incorporate regularly into its meeting rhythms. The SoJ fell into omitting the practice; however, the group has recently retrieved and now practice some form of opening and closing ritual, blessing, and/or biblical theme.

To explore further, a network has the feature of encouraging reciprocity, over time, and with sufficient dedication so that the "whole is greater than the sum of its parts." This means that an otherwise modest-sized and quite moderately funded Longhouse Ministry can both intensify in its depth and extensify by width its influence and, in turn, have its influence affirmed and challenged. A network, we are duly reminded, is a sure challenge to the "mythical truth of autonomy."[10] Networking affords a desired—and certainly needed—reality check. There is a sharing of "communicative infrastructures," or that which is already in place or becoming rooted that is worth sharing from one organization or body of associated people to another.[11] In all of the network or alliance cases discussed, the Longhouse had the fortunate role of helping to form them and, in turn, reciprocally, to be formed by these networks. Adult Educator, Michael Welton, attests, "If relations of trust and reciprocity are damaged or only thinly present, persons will not be open to each other . . . exclude any willingness to walk down a conversational road."[12] The Longhouse became involved almost from the outset with SoJ, as with ACA, at an important time when its co-founders were doing some genuine soul searching and were open to broadening its range and spheres of influence. What matters is what a minister or community worker does daily: here and there, upwards and downwards, to refer, connect, link, partner or associate, and even as possible animate. Constant goals are to reduce isolation, to move from fragmentation to possibilities of wholeness, or to engage and redress dislocation to achieve integration or a working harmony for the sake addressing and redressing indignities and inequalities of a significant issue. What endure as essential are the sheer energies that an urban minister contributes and throughout, seeks to renew. Herein is the importance of the hoping justice prayerfully triad and its practice. As noted

---

9. See e.g. Moore, "Difficult Words," 49. She comments that practicing justice " . . . describes the required relationship between God and humanity, who (at best) participate in God's purpose to restore justice in our broken world . . . ."

10. See Moss, *The Neighborhood Church*, xix–xxi.

11. Welton, e-mail Feb. 7/15. (used with permission).

12. Welton, *Unearthing Canada's Hidden Past*, 218–19

in chapters 2 and 3, the work is seldom an ordinary work week of 35 to 40 hours with overtime pay.

On Cases: Intrinsic and Instrumental

To illustrate further on the significance of networking for a steadfast ministry in the city that has a meaningful chance to dig deep, engage widely, and experience the thickness of what a hopeful realism entails, it is helpful to explore an urban ministry case with actual networks. Case studies are employed for both their intrinsic value and their instrumental or exemplary purpose (as are the three core theologians of chapters 4, 5, and 6). Speaking of the instrumental value of cases " . . . a particular case is examined mainly to provide insight into an issue or to redraw a generalization . . . " and, in any case, Robert Stake notes: "We simultaneously have several interests, particular and general. There is no hard-and-fast line distinguishing *intrinsic* case study from *instrumental*, but rather a zone of combined purpose."[13]

Case studies also help to bridge the perennially challenging gaps between (hopefully) good theory and the cantankerous exigencies and mixed motives or competing interests of actions. In the aftermath of projects launched and actions taken, there is often a sense of too much of one thing and not enough of another—too much adventure (or alas, not enough) and too little caution (or alas, not enough). Daniel Schipani writes: "(C)ases help bridge the gap between experience and practice, on the one hand, and reflection and theology on the other . . . . case studies can exemplify theoretical constructs, and the latter can also be drawn from particular case descriptions and analysis."[14]

To elaborate, the Longhouse Council of Native Ministry (LM) is a small eastside community and congregational ministry affiliated with the United Church of Canada (by way of its regional ecclesial authority, the Vancouver-Burrard Presbytery). It began in the 1970s as an ecumenically shared ministry with the Anglican Church in Canada (via the Westminster Diocese) and its first combined full-time staff were the late John and Jean Jeffries, Ontario First Nations persons. It had been previously spearheaded by a LM current elder, Jim White, in his ecumenical role of being an animator and consultant for the larger church.

The Longhouse endures despite being fragile in actual support—defying, to date, a predicted closure given the discouraging but realistic closures of several surrounding churches, not only of the United Church of Canada

13. Stake, "Qualitative Case Studies," 123. (italics added).
14. Schipani, "Case Study Method," 99.

denomination. The Longhouse regularly seeks to involve and work with local and city-wide people. It also works with those ministries vulnerable to unstable funding as the national church's mission and service grant support steadily declines (despite recent generous national and regional bequests, in the millions, that rarely get to grass-roots ministries). The LM's steadfastness is partly due to a dedicated part-time (essentially working full-time) paid staff person, one or two live-in or on-site volunteers, and clusters of oft-changing volunteers. It is also due to its heritage, the length of time it has existed, and the efforts it has made, though small, to be present and bear a faithful public and energy-and-nerve-willing, prophetic witness in a flexible manner. Its smallness contributes to its being flexibly and self-critically present (not alone among urban ministries on this[15]). The Longhouse thereby tries to engage justice as well as the more convenient and nearer at hand charity responses to people's poverty in the surrounding communities.

The Longhouse does the task of justice advocacy and sometimes actual organizing by way of networking with the likes of the "Metro Vancouver Alliance" (MVA), "Streams of Justice" (SoJ), the modest and fading "Coalition for Migrant Worker Justice", Kairos Vancouver, and "A Community Aware" (ACA). As noted above, the Longhouse has been a founding member of the first three networks and a recent supporter and frequent host of the ACA. But none of these are yet the kind of strong, widespread organization or alliance that is truly required to fulfill the sub-title theme of *Roots for Radicals*, namely, "organizing for power, action and justice."[16] MVA at least has this as part of its mission statement. Without these networks or alliances, the Longhouse Ministry would simply not be anything more than a very small, certainly fragile church with some in-house programs. It would still only include the Sunday worship service, a mid-week food bank (which we host), a small sharing circle in association with a First Nations agency (alas, now forced to close), a loose and informal drop-in center for persons looking for use of the phone and messages or a computer or a place to fetch their mail, a place to read the daily newspaper (especially the want ads); a consistent place for several 12-step meetings for recovery from or support out of addictions, and, not least, a place and time to be listened to and taken seriously.

---

15. See, *inter alia*, Tim Huff, Al Tysick, Barry Rieder, Robert Moss, Juliet Kilpin, Laurie Green, "Urban Expression" street level ministries (J. Kilpin), New Monasticism writings, and Morris et al. as further illustrations of the "small is beautiful" or a flexible reality via modest-sized ministries.

16. See Chambers, *Roots of Radicals* and its instructive sub-title: *Organizing for Power, Action and Justice*.

More programming could possibly be done if there were more than a part-time staff member and actual live-in volunteers. But as a reality check, there might not be the same level of flexibility to respond, host, and innovate, including fresh networking. Nonetheless, the dedication of these persons with their generous presence and availability mark the Longhouse Ministry as a loose kind of "new monastic" community (short of explicit vows). It thus features a steadfast presence—someone around virtually 7/24 and season-by-season—and a capacity for flexible, even generous hospitality.[17] Like the rhythm of each day's dawn and each day's dusk, every day one group or another, including as part of the Sunday worship service, prays the Niebuhr-resourced and grace-based Serenity Prayer.

Yet again, the LM would not be more than all this but for the extra, energetic effort—and synergistic outcome—to be a part of the above social justice networks or alliances. This has meant intentionality with lots of trials-and-errors. It has required patience with some humility and persistence with some peacefulness. It has required a self-critical perspective with some risk-taking in the service of exercising a manner of ministry that endeavors to be a faithful witness to what God requires of its gathered and scattered people (again evoking Micah 6:8's triad of justice, kindness or integrity, and humbleness as well as the *praying justice hopefully* triad).

A note of anxiety pervades. This is the warm or thermal-current challenge to carry on—steadfastly—when the incumbent minister of 25 years eventually retires (or plainly has to, even if reluctantly). With the minister having spearheaded, even cajoled, the Longhouse Ministry to connect, help animate, and thus contribute to the above networks, would—could—this continue following his departure? More importantly, would the critical and constructive functions of the Longhouse to these three networks or arising equivalents continue?

Enduring Responses and the Help of Response Ethics' Criteria

One ponders the various ways that a ministry can and ought to engage in hopefully constructive self-criticism. First, there is an application of the Wesley quadrilateral, whereby the uses of Bible/ tradition/ experience/ and reason are employed to make sense of issues, concerns, tasks, or a rationale for what next to do and why. This implicitly goes on. For the Longhouse Ministry this entails its mission statement of seeking the welfare or shalom

---

17. Cf. Kilpin, *Urban to the Core*, where minimal/expected commitments provide a stable basis for steadfast presence, xiii, 2, passim.

of the city wherein it lives, moves, and has its being. It means acknowledging its modest capacity due to its size, limited budget, and sole staff person. Less intentionally perhaps, there is a second task of becoming suspicious that, sometimes, the work of the Longhouse is irrelevant and/or prejudiced and/or self-serving due to class factors and frequent temptations to take short-cuts. There is a third step of a retrieval of that which matters most or is felt to be needed and adventured. This means, for the Longhouse, questioning its penchant to respond to poverty with charitable measures but stopping short of justice advocacy and support—support to at least those wider and deeper networks or alliances, as the above. Lastly, there is an intuited or direct invitation to practice hospitality, such as to non-church people or occasional users or for only those "rites of passage" users of the church (marriages, funerals, even passing through baptisms). Following Thomas Ogletree's helpful discernment (which the above has adopted), the ministry and its practitioners or volunteers are encouraged if not challenged to attend to the "stranger" and therein to the element of surprise and even a promise of change (cf. Hebrews 13: 2).[18] All of the above challenges the Longhouse Ministry to reach beyond the safe confines of its status quo conveniences—to practice an open door philosophy of availability, open to alternatives and animating where possible for mutual help and long-term social justice purposes, and willing to live in and with anguish (far easier to espouse, alas, than practice).[19]

Longhouse Ministry Nourishment

At least the following nourishes the Longhouse Ministry: weekly worship and mid-week meetings (that hopefully matter), especially a Tuesday-morning sharing circle and the penitential seasons' Bible study during Advent/Lent. The LM also participates in wider networks, such as in-house or denominational soul searching or social justice networking which includes the above-mentioned Streams Of Justice, Kairos, Metro Vancouver Alliance, as well as Advent and Lent Vigils for the Silenced, and Vancouver-Burrard Presbytery's occasional or ad hoc Faithful Public (and Prophetic) Witness Committee. In addition, the LM participates in an elders group, sometimes a Vancouver East Ministerial Association, and occasional meetings with

---

18. See Hebrews 13:2 and Ogletree, *Hospitality to the Stranger*, Pt. 2's "Hospitality to the Stranger: The Role of the 'Other' in Moral Experience" and Pt. 4's "The Activity of Interpreting in Moral Judgment."

19. Again, availability, animating, alternatives, and anguish are discerned and elaborated in Morris, *Engaging Urban Ministry*.

other United Church leaders. There are also the minister's very welcome continuing education—especially, its inclusion of major research on a *hoping-justice-prayerfully* triad within the framework of hopeful realism. The LM also benefits from other lay persons taking annual summer school courses of the Native Ministries Consortium.

The following attests to a hopefully faithful, public, and prophetic witness of the Longhouse Ministry in Vancouver and, sometimes beyond. There is an elders' involvement in higher courts of the (United) church and the felt sense of urgency that this entails and summons.[20] There is credibility with some aspects of the wider, higher church, from whence its legitimacy comes as well; there is also appreciation from the above social-justice-and-community-aware networks for extending and intensifying the Longhouse's involvements. There are invitations from district organizations or agencies to be part of their work, as formerly in the Hastings North Partners Group (though this was fraught with ambiguities, including the use of gambling proceeds for their work). There is the cultivation of respect for its relative length of time in a representative, advocacy role on behalf of the higher and wider United Church in greater Vancouver. There is a "new-monastic-like" dedication to maintaining a daily presence of one or more of us to keep the doors open, phones engaged, e-mails responded to, an old Plymouth Caravan freely loaned and maintained, and networks or alliances supported beyond but often within the building. And not least, inevitably there is a lot of money exchanged one way or another, in cash or in kind. Literally and symbolically "bread" too is a deep and widespread means of exchange, attesting to D. T. Niles' condensed depiction of the Christianity and the church as where and when one beggar tells another that one finds food.[21]

Along with ideal mission purposes, self-interests come into play in the practice of plain survival. There are the practical uses of the building space for mutual help groups as well as mutually favored rental arrangements with local social services like an Out-of-School Care program and free uses of the church for a weekly Food Bank. There are charitable donations receipted to some local merchants and sympathetic neighbours for supplying in-kind donations. There are the flexible uses, mostly free, of that reliable 1993 Plymouth Caravan. It has multiple uses and is especially useful for people moving, shopping and/or traveling to distant burial grounds, and assisting other churches with/for food pick-up/delivery. There is help to provide

20. Jim White is a founding elder of the Longhouse Ministry and remains constructively critical, given his higher-level positions in the governance of the United Church of Canada regionally and nationally.

21. See further *Think Exist.com*, http://thinkexist.com/quotation/christianity_is_one_beggar_telling_another_beggar /203369.html.

legitimacy to groups needing space for their own project or program or cause—whether the smaller and less frequent Traditional Grandmothers', the Urban Gitxsan Society, the aforementioned numerous 12-step groups, and emotional support groups by means of weekly morning or evening sharing circles. Similarly, there is free and flexible meeting space for networks like ACA or the MVA. This assists in involving the surrounding area and the Longhouse itself in wider spheres of educative influence.

The Triad, Realism, and the Longhouse

What of the evidence of the presence of the conjunctive hope/prayer/justice—and this triad as the content of hopeful realism—in the Longhouse Ministry? How do these influence, leaven, and animate its ministries and, in turn, that of its nourishing networks? Self-critically, what of the presence of any opposites such as extending mere charity without any sense of a commanded justice and the presence of frenzied ministries of mere activism apart from or instead of the disciplined practice of prayer? Extended to social justice concerns, these possibly imbalanced practices mean less pastoral and/or congregational development and acting as if an incumbent's eventual loss or retirement can be ignored with funding challenges when that happens (for now, the Longhouse has banked a year's endurance, as its UCC's Mission and Service Grant annually declines). As throughout, "balance" is the operative term for this ministry, as for its precedents and connecting networks—especially a vital balance, and, for a meaningful *telos*, an animated vital balance.

A further ministry incident illustrates the move from first aid to a prophetic kind of witness while maintaining pastoral care. In 2012, during Advent and post-Christmas, there was, in a crowded rooming house, (2862 Pandora St.), a fire with three immediate victims. The head tenant, "Bud" Barker, survived a month-long coma; also four others survived but only because two got out just in time and because one was already out looking for cigarette butts (and the last had had a premonition he should not stay that particular night!). A superbly vigilant media involvement raised questions and pressed for redress. Eventually, the Coroner's office conceded to an actual inquest. This took also the vigorous advocacy efforts of networks like SoJ. We all pressed for a public Coroner's Inquiry to root out the causes of the fire and conditions of that house—helpfully spurred on by the 5th Estate of local journalists (one TV journalist lived in the immediate area) to ask some wider justice questions.

As that Christmas season moved to closure—virtually consumed by Pandora House victims' concerns, memorial planning, continual media requests—at least three other city groups pressed the justice issue to be probed. What underlying conditions caused such a fire and loss of life and what now to redress? The minister, meanwhile, amid maintaining a semblance of ministry out of the Longhouse and a Central City Lodge chaplaincy, attended and helped with, all told, ten funerals or memorials over eight of the twelve days of the Christmas season.

Longhouse Ministry and Network Comparisons

How does the Longhouse critically and constructively contribute to and with the above-noted networks? What may be intimations of the presence of God—the biblical ground and aim of hope no matter what harsh realities exist and even prevail? Recalling a social ethics' affirmation that it is in the processes and patterns of interdependence that God may be discerned, what enables and sustains a ministry in the city?

The Longhouse Ministry is much less institutional than large-scale, urban missions across the country, such as Victoria, B.C.'s Our Place Society and the Toronto Christian Resource Centre. But the Longhouse Ministry is more established and institutionally funded than Vancouver's Streams of Justice. There is a "forced option" of having to practice charity in response to poverty at the door and in the Sanctuary with a regular food bank depot. Thankfully with the help of, again, the above networks, the Longhouse is freer to extend beyond charity measures to actual networking and even a steadfast fostering of social justice concerns. This attests to the needed reality base for such a witness—and hope therein that it can endure. In addition, there is a special, inherited, and intentional First Nations ministry with lots of practiced openness to others so that, for example, maximum hospitality is granted to families or groups or ad hoc gatherings in need of space for a memorial or funeral or an out-of-city Band Council meeting. The minister is on call for hospital and prison visits, some of them akin to the late-night or early-morning knock on the monastery's outside door (for hospitality and/or emergency aid).

Meanwhile, it is important to discern what all three urban networks in concert with the Longhouse Ministry (and vice-versa) feature in common. As fragile and impermanent as all four entities are, they exhibit features of Chapter 2's section "critical and new faithful responses"—recalling the contemplation-and-action creative tension expressing due care for a vital balance; community organizing as a strategy of engaging justice as more of a balance power; and evidence of the new monasticism's disciplines to focus on cardinal or singular themes. There are least the following:

1. An "animated contrast-awareness", rooted initially in contrast experiences of negative, aching conditions of inequality and resultant indignities that gave rise to the very origins of each network (see *Viva Voce* Appendix B) and a continuing concern for the street people and/or homeless and/or root conditions for addictions. Out of these arise an enduring concern for such justice issues as housing affordability, a living wage, due recognition of First Nations' claims around still unceded and traditional territories, and redressing the pervasive presence of fragmentation and resultant dislocation as the root conditions of addiction.

2. The networks' concern to practice advocacy, even if implicitly out of and following from their experiences of mere education on pertinent social issues. Such concern relates a personal level of awareness to social awareness—especially exercising their personal freedom to advocate apart from government restrictions on the Ministry's political activity (see below).

3. The direct and indirect responses of the networks on the dimension of current and pressing social issues such that education is regularly offered and, where possible, support to the relevant actors involved in such issues. Such support is offered to: SoJ, listening intently to groups organizing for change for illegal immigrants or migrants or the loss of affordable housing stock due to gentrification and even gentri-victions; to ACA hearing from recovering addicts as well as front-line workers in detox, treatment, and recovery homes; for MVA, intensively listening to and taking actions on the discerned issues of affordable housing, affordable and mass transportation, poverty and social isolation; and to C4MWJ/Kairos, supporting the grass-roots efforts of farm worker organizing or advocacy if only for awareness of their rights but also protection if part of unionization efforts).

4. In each network, and all together, there is an expressed presence by way of an outreach and prophetic component to move beyond merely in-house work and, even with SoJ's host church (GCBC), the earnestly offered hospitality of meals and over-night shelter for cold-weather times. Always there arises the need and task of self-scrutiny via a prophetic posture: "Gracious hosts and pleasant music could not obliterate

the differences in power and resources between those who served and those who come as needy guests."²² There is, meanwhile, a commitment to practice an ear-to-the-ground to receive and offer credibility.

5. Networking with allies such as other churches or agencies: in SoJ's case, other social justice causes and sponsoring organizations; in ACA's case, with those people involved in alcohol and drug counseling or treatment centres or teaching on the topic of addiction and social psychology; in MVA's case, reaching out to and seeking firm alliance relationships with organizations with real membership bases; and in the C4MWJ/Kairos case, connecting with sympathetic unions and churches—especially in the spheres of awareness and influence of migrant work, farm labor, or domestic labor.

6. Each network has its own critical and constructive contribution to make, ranging from ACA's special focus on challenging addiction globally as being "not about drugs" but stemming from society's fragmentation and dislocations. ACA constructively organizes regular soul-searching sessions of personal and social justice. SoJ offers a critical focus on challenging justice as a mere paltry, convenient distribution of day-old bread to food banks as well as constructively organizing regular sessions on biblical, economic, political, and cultural (especially First Nations) viewpoints. MVA's special focus is on broad-based community organizing, across sectors and on multiple issues that are carefully culled from relational meetings and listening campaigns before taking public and prophetic actions for justice purposes. The Longhouse Ministry, as a node in and of these three significant networks, is thereby challenged to take an in-depth and wide note of the above and contribute its own pastoral, community, and prophetic concerns—"in" the networks but not so much an uncritical part "of" them that it then loses its needed, independent voice.

7. Each network offers its own particular focus from time to time and thus the potential to contribute depth, width, and thickness to the whole being greater than the sum of its parts. With ACA, there is a sensible awareness of precisely what community "awareness" yearns to mean, including letting go of a persistent controlling disposition or that which precludes serious listening and the practice of acceptance (its regular mindfulness sessions assisting). With SoJ, there is a patient focus on the meaning and practice of justice advocacy, supporting but

22. Pohl, "A Community's Practice of Hospitality" with its instructive sub-title: "The Interdependence of Practices and of Communities," 126.

sensibly resisting chasing one cause or issue after another to the point of weariness and plain exhaustion. With MVA, there is a similar focus on what justice consists of and sensibly how do we get there and sustain it on a step-by-step basis. For Longhouse, there is the sense to contribute to these three bodies, recalling its founding though modest influence. At the same time, it does not forego its vocation as a Christian ministry, called to practice and hold in as vital a balance as possible, the prophetic with the pastoral and even priestly roles it is invited to engage (including the church building's function as an ageing, ailing, and yet ever-available place of hospitality).

Drawing on the focused discipline of justice from SoJ, there is more of the perspective of an animating awareness from ACA and more of the challenge of building and sustaining an alliance for the long haul from MVA. The Longhouse Ministry receives and benefits from all of the above network commonalities. If it cannot often share the practice of advocating justice making-and-keeping, the Longhouse is at least aware of how its inevitable practices of charity in response to poverty are insufficient and, as with hope, in need of helpmates to move from charity measures to affirm justice principles and practices. For example, the Longhouse's virtually daily fetching and distribution of bread to the surrounding neighborhoods, by way of drop-ins, a weekly food bank, and regular shared meals following the worship services, could not fulfill what doing justice summons. But its intentional and renewed involvements in the above networks serve as a critical and constructive check and balance, so there is continued mindfulness of the Augustinian caveat that charity is no substitute for justice withheld. On its own, the Longhouse would cave in to merely offering, at best, charity measures. In concert with the wider and deeper witness of the three networks, there can be and often, thankfully, are bolder measures undertaken even if with considerable fumbling, bumbling and stumbling.

On the other hand, it is possible that without the Longhouse's annual practices of organizing the Advent and Lent Vigils of the Silenced, the value of doing a theology of and for justice would not occur. (SoJ regularly pursues a biblical perspective on justice—a recent series of faith and justice roundtables combining a "reading of the Word" with readings of issues including poverty and homelessness, First Nations' concerns on colonization and land uses, the climate crisis, and migrant worker/refugee crises). These penitential season vigils illustrate both an intrinsic and instrumental value since to stand for the silenced is in itself an intrinsic public witness and, to advocate that others conscientiously press their politicians to take note and justly respond is an instrumental value and purpose for the Vigiling. In tune with biblical scholar, Anglican priest, and occasional SoJ participant, Laura Dykstra, such vigils hold open and energize the hopeful witness that simply to be present is warrant enough, to be present without regard for a successful outcome yet with the longing of and for praying justice, nonetheless. Dykstra's view complements the likes of Merton's theological interpretation of the meaning and practice of prayer, so she attests that: "Vigil does not ask that we accomplish something; instead it affirms our presence itself has meaning, that our *attention* is a valuable currency."[23] None of the above networks engage in such regular vigils and in tune with the liturgical rhythm of the church year. SoJ occasionally participates when another organization or project's cause hosts a Vigil or Lament, such as for a young First Nations man who died from an assault at a train station, allegedly by the transit police themselves or a Holy Saturday Vigil to note major proposed pipe-line threats to the urban environment and First Nations land claims.

The Longhouse ministry could not exercise its width and depth of involvement without it also being, to some degree, independent (especially in its funding sources or base), and thus able to be prophetic. To be prophetic requires that fundamental capacity to be independent enough to be willing *and able* to "speak the truth to those in power." Politics is a genuine vocation if independent, and so an urban ministry, to the extent it can exercise an independence, can convey its true vocation.[24] The Longhouse Ministry does not come easily to a position of even modest "independence." Financially it is relatively independent, which means that, like of lot of urban ministries its funding sources are diverse and thus less vulnerable to the arbitrariness of only one funding source withdrawing or threatening. Non-profit agencies as well as ministries become nervous about their charitable tax status with the Federal arm of the government, restricted as they are by a very limited per cent (10% maximum) of their work available to practice sorely needed and timely advocacy. The questionable distinction enforced by the Federal government is that it is okay to alleviate poverty but not prevent it or challenge its contributing causes! Recently a "public good letter" has been issued to the governing party by leading organizations including the

---

23. Dykstra, *Set Them Free*, 202, (italics added). See also Merton, compared to and perhaps drawing upon Simone Weil, on prayer as an unmixed, focused attention in Waldron's thoughtful *Thomas Merton* with its instructive sub-title: *Master of Attention*, 20–21.

24. For an important notion of politics as a vocation with obvious reference to the ministry as a vocation and the affinity of *living off* of, or with independence or *living for* one's vocation (albeit it is often and realistically both in the actual life of power politics), see Weber, "Politics as a Vocation" http://anthropos-lab.net/wp/wp-content/uploads/2011/12/Weber-Politics-as-a-Vocation.pdf., see especially 5–6. See also Brueggemann, *Truth Speaks to Power*, passim.

Canadian Centre for Policy Alternatives and the Ecology Action Centre reminding the governing party of the past contributions of the non-profit and charitable sectors and thereby questioning the apparent political motivation to investigate if not curtail their activities.[25]

Noted above, the Longhouse Ministry is also assisted in its indispensable independence by live-in volunteers who exhibit aspects of the new monasticism in terms of living simply (so that others may simply live) and with its only paid staff person living and working likewise. "Living simply" relates to attaining a degree of stability and another classical monastic vow, that of a life-long "conversion of manners" or conversation to engage with one's ministry and place of ministry for life (see Appendix A). To be independent, even relatively, is to be afforded a prophetic possibility—not being in fear of "the powers" and their funding influences—so to speak the truth to those in power and not be unduly and arbitrarily incumbent to them. This means that the Longhouse reluctantly challenges the temptation of making exaggerated claims of even one of its participating networks. The Longhouse has already questioned the MVA claim to represent hundreds of thousands of total members when, at best, it is but a small percentage of the organization's gross numbers on paper that really could and would respond to an issue or a campaign on a major issue such as improving mass and affordable transportation and housing in greater Vancouver.[26] It is thus vital to be aware of the subtlety and triggering lures of power. One must be humbly prophetic enough to be willing to profess and practice the second plank of the Micah 6:8 triad wherein modesty and loving tenderly are hallmarks of obeying and serving thy God—what the late mission theologian Bosch succinctly named as bold humility and/or humble boldness. Paralleling Paul's I Corinthians 13's conclusion, Bosch professes: "We know only in part, but we do know and we believe that the faith we profess is both true and just, and should be proclaimed . . . not as judges or lawyers, but as witnesses' not as soldiers, but

---

25. See e.g. Vandergrift's "CRA Audits: Six Questions," 10 and Jenny Uechi, "Charities Rebel Against CRA Targeting" March 5, 2015 http://www.vancouverobserver.com/national-observer/charities-fight-back-calling-clarity-rules-contributing-public-policy and http://www.scribd.com/doc/257718331/Public-Good-Letter-E-Dubourg. With a recently, newly elected Liberal Federal Government there are modest signs that some of this hard-line scrutiny of registered charities may lessen.

26. The Longhouse Ministry has raised this challenge internally, but so far in vain. Meanwhile, recent research by a member organization of MVA which loaned nursing students to do an inventory of MVA members and concerns reported that of the possible 63 MVA member organizations .75 million people are claimed to be represented (another states .25 million) a significant proportion of the population of the city of Vancouver, indeed! From an unpublished Demographic Grid Summary Feb 2015 power point.

as envoys of peace; not as high-pressure salespersons, but as ambassadors of the Servant Lord."[27]

The Longhouse Ministry's mission purpose of "Seeking Shalom of the City" is stamped on its free hand-out pens.[28] It arises, of course, from the prophet Jeremiah 29's animating *raison d'etre* brought to his exiled people: pray and seek the shalom of the cities you are now in, for therein and thereby, is your justice too (verse 7). Key is the twinning of prayer and the mission goal of shalom or justice. Not specifically named in the Longhouse's mission credo, hope is pervasively implicit. These are all basic signs of hope: to have been formed at all by the earnest steadfastness of its First Nations' founders (the late John (Cree) and Jean (Mohawk Jeffries thirty-five years ago); to have been sustained by a host of backroom and low-key volunteers in and out of season (not merely Christmas); to have been supported by surprising benefactors, some of whom have appeared with an envelope of crisp $50 bills for whatever was needed and not merely for the Christmas time splash of charity. When thought of as "Christ's mass", the season conveys a prophetic-priestly poignancy that is a helpful counter-cultural measure. Meanwhile, vigiling and dedicated involvements in the above networks arouse and stir hope to be fed by the necessary ingredient of waiting. This entails waiting, with the helpmates of the other virtue disciplines of faith, love, and, via Aristotle's and Aquinas's cardinal virtues, especially, justice. To these some social ethicists would further add, at least, integrity.[29]

Triad's Conjunctive in the Service of Hopeful Realism

It is pertinent to press for clarity of what makes for a vital balance of factors for a sustainable, faithful, public, and prophetic ministry. We continue to press for what an urban ministry would look like if one or even two of these *hoping-for-justice-prayerfully* ingredients are missing—even perhaps latent, perhaps suppressed? With an emphasis on explicit considerations in the following, inferences are ventured. Implicit understandings of prayer include attentiveness to a concern, an issue or cause and, of course, people: the one praying and the others. It implies understandings of justice that start with a plain grasp of fairness in due process and outcomes (while moving beyond to include organizing power to contribute to negotiating for fairness via

---

27. See Bosch, *Transforming Mission*, 489.

28. Cf. Kilpin, *Urban to the Core*; Villafane, *To Live in Peace*; Gornik, *Seek the Peace of the City*; and Dickau, *Plunging into the Kingdom*.

29. See MacIntyre, *After Virtue*, 3rd edition, 203.

a balance of power). It also implies understandings of hope that include, again, the "hop" of adventure.[30] Students of hope once again affirm the relativity of hope and its need for the helpmates that justice work brings to the task. There is as well a recognition of the inherent aspect of "a patient waiting" in the very nature of what it means to hope.[31] With Moltmann, such a tone of waiting is vitally complemented with hastening the very conditions sought—indeed, with practising parables of the coming of the Kingdom that could be anticipatory (proleptic) illustrations of that reign of the Kingdom and therein the coming of God—for the arousal of the intentions and possibilities for practicing hope.[32]

If Only Justice Is Present

Although justice is a strong biblical, church history, Niebuhrian, liberation theology,—and is an enduring evangelical and ecumenical mandate, it could not be long before self-righteousness arises and/or burnout occurs. Or, the practice of justice could dwindle into mere charity aspects of the practice of ministry to the poor and be thus viewed as part of the "poverty industry." There have been challenges to this poverty industry recourse. These challenges include: Steams of Justice (as above) and, in decades past, at least in Canada, the Just Society Movement in 1970s Toronto (a challenge to the then Prime Minister's campaign slogan); the Parallel Institute of Montreal and/or the Greater Riverdale Organization in 1970s Toronto, via the late Don Keating (organizing for grass-roots alternatives to power on high). Also should be added, with ambiguity, First United Church of

---

30. Further, Norris writes: "To hope is to make a leap, to jump from where you are to some place better
[. . .] (and helped via imagination and daringness) no matter how hopeless your situation may appear" *Acedia and Me,* 221.

31. On the "relativity" (vs. an absolute) of hope, see again Lynch, *Images of Hope* and on the need of the virtue of hope summoning the helpmates of faith and love, in trust, see Tinder's *The Fabric of Hope,* 2nd edition, vii–ix. On the necessity of waiting with the discipline of hope lest what is prematurely hoped for be for the wrong thing, see T.S. Eliot's "East Coker, Part III" of the *Four Quartets.* Finally, see McCarroll's *Waiting at the Foot of the Cross* for a central and consistent emphasis on "waiting" as the indispensable ingredient of hope, both passively and actively, especially 197-9.

32. See Moltmann's *Ethics of Hope,* 6–8. Cf. Moltmann, *In the End—The Beginning,* 91–92. As with Barth, Moltmann employs "parables" to denote exemplary Kingdom signs and is akin to Schillebeeckx's contrast experiences, both affirming the value of "critical negativity" or a negation of the negative. "Proleptic," an advance anticipation of things/Kingdom to come, is recalled from Pannenberg's writings; e.g., "Appearance and the Arrival of the Future." *The Coming of God* is Moltmann's later work on Christian eschatology.

Vancouver as it stoked the potential funding coals to take advantage of temporary revenue for emergency shelters (made available for the 2010 Winter Olympics, if only to avoid anticipated tourist reactions to urban core poverty). Nonetheless, the collapse of justice into mere charity measures is feared in some dimensions of the life and ministry of Victoria's Our Place Society. Its former head minister, Rev. Al, took with him the indignation he encountered from the raw hurt of the streets and translated it into regular board meetings, staff retreats, and monthly newsletter stories. He carries on with this mission in his newly formed Dandelion Society. The current Metro Vancouver Alliance (as above) risks a reduction of its justice aims, and its strategies to attain them, in providing safe and convenient support for its already-organized member groups but not also including the less organized or plain unorganized so that they could join such an alliance. This dashes the hopes of some Vancouver urban ministry practitioners. As a participant-observer of the Streams of Justice, I worry about an isolated focus on justice apart from the disciplines of prayer and hope. It has been noted that the analysis and work of justice making and keeping is complex; it also requires dedication and courage.[33] The practitioners of justice invariably need the witness of what it means to behold and practice hope as well as prayer (thus Niebuhr's witness). Again, with the conjunctive presence of hoping justice prayerfully, there is the leaven of a nourishing and thus animating check-and-balance dynamic.

If Only Prayer Is Present

For Merton the discipline of prayer, however practiced, is primal—the *spring* source for the streams that arise to flow. If people and their faith community attempt to fly solo, to look only after its own household, then it would not be long before an inward-looking or in-house urban ministry or network community formed. This community could develop apart from, if not become indifferent to, the world and its challenging summons. On the one hand, there is the faithful public and prophetic witness and promise that, for example, abides in Kathy Bentall's founded urban retreat oases of Vancouver's Main Street's "Listening Post" and her former Salsbury Street house basement. This basement is conveniently near to and a resource for both the Stream of Justice and its host church, Grandview Calvary Baptist Church (where its lead pastor lives and his partner, Mary, conducts spiritual direction and healing). There is, as well, the Bentall extended family's founded

33. On engage as also a "pledge," "dedication" and/or "devotion," see Tracey, *The Earth Manifesto*, 57–59.

and funded Rivendale Retreat Centre on the nearby, enviable Bowen Island. On the other hand, there is a perceived irrelevance of monastic-like living/working in the Greater Vancouver Regional District by hard-core, seasoned political activists. While these retreat places could well be helpful—and indeed have for many ministers, lay-people, and street people—they seem less helpful for bearing an actual witness to the public/common good.[34] Though seemingly limited to his strict monastic life, Merton strove for a consistent witness of integrity through writing and correspondence, and occasional on-site retreats. He reflected:

> One of the worst illusions in the life of contemplation would be to find God by barricading yourself inside your own soul, shutting out all external reality by sheer concentration and willpower, cutting yourself off from the world and other men by stuffing yourself inside your own mind and closing the door like a turtle.[35]

When thus prayer is conjoined with the practice and realism of justice making and keeping, then the testimonies of those who hunger and thirst abiding in the leaven of hope will arise even in the conflict and contradictions of collective life. With Merton's witness as background, it is valuable to recall Moltmann—a virtual testimony to the necessity of twinning realism with hope:

> Propositions count as true if they correspond to the reality which can be checked. But hope's assertions of promise often enough stand in contradiction to the reality of the present experience. These assertions are not the outcome of past experiences they are an invitation to new ones. Their aim is not to illuminate the reality that already exists; they want to explore the possibilities ahead [. . .] they do not aim to be reality's train-bearers; they want to run ahead with the torch.[36]

If Only Hope Is Present

As basic as Moltmann's virtue discipline of hope is, it could be but an abstraction, especially apart from the realism of ministry in the city, day in and day out. Hope could be so general and generic that real injustices are neglected. Such neglect might be the situation even for the A Community

---

34. Helpful are Brueggemann and Wallis' writings on the common/public good. Respectively, see *Journey to the Common Good* and *On God's Side*..

35. Merton is cited from *New Seeds of Contemplation* found in *Through the Year with Thomas Merton*, ed. McDonnell, March 23 entry.

36. Moltmann, *In the End—The Beginning*, 89.

Aware network and earlier "think tanks" such as the Hope Foundation (recently renamed Hope Studies Central) in Edmonton, Alberta, despite its retired founder, Ronna Jevnes', original purpose and hope![37] Hope, apart from prayerful justice or just prayer, may well fall short of animating and sustaining the long haul of, and in, urban ministry. The late Lawrence Moon practiced prayer on the very first day of The Open Door's 1990 opening in Victoria, B. C. Streams of Justice steadfastly insists on a predominantly justice focus while welcoming at least occasional check-ins to affirm the accompanying centeredness, even energy, of contemplative prayer. A Toronto Christian Resource Centre (CRC) key community-and-program staff person of many faithful years, Phil Nazar—recently all too quickly departed from the CRC—carried on his inherited monastic and religious-ordered traditions of faithfully gathering and committing to quarterly, personal, renewal retreats. He illustrates the contemplation-and-action tension noted as a warm current of a burning ember in Chapter 2. When those practicing hope commit to learning from trials and errors, mistakes and the host of inevitably miscalculated ventures—in a word, *praxis*—then hope could well be present as its conjunctive part of the triad—bearing with and fuelling endurance. The examples of this Chapter 7's networks, along with the grounding theologians' own stories, attest to how they work together to provide a check-and-balance realism and how hope is an intimate aspect of what sustains a long-haul, faithful, public, and prophetic witness, and yet hope is not on its own.

If Two Discipline Terms Are Present but Not the Third

If both prayer and justice are present, as *praying justice*, but not hope, then eventually, one senses that the long-haul nature of an urban ministry's faithful public and prophetic witness is compromised, weakened, and/or depressed. The wider "horizon" of God "for all, in all" is compromised if not forsaken for mere self-interests so that, despite the earnest efforts of a Metro Vancouver Alliance (MVA) to organize across neighborhoods on multiple issues and with the disciplined alliance (to the extent possible) of organized labour, churches, and community groups, the MVA's horizon would be drastically curtailed. It could be limited merely to its political interests and funding needs and succumbing expediently to exclude the inconvenience of the un-organized poor (as above). While entertaining the default absence of hope, Bonhoeffer poignantly challenges:

37. Such a dedication to studying hope, I recall from Ronna Jevne's VST summer school attendance and the early reflections leading to the beginnings of Edmonton's Hope Foundation. See also Jevne, *Finding Hope*, *The Voice of Hope* and *The Inspiration of Hope in Bereavement Counseling* (with Cutcliffe).

> [T]he series of steps from perseverance to hope is no self-evident truth gained by worldly experience. Luther said that it might very well be put in an entirely different manner (contra Romans 5: 1–5 affirmations), namely: suffering produces a lack of perseverance; a lack of perseverance, impenitence; and impenitence despair. And despair utterly disappoints.[38]

There is a caveat of realism here. With hope, however, the praying-justice partnership is stretched and even fortified. Hope thus does not disappoint. Prayer and justice are necessary but not sufficient for the purpose of an urban ministry's faithful, public-prophetic, witness. Hope is needed to behold the inclusive horizon of God's reign that all be in all—spurred by that restless goad that, again, stabs inexorably in the flesh of every unfulfilled present.[39]

If, secondly, both hope and justice are present, as *hoping justice*, but not prayer, then eventually one anticipates that compassion wanes and spiritual fatigue arises. Again, a long-haul ministry would be compromised. In any case, a shift from a spiritually oriented, church-based ministry to mainly a mere social service agency could emerge. If only to attract and sustain much sought-after secular funding, this could be the temptation of Toronto's Christian Resource Centre's recent and likely current phase, in which even the "Christian" in its name is anxiously expressed though recently also reaffirmed. One of their recent Board members and conveniently an active Emmanuel College/Toronto School of Theology theologian, Michael Bourgeois, helpfully attests otherwise:

> We are the Toronto *Christian* Resource Centre, not because we are necessarily all Christians or because we serve only Christians, but because the work that we do can be called *Christian* work. This defines not only what we do, but also why and how we do it. Perhaps most importantly, it defines who we serve.[40]

Crucially, prayer yokes a humble willingness to begin again or begin anew with the courage to relocate one's centre of gravity; that is, to "reclaim and root ourselves in our place on earth and in heaven."[41] Merton professed that we are always, truly, beginners—beginning anew or again.[42] Moltmann similarly affirms this, adding a significant note of solidarity that one's contributions

---

38. Bonhoeffer, "The Secret of Suffering," 292.

39. Moltmann, *Theology of Hope*, 21.

40. E-mail communication to Morris of a committee's draft on the CRC's name et al., January 28, 2011; (italics added).

41. McEntyre, *Caring for Words in a Culture of Lies*, 213.

42. Again, *inter alia*, see *Contemplative Prayer*, 37, 69. Also, see *A Year with Thomas Merton*,
ed. Montaldo, 313.

overlap and sow the seeds for those who follow.[43] Prayer enacts this time and again as prayer also evokes the response to praise, the will to sing or chant, and, while celebrating ourselves as works of art, to render ourselves worthy of being saved, as God, the covenanting partner, needs our help.[44] Justice and hope are necessary but not sufficient for an urban ministry's faithful public and prophetic witness. Prayer is needed to enable that willing, patient, and synergistic collaboration with the covenant-making God.

Prayer is needed to save a ministry or a network from self-righteousness. Even surmising that one and one's ministry need not be prayed for, prayer is needed precisely for one's privileged position and protected perspective. Alas, the poor may well intercede for those of us in this position and perspective, as an East Harlem Protestant Parish storefront lawyer came to confess.[45] One may also profess that prayer attentively moves a ministry and its practitioners from the periphery to the center of where it needs if not longs to be, something that could well invite and require a conversion process (as William James attests).[46] In the case of the above three networks, it is good for the Longhouse to be a base of prayerful centeredness so that at least its contribution as a node to the associative networks is intentionally nourished—although ACA has come to host, at the Longhouse Church, regular mindfulness meditation sessions (of nine weeks duration) so as to contribute to the contemplation or meditation and action tensions. This crucial tension, so as to be creative, and through the influences of Merton, is presented often to ACA by the Longhouse's minister.

If, thirdly, both prayer and hope are present, as *hopeful prayer* but not justice, then the ministry may well be oriented only to an inner circle or merely a one-dimensional level of charity ministry, however well-intended and even long-lasting. The ministry may be short of a biblically sound,

---

43. Moltmann thusly reflects on a significant body of life experience and writing, "Since I cannot 'start all over again,' I will hopefully bring to a good end what was hidden in my beginnings. In every end is hidden a new beginning. Others have already begun where I have left off." Moltmann, "The Adventure of Theological Ideas," 105.

44. Paraphrasing Heschel's remarks in "The Spirituality of Abraham Joshua Heschel," December 6, 2012 with Arnold Eisen, via *On Being with Krista Tippet,* December 8, 2012, http://onbeing.org. Cf. " . . . the important thing is not that theology should *look like* prayer, but that it should *be* prayer, namely prayer in this most rudimentary sense of an earnest, hard-headed, Jacobean struggle for the blessing of understanding" in Hall, *Thinking the Faith,* 289 (italics original).

45. Again, "The travail of the poor is intercessory for the rich—for them, in their behalf, in their place. It substitutes for their own suffering. They would suffer if the poor did not purchase for them some immunity from suffering"; Stringfellow, *My People is the Enemy,* 29, cf. 22, 97.

46. James writes: "To say that a man is 'converted' means [. . .] that religious ideas, *previously peripheral* in his consciousness, *now take a central place* and that religious aims *form the habitual centre of his energy,*" *The Varieties of Religious Experience,*162. (italics added).

social-justice integrity and disciplined practice. For the Longhouse, the SoJ remains indispensable in order that it remain focused on justice—amid all of the myriad, "busy-work" temptations to attend to anything but justice making and keeping. The literature review in Chapters 2 and 3, the theological groundings for the triad in Chapters 4, 5 and 6, and the three urban networks in conjunction with the Longhouse Ministry case study in this Chapter 7 all combine to induce a core category or over-all story-line of *an animated contrast-awareness* (of the experience of the world as it is versus what it ought to be). This contrast-awareness is discernible in Appendix B wherein some vivid testimonies from the networks' founders are duly noted and drawn upon. This integrating central story-line category demonstrates that if justice was intentionally present in an urban ministry's mission, then it could practice a faithful, public, *and* prophetic witness. Hopeful praying—that is, praying in the hope that a contrast-awareness experience can lead to serious and sustained justice advocacy and organizing—is stretched to include the concrete trial-and-error work of justice.

Summary Conclusion

When combined with the leavening discipline of justice, prayer in the practice of hope—or, hope in the practice of prayer—provide indispensable help to animate and sustain what it means to petition and bear an urban ministry's public witness. Thus, prayer and hope enable a prophetic response to the Lord's Prayer reign of God dawning, time and again.[47] That is, with the resounding imagery imperative of the prophet Amos' and the Streams of Justice adopted mandate: "Let justice roll down life waters and right-wising like as ever-flowing stream" (Amos 5:24). Prayer and hope are necessary but not sufficient, as a theological reality base for an urban ministry's faithful public witness. They are insufficient because justice is needed to provide the social-ethical and realistic content and the commanding resources for revision—in the service of a *prophetic* witness—for when an urban ministry's work is tempted to succumb or retreat to short-cut practices and disciplines.

---

47. See also Kamergrauzis' "Ronald Preston and the Future of Christian Ethics," 80, where Merton-like he cites Karen Lebackz: "Because justice emerges out of protest against injustice, justice is not so much a state of being as a struggle and a constant process [. . .] It is the process of providing new beginnings, not an ideal state of distribution," *Justice in an Unjust World: Foundations for a Christian Approach to Justice.* Minneapolis, MN: Augsburg, 1987, 152

Chapter 8—Summary Considerations and Conclusions

Besides the debilitating sense of futility which comes from wherever, I also have the refreshing tonic of reality. This is a real world: real people with real needs. I need travel no further than the school next door at lunch time [. . .] having fast-food, mean-looking government lunch, which might be their best meal today [. . .] I bring such hope to the Church. I have never outgrown that vision acquired in seminary days that the Catholic Church is the full realization of that vision of the Psalms: 'for all shall be her children'.[1]

. . . (U)rban ministry is gritty, demanding and hard work. None of the Christian communities we have pioneered look that successful according to common standards—they remain small, fragile and highly aware of their weaknesses and imperfections. Life often appears chaotic [. . .] People's lives are astoundingly resilient yet deceptively delicate—too many people die early in the inner city. Urban life is so diverse, causing migraines and ecstasy in the one brain at the same time. However, in the rawness and grittiness of life there is creativity and freedom which is celebrated.[2]

Introduction

THIS BOOK'S EARLY CHAPTERS on key precedents in the practice and dynamics of urban ministry have sought to provide a realistic perspective. These practices and dynamics have invited a response-ethics kind of

---

1. McNamee, *Endurance*, 123, 204.
2. Kilpin, *Urban to the Core*, xiii.

query: what has been occurring in ministries and what of their responses in the cities over generations, particularly in North America and the United Kingdom? Chapter 1 sought to balance realism with hope: that is, to offer a hopeful realism. Indeed, the whole first chapter has in mind this necessary balancing act—and subsequent chapters at least implicitly recall and apply the interpretive value of hope with realism or, realism with hope. These are dialectical interplays toward creative tension so that such a balancing act is vital. This dialectic also warns of the risk of falling into one extreme or the other—given the inevitable tensions, apparent conflicts and/or contradictions in an urban ministry and the resultant paradoxes that several writings employ to give a mature account of urban ministry. On one level, the book seeks an overview that is comprehensive if not compelling. On another level, it confesses that such a perspective is only possible for the short-run, or in hindsight, for a portion of an era, decade, or ambitious body of writings on the subject. It defies a permanent accomplishment in and over the long run. Nevertheless, the twinning of hope with realism offers a vital balance. Such a mature balance arises from out of hope itself, especially when its needed helpmates of prayer and justice are animated.

The evidence and need for a *hoping-justice-prayerfully* triad is revealed in the urban ministry and theology literature. This triad is clarified in the works of the three theologians employed in these chapters to ground each of the triad terms—especially as the origins and means by which hope for Moltmann, justice for Niebuhr, and prayer for Merton are elaborated. These chapters are as much an exercise in biography-as-theology as they are an historical retrieval of what makes the best sense for what an urban ministry can draw from. From these three theologians' lives, thought and legacies, there is hope and a basis for their contributions in their lived realities.

It is one task to aim to adhere to a broad mission vision like practicing a faithful public and prophetic ministry. It is quite another task to elicit the discipline and accompanying encouragement to stay the course to do this—to hear again and again and yet freshly, the Micah command to do justice, love kindness, and walk humbly with thy covenant God. To hear, pray, and actually respond to the grace-based serenity prayer is always more than personal. To know that these three biblical virtues of hope, justice, and prayer are also time-tested, and thus classical, and yet that the practices of these virtues are hardly possible on one's own, as Merton and the new monasticism gratefully attest (detailed in Appendix A).

The Longhouse case study, with its trio of significant networks, provides concrete ways to illumine the meaning and power of hopeful realism in urban ministries, and this case study is assisted by the triad—through which it clarifies where urban ministries can be difficult, wearying, disillusioning

CHAPTER 8—SUMMARY CONSIDERATIONS AND CONCLUSIONS 129

and temptingly self-righteous or pretentious. There seem never enough examples to document and analyze—one misses current anthologies of urban ministries and theologies as past generations' contributions. On this score, the previous chapter remains incomplete. A more thorough employment of multiple cases would have been illuminating. Perhaps an application of a qualitative research method such as grounded theory would have yielded more from the case study and its networks.[3] Nonetheless, the chapter ended on the note that there is helpful evidence in the witness of even a modest urban ministry such as the Longhouse Ministry wherein a faithful public and prophetic witness is possible, especially when additional and farther networks are sought out or initiated.

The introductory chapters bore witness that there is hardly a single urban ministry that can fly solo for very long if it is to be meaningfully, faithfully sustained. Though mention was made of urban theologians who bequeathed a significant body of material to our generation, they hardly ever practiced or honored their vocations isolated from other ministries. Kenneth Leach is representative of a well-networked, urban theologian in the UK, as Harvey Cox is as a theological, urban commentator or the late William Stringfellow is in the USA, and, more as an actual Anglican parish priest, Norman Ellis and the late Presbyterian/United Church's Stuart Coles or Bob Lindsey are in Canada. Their urban, theological legacies convey a sense of shared space. Similarly, the chapters on the three time-tested theologians and their sustaining hope, grounded in realism, attest to their legacies—with intimations and implications for urban ministry. Similarly, the prior Chapter 7 on the Longhouse Ministry and its networks deepen and widen this otherwise small and perhaps insignificant ministry in the east end of Vancouver, B.C. We are reminded that "nodes" are the significant links to networks as, in turn, networks are to community ministries to practice this book's chosen mission vision of a faithful public and prophetic ministry.[4] A network's nodes provide its actual sources and binding ele-

---

3. There is, again, a description and application of grounded theory to analyze Canadian urban ministry case studies; to discern each of their core or central story-line categories and then all together, see Morris, *Engaging Urban Ministry*, Appendix C and Appendix A of this book.

4. Again, it is important to note that this book adds to the author's denominational web site purposes the "prophetic" to merely a "public" witness since the latter does not always or intentionally draw upon the biblical and church tradition of the prophetic. Vital also are biblical notions of the prophetic, an enduring resource being Abraham Joshua Heschel's reflections. Unsurprisingly, Sifton's unearthing the Serenity Prayer's origins of her father dovetails with his close theological friend, Heschel, as she cites him: " (Prophecy is) the voice that God has lent to the silent agony" to those who are willing and able to "draw upon themselves the excess poison in the world"; Sifton, *The*

ments allowing it to arise and, critically and constructively, flourish—often bearing witness (as *telos*) beyond its eventual demise (as *finis*) for others coming later. To the extent that hope is the future aspect of faith (Niebuhr) there is a sense of end as an eschaton or God's fulfillment. To the extent that hope, like peace, is a goad that incites and excites possibilities to transcend fate (Moltmann) then there is purpose. To the extent that hope is like despair in that both may eventually lead to a humble dependency on the Ultimate, Holy One (Merton), there is realism. In all these senses and functions, urban ministries are not alone (as *eschaton*).[5] These three Greek term senses of "end"—*finis, telos* and *eschaton*—will conclude the book.

A Singular Prayer in Focus

It has been stated throughout this book that it is the grace-based serenity prayer that vitally provides a realistic chance of the working triad to become operative and hopeful. It is the vital balance of this prayer that conveys a hopeful realism. Balance is the operative, indeed, indispensable word. It is realistic in its humility that prayer invites the discipline virtues of justice and hope. That it is an animated and vital balance is crucial. Is it in the prayer itself and the praying of it that one is prepared and rendered ready and fit to become the answer—the animating means—to the prayer?[6] Building on and paraphrasing others' apt reflections of the connection between prayer and justice—or contemplation and meditation, with prayer and justice[7]—I pose the following affirmation:

Serenity Prayer, 337.

5. I am also mindful of my own United Church of Canada's creed that indeed we are not alone for we live in God's world and that "in life, in death, in life beyond death, God is with us. We are not alone. Thanks be to God." See *Voices United*, 918.

6. E.g., "We often find relief as soon as we pray, because our attitude toward the situation has changed through the act of praying," *Sex Addicts Anonymous*, 44.

7. Elaborating, one thinks of Dietrich Bonhoeffer, Eberhard Bethge, and Thomas Merton (also Sr. Joan Chittister) as examples of inspiration. In Bonhoeffer's groundbreaking *Letters and Papers from Prison* there is a sermon for the baptism of a nephew (Bonhoeffer was executed by the Gestapo just days before his prison camp was liberated).The sermon included his mature sense that Christians/the Church would have a minimum role to play post-WW II, other than, crucially, to pray and do justice/action, while waiting and hoping for more of an opportunity later (p. 300 in enlarged edition of 1971 via SCM Press). His biographer, Bethge, eventually summarized and enriched this in a short book aptly called *Prayer and Righteous Action,* and his summary of prayer with righteous action or justice can be found on pp. 26–27. From this work, I borrow most of the terms named to depict the interplay between prayer and justice. Merton's summary description of the relation between contemplative prayer and action can be found in *No Man Is an Island*: "[. . .] action is charity looking out to other men, and

CHAPTER 8—SUMMARY CONSIDERATIONS AND CONCLUSIONS   131

Prayer saves justice from self-righteousness, resignation, and ideologizing, and prayer keeps justice in the realm of "honesty" or truth. On the other hand, justice saves prayer from hypocrisy, piousness, and pessimism, and keeps prayer in the realm of action. A third virtue discipline is needed and that is hope. Hope saves prayer and justice from a premature closure, a foreclosure, when a more inclusive horizon is needed and possible for humans and their host planet; and, hope keeps prayer and justice in the realm of God's being. Haiku expressed:

> *Hope animates contrasts/ Contrasts goad* [8] *just prayer/ Steadfast Horizons* [9]

The Original Serenity Prayer Clause-by-Clause

Does the grace-based serenity prayer convey the meaning of this haiku and at the same time aptly illustrate the meanings of hopeful realism? By examining the prayer, clause-by-clause, I will demonstrate that the prayer incorporates steadfastness by way of an animated vital balance (*animated* by the very praying engagement of it). Therein is the hope of the prayer's grounded realism. This is a move deeper than the popular prayer's rendition which omits "grace", with serenity itself as the first petition. To pray for the serenity to accept the things that one or a community cannot change illumines the Buddhist notion of change and suffering being inevitable. A radical acceptance is thus prayed for and commended.[10] How often an

---

contemplation is charity drawn inward to its own divine source. Action is the stream and contemplation is the spring," 7. Chittister's several thoughts may perhaps best be summarized as: "Contemplation is a very dangerous activity. It not only brings us face to face with God. It brings us, as well, face to face with the world, face to face with the self. And then, of course, something must be done. Nothing stays the same once we have found the God within [. . .] We carry the world in our hearts: the oppression of all peoples, the suffering of our friends, the burdens of our enemies, the raping of the Earth, the hunger of the starving, the joy of every laughing child," http://30goodminutes.org.

8. Here one is again reminded of Jürgen Moltmann and his early *Theology of Hope* when he speaks of peace and hope being like a "goad" which "stabs inexorably into the flesh of every unfulfilled present," 21–22.

9. Sebastião Salgado's social photography, spanning continents and now generations, expresses much of this haiku intention. See especially the mixed/multiple media presentation in his recent *The Salt of the Earth* social documentary—from curiosity to despair to mature hope grounding in realism—via the director, Wim Wenders and the son, Juliano Ribeiro Salgado. See further http://www.imdb.com/title/tt3674140/ .

10. See Brach, *Radical Acceptance* and its instructive sub-title: *Embracing Your Life*

urban ministry simply cannot change what is before it at that moment or indeed, for a long time. For an urban ministry (as for twelve-step groups), the prayer for and practice of acceptance expresses that to accept what is now before a recovering addict is part and parcel of what it is to let go—to let go, for example, of resentments, fears, the hankerings for the familiarities of addictive indulgences to numb pain, or "chasing the dragon" yet one more time[11] and even, to let go of there being no hope. In short: to let go and let God. An urban ministry must often accept that giving bread or cup of soup or a bus ticket and maybe a ride to (and from) a hospital or even, at long last, to a detox and treatment centre or recovery house has to suffice. There are those, however—even academics and urban ministry veterans—who claim that even charity responses are a measure of justice in that there is at least a bit of redistribution of resources, otherwise withheld or trashed as waste food or clothing. However, to remain at such a level of a ministry response does not redress the raw indignities and underlying inequalities of poverty (often accompanied by addictions—and their frequently associated histories of abuse). No matter how many petitions signed or rallies attended by urban ministry workers, these are not enough and the ministry tends to stay virtually stuck at a level of mere charity.[12]

The second clause of the prayer is hence ever so welcome as indicative of the balance that this prayer so sorely expresses: the prayer for courage to change the things that not only can be changed, but imperatively ought to be changed. The previously cited caveat, attributed to Augustine, is pertinent here—that charity is no substitute for justice withheld. This is the burden of Niebuhr's coming to justice—via his Detroit pastorate with its many networks pertaining to racial and economic injustice. This was, to remind ourselves, complemented by biblical readings of the prophets as well as Augustine in the subsequent years following Detroit for his teaching and

---

with the Heart of the Buddha.

11. "Chasing the Dragon" may refer to an original "high" when first taking heroin or some other strong opiate but alas, never quite attaining such a level, though not for lack of repeated trying. One recovering heroin addict spoke to me of her eventual acceptance of this as key to her willingness, finally, to engage healing (via the harm reduction of methadone, blessed be Jackie's memory). There are many reflections on "letting go." See an earlier classic, Keller, *Let Go, Let God* with its instructive subtitle, *Surrendering Self-centered Delusions in the Costly Journey of Faith.*

12. An abundance of literature on this charity-and-justice tension could be cited, and some have in Chapters 2, 3 and 4, but also see a relatively unheralded account of at least several USA urban ministries in Harper's *Urban Churches, Vital Signs* with its governing sub-title, *Beyond Charity toward Justice*. Vancouver's Streams of Justice, in my view, remains the single best example of an enduring focus on this challenging and—to have a chance—consistent, faithful move.

CHAPTER 8—SUMMARY CONSIDERATIONS AND CONCLUSIONS 133

circuit-riding vocations. All this sustained him in justice. Justice, we recall for Niebuhr, is rooted and informed by love in all its deep and inclusive implications. However, justice is not simply a love expressed one-on-one and then possible spreading to everyone. This imperative is not limited to what merely one person or a community can conveniently achieve. This clause of the prayer summons a whole lot of imagination (more than one's own limited imagination). It risks to begin to give justice making and justice keeping an adventuresome chance. The implications of Niebuhr's theology of justice for broad-based, multi-issue community organizing are a consistent exercise of imagination—by way of engaging "the possible" in the face of skeptical, precluded impossibilities.

To be sure, more than Niebuhr's written insights inspired Saul Alinksy to undertake many trials and errors, including imprisonment. In prison, Alinsky penned *Reveille for Radicals* and later drew on and applied Niebuhr's theologies and the social-ethical implications of justice. In addition, Alinsky based his insights on John Lewis of the early organizing days of the United Mineworkers and the Congress of Industrial Organization,[13] and later supplemented this body of hard-won collective bargaining experience with Niebuhr's reflections.[14] As Chapter 7 depicted, the modest Longhouse Ministry could not possibly continue seriously with social justice causes without its links to networks and alliances. Streams of Justice maintains a consistent focus on justice, albeit remembering what it took to shift away from charity responses to poverty, including homelessness, and raw addictions. The Metro Vancouver Alliance demonstrates the adoption of Alinsky styles of community organizing via the Industrial Areas Foundation.—which we recall was partly sparked by the Longhouse Ministry at a time when few thought it possible to move beyond Vancouver styles of calling forth for justice by mere public demonstrations or short-lived, chiefly single-issue coalitions. A Community Aware illustrates what it means to focus on the discipline of "awareness" (especially as it relates to a "poverty of the spirit") as the animating task for redressing at least some of the causes and conditions of local and global addictions. All of these operate in the context

---

13. See Alinsky's unauthorized biography, *John L. Lewis*. Niebuhr also tried to resource earlier Congress of Industrial Organizations' organizing attempts by way of his Detroit pastorate and pulpit, sharing these with labor organizers. See further Luke Bretherton's *Christianity and Contemporary Politics: The Conditions and Possibilities of FaithFul Witness*, Chicester, UK: Wiley-Blackwell, 2010, espec. 88–91.

14. I vividly recall Alinsky brandishing a volume of *Reinhold Niebuhr on Politics* as a virtual training manual during a week-long seminar for clergy in California in the late 1960s.

of a contrast experience which, when aroused by unjust negativities, often becomes animated. Indispensably, prayer and hope are instrumental. .

The third clause elicits the resolution to the contrast of the difference between what can/ought to be changed and what for the time being must be accepted. Wisdom is partly the outcome of wrestling with a prior acceptance while yet working to change what is still possible, to change the "can"—always drawing on the limits of realism and the possibilities afforded by hope (Chapter 1). Wisdom is also partly the outcome of attending to the discipline of contemplative prayer or centering prayer or Christian meditation, wherein a quiet center is sought, a "resting in God."[15] Herein the Moltmann and Merton chapters are resourceful (Chapters 4 and 6). Moltmann notes that conditions of hopelessness often indicate justice making-and-keeping issues; namely, that one may move from being mere recipients of menial hand-outs and occasional turkey dinners fit for temporary kings and queens to possibilities of change, however initially incremental. From the spirituality of his monastic cell, Merton continually counsels through his copious journals and letters—that beneath all of the burnout outcomes of a frenzied (if not "demonic activism")[16] there is the place for disciplined grounding in intercessory prayer, personally and politically. Implicitly addressing this third Serenity Prayer clause on wisdom, he attests: "A certain depth of disciplined experience is a necessary ground for fruitful action. Without a more profound human understanding derived from exploration of the inner ground of human existence, love will tend to be superficial and deceptive."[17]

There is at last the fourth (in the original the first) clause of the prayer—the admission that grace is needed. For some, the affirmation of grace is not needed; for "serenity" already conveys the notion of grace. The very willingness to pray and be open to eventual responses is itself a sign of God's presence and thus grace—with ourselves as responding answers, as some new monastics affirm.[18] For others of us, the explicit affirmation of grace is indeed needed. Perhaps in the heat of moments of frustration or

---

15. Cf. Rohr's opening reflection to this chapter. See also "There's a Quiet Understanding" hymn which title is expressed " . . . when we are gathered in the spirit, it's a promise Jesus gives us when we gather in his name," *Songs for a Gospel People*, Hymn # 66, words and music by Tedd Smith.

16. See Merton, *Peace in the Post-Christian Era*, 102–8.

17. Merton, *Contemplation in a World of Action*, 154.

18. See Claiborne and Wilson-Hartgrove, *Becoming the Answers to Our Prayers*. See also

Abraham Heschel's rendering of prayer as the answer, our response to the inconceivable surprise of being alive, cited in *Answers in the Heart* meditation reader, July 7 entry.

even rage, one simply refuses to "accept" the serenity as "being exactly the way it should be at this moment."[19] Grace is also needed to assist recognizing that all of life is a gift, and within it the tasks that arise to summon our engagement, beginning with ourselves and, of course, including others. Prayers of thanksgiving and confession are dimensions of the engaged reality as are the prayers of petition and intercession. The latter ache to be brought "into the light"—here evoking a Quaker spirituality. Therein, apart from grace, it can be no simple or easy task to accept the serenity of the situation to work with some one or some body of people suffering the indignities of inequality or evil—when a being is thwarted, denied, or starved in their very beings[20]—and for that matter, working with allies or associated networks where personalities, alas, may prevail over principles (and thwart the latter).[21]

Grace Hi-lighted

Niebuhr has helpfully written of grace as that which empowers, but also grace as that which is the presence of mercy towards and in our actions or helplessness in the face of blocked or totally denied action. [22] He has aptly flagged that justice "without the grace of love always degenerates into something less than justice."[23] There is also Niebuhr's strong profession of the application of justification by grace through faith, previously cited, that invites as it reminds social justice activists, with others, to remain involved for the long haul.[24] Within, and as a part of the practice of the grace-based serenity prayer, there is profound hope; a hope that the ones praying are indeed not alone and that change is possible as it is desirable. The Augustinian confession that restless hearts remain unfulfilled apart from finding rest or stability in God resonates—the restlessness of desire or hunger is realistically primal and hopefully renewing.[25]

---

19. See such a closing in the twelve-step fellowships of AA and other spin-offs, even adding, "nothing is there or here by mistake in God's world"; *Alcoholics Anonymous*, 449.

20. See H. Richard Niebuhr's *Radical Monotheism and Western Culture*, 103, cf. 37, 47.

21. See the caveat of "Tradition 12" in the AA and related fellowships' literature.

22. Niebuhr, *Nature and Destiny of Man*, II, 107.

23. See Niebuhr, "The Ethic of Jesus and the Social Problem," 28.

24. See again, Niebuhr, *Human Nature & Destiny*, II, 284.

25. See Augustine's *Confessions*' first paragraph and L. Cohen's song lyric "when the hunger for your touch rises from the hunger" from "You Have Loved Enough."

For urban ministries there is the realism, however reluctant, of charity measures being the virtually normative practice of alleviating the symptoms of poverty—reinforced, as elsewhere mentioned, by the Federal Government's heavily curtailing political or advocacy activities of registered charities. There is realism in that few ministries are likely to cast their energies and weight into the organizing of power to take action for the sake of justice. As previously noted, justice advocacy is rife with complexity; there is a need for courage, and people are bound to weariness. Almost inevitable signs of self-righteousness are looked for by by-standers of social justice ministries or ministries joining in meaningful shared efforts such as the Metro Vancouver Alliance. Yet, when hope and realism are combined—that is, meaningfully yoked and serving as a creative balance to one another—then hopeful realism can indeed provide critical and constructive ways to practice a steadfast, faithful, public, and prophetic witness. It is critical for the prophetic capacity of hope, when its helpmate is justice, to counterbalance the tendencies of ministry to engage in mere optimism or worse, wishful thinking. It is constructive, when hope's helpmate is prayer, to deepen the contemplative aspects of what being a faithful witness means and what it means for the long haul when prayer with hope for justice is pacefully grounded in the presence and power of God's being.

In an earlier reference to a phenomenology of hope, James Smith was representatively cited to ground the aims of hope in God. The above exegesis of hope attests to some theologians' and social ethicists' discerning God in the making and keeping of human life or, cited earlier, God discernable in the patterns and processes of interdependence. This is aptly possible, even resourced, in the grace-based serenity prayer. As Merton has prayerfully encouraged, we pray for our own discovery [26]—akin to the late Abraham Heschel's book title *God in Search of Man*. The implications of this include our willing participation in the patterns and processes of interdependence—a willingness to take our due share, while we can, in the second part of Augustine's paraphrased axiom that while without God, we cannot do anything, without us, God will not.[27] As Niebuhr as oft prayed with a deep sense of grace in addition to his serenity prayer, we pray with the petition and hoped-for assurance of God's grace.[28] Recalling the previous chapter on

---

26. See Merton 's chapter title "Pray for Your Own Discovery" in *New Seeds of Contemplation*, 37–46.

27. See further www.beliefnet.com/...Augustine/Without-God-I-Cant-But-Without-Me-.

28. See Niebuhr's frequent references to and uses of "grace" in his prayers. His wife, Ursula Niebuhr, has helpfully collated these prayers, with grace, from his sermons, *Justice and Mercy*, 46, 48, 96, 101, 104, 112, 113, 115–18.

networks and the Longhouse Ministry, all of which embody fragility, we read from Niebuhr:

> Give us grace to walk humble and save us from pretension and every arrogant folly [. . .] to remember the limits of our power and our wisdom, but help us, too, to do our duty within the limits of our power and our wisdom [. . .] Give us grace in this fellowship to be helpful to each other in our several responsibilities [. . .] Grant us to bear each other's burdens, and so fulfill the law of love.[29]

Moltmann too has prayed for the grounding of hope, that its practices be supported by and empowered with the mutual communion of the Triune God itself. We pray: "God, Father, Son and Holy Spirit, /Triune God, / unite with yourself your torn and divided world, / and let us all be one in you, / one with your whole creation, / which praises and glorifies you."[30]

Conclusion

No vast and comprehensive literature survey and no case study focus on innovative and passionate networks could provide all that is required for an urban ministry to bear a steadfast, faithful, public-*and*-prophetic witness. If only they could! Meanwhile, each generation of urban ministry practitioners and dedicated theorists contribute—especially as animated and extended networking occurs out of the spheres of influence and risk-taking, trial-and-error adventures that are possible for urban ministries. Hope depends on the discernment and practice of possibilities—in the inevitable face and challenge of limitations (realism). Theologically expressed, God acts and governs, *inter alia*, in the processes and patterns of interdependence, and thereby to "make and keep human life human."[31] This is also expressed by Paul in his poignant Romans 8 credo and possibly last testament that all things work together for those who love God and are "called according to

---

29. Ibid., 116.

30. Moltmann, *The Source of Life*, 160. Cf. Moss, *The Neighborhood Church*, 4–6 with a similar emphasis on the mutual in-and-out dwelling fellowship, *perichoresis*, " . . . when we who are creating in the image of God are primarily relational beings, too," 4.

31. For a theistic discernment of patterns and processes of interdependence see again Gustafson, *Ethics from a Theocentric Perspective*, Vol. II, 146, cf. 304. See also his *A Sense of the Divine*, 12, 48–49, 58, 72, 92–94, 103–5 and 148–49. See further Paul Lehman, a Niebuhrian-rooted Frontier Fellowship participant, for the instructive sub-title to *The Decalogue and a Human Future*, namely: *The Meaning of the Commandments for Making and Keeping Human Life Human*, Grand Rapids, MI: Eerdmans, 1994.

his purpose" (v. 28). Ideally, the depicted networks of Chapter 7 synergistically work together. This occurs if, when, and as the nodes of these dedicated networks contribute to and provide creative and critical substance to the processes and patterns of interdependence. It is critical when not just any kind of interdependence is endorsed but rather when such interdependence creatively fosters a faithful prophetic witness—informed and nourished by hoping for justice prayerfully.

Realistically, it has become among the Longhouse Ministry's tasks to help foster and facilitate the mutual networking among and between these networks. The SoJ, ACA and MVA networks—and also the Coalition for Migrant Worker Justice network via Kairos—do not naturally or predictably practice this, albeit several social justice concerns are shared much of the time at large. To date, only rare gatherings of all of these networks actually occur at the same time and place—but not without the pushes and pulls of persuasion. So far, this does not occur without the animation of the Longhouse's minister—and this with the odds that the more intentionally the Longhouse tries to animate a mutually synergistic connecting, the more possibly resistant any or all these networks or alliances become! At the very least, the networks share in common the contrast experiences and awareness that aroused their very beginnings and fuel their enduring energies—the moves from the world as it is to the world as it ought to be, and with prayerful justice, hopefully can be. In the end (as *finis*) and to the end (as *telos*) and thinking of the eventual demise and death of virtually all finite and flawed ministries and networks, God will nonetheless be all to all that which matters most and cannot thus be lost, as the biblical vision of the *eschaton* professes (cf. again I Cor. 15:26 as well as the contributions of Liberation, Process Thought, and Moltmann scholars[32]). The implications of eschatology for urban ministry are significant and, in my view, have been barely scratched—though there are promise in others' reflections, in particular my theological teachers of Seminary and post-graduate years, Thomas Ogletree and Terence Anderson.[33] They inspire content to all that

---

32. Process theologians include John Cobb, Jr, David Ray Griffin, and of course, their mentor, A. N. Whitehead. They attest to human and other entities' contributions not being lost but received, preserved, and offered back for future occasions, by God. See Whitehead, *Adventures of Ideas*, 176, 237–38 and *Process and Reality*, corrected version, eds. Griffin and Sherburne, 346–47. See also Ansell, *The Annihilation of Hell* and its illuminating subtitle: *Universal Salvation and the Redemption of Time in the Eschatology of Jürgen Moltmann* and Bauckham, *God Will Be All in All*.

33. See Ogletree, *The Use of the Bible in Christian Ethics*. Like McNamee, he relates the eschatological nature of ministry to endurance and affirms, similar to middle axioms (below), favored postures and practices (equality, plurality, and forbearance, even forgiveness) that "bear something of the promise of the new age," as well as conditions which movements, organizations, and institutions need to call into question and challenge fixed hierarchies, marginalization of social groupings, and resolution of conflict

CHAPTER 8—SUMMARY CONSIDERATIONS AND CONCLUSIONS 139

inspires, enables, and sustains one to the end of an urban ministry vocation, when purpose, death, and yet a witness to fulfillment beyond death converge. Their reflections, along with those of Moltmann, Niebuhr, and Merton—especially for what kept them dedicated—attest to a bold modesty. Ogletree representatively professes:

> An eschatologically determined ethic gives primary weight to the issues involved in building up and sustaining [. . .] communities bearing authentic alternatives to the cultural norms and institutional arrangements of the larger society [. . .] They concern as well the disciplines which enable individuals and communities to detach themselves step by step from needs, desires and gratifications that hinder their full participation in the coming new age. The vision is grand, even breathtaking; but *the ministry it calls forth has its tough and realistic dimensions*. It is a summons to new life, which includes a readiness to let go of the old, with its special securities and gratifications.[34]

Eschatology heralds a vision hopefully to behold, even as it realistically cautions that virtually all of urban ministries' own visions, policies and programs are at best, provisional.

If only one theologian and his or her prayers could be summoned to summarize and exemplify the animating core for all this, then it would be what is confessed and professed daily in and out of the modest Longhouse dwelling, again, the original version of Niebuhr's (grace-based) Serenity Prayer. It is so vital for the whole pervasive understanding of a balance in this book, that it has been caringly exegeted in this chapter. At the Longhouse Ministry, it is prayed at least eight times per week including accompanying the Lord's Prayer on the Sabbath. Herein, the *praying justice hopefully* triad in the service of a hopeful realism resides and arises: "God, grant us the grace, to accept with serenity, the things we cannot change; the courage to change the things we ought to; and, the wisdom to distinguish the one from the other."[35] The conjunctive dynamic of such a triad indeed functions as a connecting node. Hope has that fundamental need and creative capacity as a relative term to ask for and perseveringly work with helpers. Hope's helpmates of prayer and justice or just prayer function as nodes of a network every bit as much as the mutually reciprocal networks depicted in Chapter 7 do for and with the Longhouse Ministry.

Summarily, urban ministries take note of reality. We live in reality as we are challenged, shaped, and constrained by the warmth of human reality in the city, its core, and indeed its peripheries, yet which includes

---

via violence 191–92. Cf. Anderson, *Walking the Way*, "A Concluding Word," 273–74.

34. Ogletree, ibid., 186. (italics added).

35. Sifton, *The Serenity Prayer*, 292–93.

the city's colder "slings and arrows of outrageous fortune."[36] We often face nigh despair if not defeat, weariness if not burnout, and temptations to inhabit isolated compartmentalization if not a devouring self-righteousness. Nevertheless, urban ministries pray for a willingness to practice steadfast faithfulness in and for the mission purposes of bearing a public and prophetic witness. The willingness to aspire to and practice such steadfastness is important since a mere vision statement of a ministry's mission cannot suffice. A public and prophetic witness would be left hanging apart from the helpmates (or "middle axioms"[37]) that Christian realists and their social gospel predecessors have long called for, so that the implementation of a vision can be worked for and hopefully implemented, all along the way.

The move from theological affirmations and principles to urban ministry practices are enabled by the hope-justice-prayer triad. Prayer engenders hope, as hope in turn, summons the helpmates of justice making and keeping. An awareness of negative experiences and an emerging contrast experience [38] catalyzes the "hop" for bold adventures. Therein, we come to hone a fine-tuned balance, really a time-and-again willingness to be (ever) beginners. The limits of an urban ministry are humbly accepted as the possibilities are engaged of hoping for justice prayerfully. Haiku summarized:

Finis, we labor (in hope)

Eschaton: endure (for justice)

Telos beckoned (via prayer)

---

36. Shakespeare, *Hamlet*, Act 3, Scene 1.

37. The networks and alliance in Chapter 7 provide kinds of structural middle axioms for the Longhouse. Middle axioms arose from the deliberations of World Council of Churches gatherings such as the world conference on practical Christianity at Oxford in 1937 by the ecumenist and social thinker Joseph H. Oldham (1874–1969 and the Amsterdam Assembly of 1949. See also the writings of Christian realists such as Bennett and Niebuhr and noted British social ethicists and social theologians such as Ronald Preston and the William Temple Centre in Manchester, UK. Such axioms are vital to bridge the gap between generalities (visions or common sense moral principles) and praxis; they serve as directives "for actual Conference work" which my own court of BC Conference of the United Church sorely lacks, as acknowledged by its ED, Doug Goodwin (e-mail of Nov. 16, 2015). Chapter 7 notes and elaborates directives via the networks associated with the Longhouse Ministry which are enabled by middle axioms. See further Niebuhr on a criticism of abstract idealism in "Christian Faith and Social Action", 234–36, "Development of a Social Ethic in the Ecumenical Movement," 178; also, Lee, *The Promise of Bennett*, 51–52; and Bucher, "Christian Political Realism after Niebuhr," 52, passim.

38. Also named "negative dialectics, as Schillebeeckx, drawing on Theodor Adorno, in *The Schillebeeckx Reader*, ed. Schreiter, 45, cf. 18, 54–59.

Appendix A: The Merton and New Monasticism Check and Balance

The New Monastics' Vocation and Challenge

NEW MONASTICS DRAW FROM Alasdair MacIntyre's call for a "new St. Benedict". MacIntyre's professes: ". . . the barbarians are not waiting beyond the frontiers they have already been governoring us for quite some time [. . .] we are waiting not for a Godot, but for another—doubtless very different—St. Benedict".[1] Jonathan Wilson-Hartgrove comments on the indispensable precedence of the classical monastics' "desire" to live, work, and minister differently.[2] To retrieve the classical monastics' major vows/promises, there are the usual three vows of obedience (with poverty and chastity), stability, and conversion. It is likely more than a charismatic figure (a St. Benedict) that is waited for. What is needed is a community-supported and nourishing cluster or organic network of figures (writers, competent editors, and sympathetic publishers; growers of food and surely the cooks; in-house and community organizers; child-minders; fund-raisers, and publicists; etc.). Elaborating on the vows/"promises", the new monastics name the following:[3]

a. The vow of poverty: to live simply so that others may simply live and, as important, so that one is less likely to be preoccupied with possessions and their protection (i.e., freed from to be free for, Gal. 5:1ff).

---

1. MacIntrye, *After Virtue*, 263.

2. Wilson-Hartgrove, *New Monasticism* with its instructive subtitle: *What It Has to Say to Today's Church, An Insider's Perspective*, 37–38. His father-in-law, Jonathan Wilson, a Vancouver Carey Baptist College theology professor, has also influenced the new monastics to MacIntyre's summons for a new Benedict from *After Virtue*. In his own *Living Faithfully in a Fragmented World*, with the suggestive subtitle of *Lessons for the Church from MacIntyre's After Virtue*.

3. See Wilson-Hartgrove, *The Awakening of Hope* with its instructive sub-title: *Why we Practice a Common Faith*, 67–86.

b. The vow of stability: to commit to stay, to remain, so to learn and live with the community (versus fleeing to supposedly greener, more enviable pastures elsewhere);

c. The vow of conversion (of manners or life): to commit, to the end, to an on-going life with others in conversation and conversion in and with the Kingdom's claims, gifts, and obligations.[4]

As one participant-observer and student of the older and newer monasticism sensitively affirms:

> A commitment to stability does not mean that I must live forever in the place where I was born, but that I take the trouble to learn and respect the particular characteristics and needs of the place where history has put me. A commitment to obedience does not mean blind adherence to the pronouncements of authority but devoting time and effort to cultivating, then heeding my conscience, that interior and intuitive guide that I so often ignore. A commitment to conversion of manners does not require me to sell all and retire to the desert or to refrain from sex. It requires rather that I accord the spiritual equal weight with the material, that I practice not poverty but frugality, that I recognize the power of intimacy—the power of the body—and that I inhabit that power responsibly.[5]

New monastics add the retrieval note of "the monastic impulse to relocate and reimagine our role from the margins of society."[6] This is important

---

4. Wilson stresses the "telos" nature and dimension of what characterizes the new monastics or what they need to draw from classical or older monasticism—*telos* being the very purpose goal that our fragmented world now lacks. See *Living Faithfully in a Fragmented World*, where the first of four characteristics is described thus: "The commitment and struggle necessary for a recovery of the gospel *telos* has little chance of occurring in the larger church. This task will be accomplished only in small, disciplined groups, in other words, in a *new monastic movement*", 73.

5. Fenton Johnson, *Keeping Faith* and its illumining subtitle: *A Skeptic's Journey Among Christian and Buddhist Monks*, 297; cf. 51–52. For creative elaborations of these three vows, especially of the vows of conversion of manners (where the vows of poverty and chastity are implicit) and of stability (with obedience as an attentive listening to trusted authority) being core, see Merton, edited by McConnell, *The Life of the Vows* with the instructive subtitle: *Initiation n the Monastic Tradition 6*, 183–92 and 478–79 ("Finale") on "the nature of religious vows"; 237–74 on the vow of obedience; 274–311 on the vow of conversion of manners (with 311–447 devoted to two aspects of this vow, namely chastity and poverty); and 447–78 on the vow of stability ("to live and die in the community of [one's] profession"). See below for Merton's implications of the vows of poverty and obedience for a public-prophetic witness.

6. Wilson-Hartgrove's *New Monastics* and p. 55 for meaning of "mono" in monastic which is 'singleness of heart', 42 and "the first task of any monastic movement is to

to their choice of actual places to take root and minister—clearly expressed in "Why it matters where we live" and "Why we live together" reflections.[7] They proffer a compelling list of "marks" that denote what it is about the "new monasticism" that commands attention and practice. Six of these twelve such marks include: #1 relocation to abandoned places of empire; #2 sharing economic resources with fellow community members and the needy among you; #5 humble submission to Christ's Body, the Church; #6 intentional formation to Way of Jesus Christ and the Rule of Community along the lines of the old monastics or Novitiate; #11 peacemaking in the midst of violence; and #12 commitment to a disciplined contemplative life (wherein Merton is drawn on).[8] Enduring is Wilson-Hartgrove's caveat that living in community is hard work and not a convenient, romantic dream (drawing from Dietrich Bonhoeffer's *Life Together's* monastic experiment and experience[9]). Thus the need for these set of disciplines to stay the course—remain, stay put, live and love, serve, do justice, and yet again, via Merton, prepare to begin anew/again.[10]

Probing a Constructive Criticism

However earnest the moves from Merton are as a bridge to the new monasticism, what invites critical evaluation are the following.

a. Is it possible to "have your cake, and eat it too"? How much of the old monasticism can one extract and still do it justice? When in a family situation, with its inextricable set of dynamics that compete (i.e. conflicting obligations), this situation could distract from the earnestness of consistent discipline to practice the "singleness of heart" and purpose in "mono" (as Wilson-Hartgrove names it)?[11]

---

remind the church that our story is the *adventure* of God's relationship with a peculiar people". (italics added).

7. Wilson-Hartgrove, *The Awakening of Hope*, Chapters 5 and 6.

8. From the Rutba House, *School(s) for Conversion* and its instructive subtitle: *12 marks of a New Monasticism*, xii–xiii.

9. Ibid, 26.

10. Again, see Merton's last published volume while he was still alive and hence could approve it, *Contemplative Prayer*: "We do not want to be beginners. But let us be convinced of the fact that we will never be anything else but beginners, all our life!" 37.

11. I remain confounded as to how to do full justice to this inevitable dynamic, having witnessed many marriages or covenants, including my own, fall apart amid the stress and strains of competing claims upon one's "personal"/family life and the ongoing demands and challenges of the vocation of ministry. Merton conveys his own confessional insights out of his gift of a relationship to "M" albeit, with considerable

b. How much of the classical monastics' practices/disciplines can be retrieved and with what adaptations (Merton's challenge), thinking of all of the vows' 'realistic applicability to the new monastics' situation?[12]

c. Similarly, what tangible resources for justice making and keeping are there in the old monasticism (their very example and works of mercy/hospitality are present, of course, along with a life-long dedication to implement them) that could be deemed germane to the new monastics and those of us seeking an understanding from one or both?

d. What could be the critical contributions from the older and enduring posture of "Christian Realism"? Is it the reasons for a Reinhold Niebuhr-like critique of mysticism as a perceived flight from reality (Merton et al. help to change this view by way of an engaged mysticism, similar to an engaged Buddhism)?[13] Is it to demonstrate the inadequacy of works of mercy or charity on their own, given the awesome weight of the immorality of society in distinction from persons in society?[14]

---

anguish. See, *The Intimate Merton* with its *raison d'etre* subtitle: *His life from His journals*, eds Hart and Montaldo, 293–304. He reflects: ". . . the whole thing with 'M' was [. . .] an attempt to escape the demands of my vocation [. . .] a substitution of human love (and erotic love after all) for a special covenant with loneliness and solitude, which is the very heart of my vocation," 303.

12. Again and often, see Merton's *The Wisdom of the Desert*, 23–24. I especially puzzle over the vow of obedience's realistic applicability, albeit with Fenton Johnson's rendering (note 5) and Merton's including this vow as part of the over-arching life-long vow of conversion-and-stability, there is creative pacing and space for long-term reflection and praxis; see his "The Place of Obedience" essay in *Contemplation in a World of Action*, 135–45 wherein dialogical imperatives and principles are affirmed, between the "superiors" and novices/monks. I wonder if biographers have done justice to this vow and its apparent necessity. Though kept with occasional anguish and possibly latent resistance by Merton, the vow might well have "saved" Merton from a fatal attraction to and with 'M'!.

13. Merton challenges the temptations of some prayers to evade the "problems and anxieties of contemporary existence" including the hard work of advocating justice making and keeping; see *Contemplative Prayer*, 112–14. An engaged Buddhism is evident in David Tracey's *The Earth Manifesto* with its illumining subtitle: *Saving Nature with Engaged Ecology*.

14. Niebuhr's contributions to the social ethics conversation are mammoth, but see his earlier *Moral Man and Immoral Society* with its *raison d'etre* subtitle: *A Study in Ethics and Politics* classic, which he would have entitled in hindsight, "Not so Moral Man in Less Moral Society". See also Niebuhr's apt introduction: "Teachers of morals who do not see the difference between the problem of charity within the limits of an accepted social system and the problem of justice between economic groups, holding uneven power within modern industrial society, have simply not faced the most obvious differences between the morals of groups and those of individuals", xxxi. See Niebuhr's own depiction of these differences, 9, 17–18, 29–30, 47–48, but especially: "In every group there

The Praying Justice Hopefully Triad

The above resources help provide a constructive critique by way of a professed *praying-justice-hopefully* triad in the name of a faithful prophetic-public witness for the long haul.[15] How do both an old and new monasticism contribute to and helpfully critique such a commended triad of justice resourced by prayer and hope? Why and how is such a critique needed?

The following points arise:

a. The vows' relevancy in the service of a basic need for promise making and promise keeping, while noting how literally and even stubbornly adhered to are the vows—or, how such vows could be so liberally interpreted and applied that they are barely discernible and operative (for if the vows of celibacy and poverty, as part of the Benedictine understanding which is part of the over-arching vow of conversion of manners,[16] are not adhered to, then what, besides plain burnout, would be the sad or disappointing outcomes?)

b. While felt necessary, is it *sufficient* to summon and incorporate an old/er monasticism into urban ministries even if the ministries are called "new" (with their qualified adaptations)? If not, what else is needed? Would regular ties to and retreats with actual monasteries for some check-and-balance reality study and spiritual direction assist?[17] This could include a retrieval and critical grasp of urban ministry models like the East Harlem Protestant Parish (EHPP) and its four earliest, formation disciplines. These discipline are the of sharing in worship, economics, political witness, and perhaps above all, their very vocational

---

is less reason to guide and to check impulse, less capacity for self-transcendence, less ability to comprehend the needs of others and therefore more unrestrained egoism than the individuals, who compose the group, reveal in their personal relationships", xxv.

15. Thankfully, the resources of Reinhold Niebuhr on justice, Merton on prayer and Moltmann on hope further assist.

16. Merton's best source could be "Conversion of Life," 145–61. Therein, he affirms this vow, which contra evasion and/or rebellion, connotes: "the persevering determination to bear with patience and courage all the trials that one may meet in the monastic life", to be the essence of all the vows, adding ". . . and monastic renewal is only really comprehensible in the light of it," 149, 145.

17. Making monastic connections is what current and long-time Baptist pastor and student of the new monasticism, Tim Dickau, engaged in a due Sabbatical as he and his life-partner, Mary, visited and reflected in European and U.K. monasteries and a Fraser Valley Benedictine Monastery in Mission, B.C. The new monastics wisely lean into and draw from the likes of Jean Vanier and Kathleen Norris as mentors and soul partners in their life and work.

call and mission purpose.[18] And yet, what came to hinder some of this being consistently being put into practice, from participant-critic's points of view, such as in the case of their once store-front lawyer, William Stringfellow, eventually taking leave of the EHPP group, sensing an abandonment of some of its founding and sustaining purposes or principles?[19]

c. Further participation-and-observation research of the old and new monastic themes and convictions could be undertaken by working with current Vancouver network and monastic-like endeavours such as A Community Aware (ACA), Streams of Justice (SoJ), and the Metro Vancouver Alliance (MVA). Chapter 7 depicts these three networks or alliances, and also Appendix B offers some actual testimonies attesting to their story line.

Each of the above intimates and illustrates the transfer of aspects of the "old" into the "new monasticism", especially regarding the matters of a attending to *determination* and *dedication* (thus an "intentional formation" from the above six of the twelve marks cited) amid *counter-cultural* efforts to challenge status-quo inequalities and accompanying anxieties.

- There is with the ACA, a determination and dedication to discern, educate, and stay focused on the "aware" or soul dimension of the globalization of addiction (as aptly noted in co-founder Bruce Alexander's lifetime of academic and community research work and implied in the sub-title of his book, *The Globalization of Addiction: A Study in Poverty of the Spirit*).[20]

- With the SoJ, one notes a determination and dedication to discern, educate, and stay focused on the "prophetic praxis" of justice retrieval, making, and keeping in urban and greater Vancouver (see its *streamsofjustice.org* website).

- With the MVA, there is a determination and dedication to discern, network and build, in the midst of increasing fragmentation and

---

18. See, among others, Webber, *God's Colony in Man's World* and "The Habits of the Christian Life", 138–43 and Benedict's *Born Again Radical*, Part II's "The Group Ministry", especially the "four major disciplines", 61–63.

19. See Stringfellow, *My People is the Enemy* with its instructive subtitle: *An Autobiographical Polemic*, 96–99 on slothfulness of the EHPP group toward the role of the Bible in their work and prophetic/pastoral witness.

20. Alexander, *The Globalization of Addiction* with its instructive sub-title: *A Study in the Poverty of the Spirit* and ACA's on-going sessions on the meaning of "soul" as well as "spirit in society, self, and the earth."

dislocation, a broad-based greater Vancouver alliance of membership organizations for power, to take action, in the name of and in the service of a common good.[21]

Steadfast Insights and Guidance

The above examples illustrate aspects of serving the common/public good, especially by way of a prophetic perspective that critically serves and constructively nourishes urban ministries and networks. As part of the practices of public education, social justice advocacy, and/or community organizing, what is needed is a set of disciplined practices such as those of the classical and neo-monastics. It is needed for what Merton drew out of his study of the "Desert Fathers/Mothers"—augmented and developed by novice teachings at the Trappist monastery, teachings so well culled and published by Patrick O'Connell.[22] It is encouraged and strengthened by the life example given by Thomas Merton to the new monastics—assisted by his biographers, patient Abbots, many correspondents and visitors to the monastery, the mutual forbearance of his fellow monks and confessors, and outside witnesses to the struggles for peace which arose for Merton and those coming later, the deepest witness possible by another human being, the Christic witness of those giving their life for the Kingdom, as in martyrdom.[23]

Further questions and responses serve this concluding reflection. What does Merton provide in the important link between his classical or older monasticism and that of the new? How does Merton provide this? And thirdly, what is the credibility of all this?

First then, Merton helps to provide the resources or contours that a disciplined set of practices needs in order to bear a faithful witness to the

21. See former theological student, priest-in-training, and life-time Industrial Areas Foundation community organizer Ed Chambers' *Roots of Radicals* with its illumining subtitle: *Organizing for Power, Action and Justice* and the Metro Vancouver Alliance web site.org.

22. O'Connell's culled and edited retrieval, plus compelling introductions to Merton's novice teachings are noteworthy. For his reflections, see especially volume 6 in the series with its instructive subtitle: *The Life of the Vows: Initiation into the Monastic Tradition 6*.

23. See Wilson-Hartgrove on Jim Douglass' appeal to Merton as now intercessorily accessible within and as part of the "communion of the saints". See his "Mark 12: Commitment to a Disciplined Contemplative Life" in *Schools for Conversion,* 163–64. See also Merton's *Disputed Questions,* 222 on monastic life as witnesses as martyrs are witnesses, albeit the monastic as a prophet does not give one's life in martyrdom as much as "shoulders the burden of 'vision" (laid) upon him (or her)". See also his "The Primitive Carmelite Ideal", 218–63.

Christian Faith in ways that are both personal and public, pastoral and prophetic. It is not enough that *The Wisdom of the Desert*'s introduction by Merton named dedication and determination as such required marks. Further study and reflections are needed to gain the fullness of Merton's contributions. From the "Contemplation in a time of Action" essay to the collection of post-humus essays by Bro. Patrick Hart, *The Monastic Journey*, and on to the last volume of *Contemplative Prayer* of Merton's as well as his very last day address "Marxism and Monastic Perspectives", all are needed to help complete the offering. They are needed even though they are embodied in the vows of the conversion of life and stability; this is life-long.[24] These several Merton additions (to *The Wisdom of the Desert*) add to those of dedication and determination. They carefully provide the depth and width of discipline required for living out a monastic way of life—that it indeed is a faithful witness of an intensely personal nature and of an extensive public-prophetic nature, which includes inter-faith and inter-disciplinary resources and examples. Merton's personal and inner renewals serve the hopeful possibilities for a faithful witness in the public and prophetic arenas of life.

Secondly, Merton provides the way by leaving to us his earnest studies which supplemented his way of clarifying and correcting his vast autobiographical writings (especially his journals and letters). The research and publications about Merton pour forth like ever-flowing desert streams. These poignantly revealing reflections convey an intimate portrait into the "work-in-progress" nature and manner of Merton as a monastic, whose writings, including letters, served as prayerfulness. This was prayer in the service of renewal and intercessory activity, including his "apostolate to intellectuals (and/or friends)" and writers at large.[25] New Monastics are part of this quest and the arising tasks as they reflect and draw from the Merton legacy.[26]

---

24. Found first of all but via his last public address "Marxism and Monastic Perspective" in Merton's post-humous *The Asian Journal of Thomas Merton*, 326–43.

25. See James W. Douglass' forward and Patrick Hart/Jonathan Montaldo's introduction, respectively, to the *Cold War Letters*, xv and xvi, and *The Intimate Merton* and also Merton's Dec. 5, 1964 entry: "One prays to pray [. . .] In the hermitage one must pray or go to seed," 229. It was in the hermitage where doubtlessly so many of Merton's letters were written, as prayers or by way of prayer (as Douglass, above, aptly discerns: "He knew his Cold Wars letters were a form of praying in darkness, a search for light with the companions he addressed, in a night of the spirit when everything seemed lost").

26. In addition to above-cited new monastics, see Dekar's *Thomas* Merton with its illumining subtitle *Twentieth-century wisdom for Twenty-First-Century living*, being part of the "new monastic library: resources for radical discipleship series".

Finally, one probes the credibility of engaging Merton as a key resource for the new monasticism. It is in the evidence of the "fruits" of both Merton and the new monastics—yet barely mined—that there is an attestation. The inspiring courage of the new monastics to adventure world-wide as well as North American conveys the hope that the work of justice making and justice keeping is worth the life-long, vow-enabled dedication and disciplines necessary (as well as the parallel or counter structures and strategies against dominant society necessary for justice rooted in the Kingdom of God).[27] Hope nourishes such a dedicated discipline.[28] To act on the hope that the love of God in Christ is possible—as it is commanded—is to practice the depth and width of the monastic virtues (then as now) with their guides to helping frame and provide content to a faithful public and prophetic witness. Such is needed for the long-haul practices necessary for a public-prophetic witness.

---

27. One thinks of John Dominic Crossan's post-Jesus seminar work, whereby he retrieves from the classical monastics something akin to an exemplifying *hoping justice prayerfully* triad deemed necessary for our generation's faithful prophetic-public witness. See his *God & Empire* and its instructive subtitle: *Jesus against Rome, Then and Now*, especially 37–48 where "normalcy" is not inevitable and monasticism critically/constructively models "the great Divine clean-up" via a "collaborative eschatology." He professes: "Any monastery is a *paradox* [. . .] of being beyond or even against the standard view of things or the normal opinion about them," 47.

28. Napoleon professed that courage, like love, needs the nourishment of hope, cited in *Answers from the Heart* with its suggestive subtitle: *Daily Meditations for People Recovering from Sex Addiction* entry for July 20. Mirroring new monastics' testimony, see Merton's preface to *Seeds of Destruction*: "To have a vow of poverty seems [. . .] illusory if I do not in some way identify myself with the cause of people who are denied their rights and forced [. . .] to live in abject misery. To have a vow of obedience seems to be absurd if it does not imply a deep concern for the most fundamental of all expressions of God's will: the love (of) His truth and of our neighbor," xiv.

Appendix B: Networks' Viva Voce Testimonies and Inducing Central Story Line

THE FOLLOWING STATEMENTS CONVEY testimonies (a *viva voce* via italics) from representatives of the three main networks or alliances employed in Chapter 7. The MVA and ACA excerpts are gratefully included with permission from then First Nations Studies Program research student, Andrea Reid. The appendix concludes with a brief grounded theory application of discerning a central or core-category phrase which summarizes the story line or the networks' *raison d'etre*—induced from quoted material.

From the Streams of Justice (SoJ) network's co-founders:

There is first Teresa Diewert's founding awareness:

> "*I think when you look at these three—charity, advocacy, justice—you see the futility of charity and it in my mind another form of bondage—it is just another dependency that becomes engrained—there does not seem to be any movement from it. For me, giving people things is important on one level, but you are never going to get out of that if you don't go to the justice part. The advocacy part I find really difficult because advocacy is me still in this helping role, and I haven't found that to be very helpful—I don't think I have really helped anybody by giving them places to look up or access to different places and different times when I have advocated for other people it hasn't gone very well. In some ways I feel like my role—my place—more and more I am coming to see in this position of obvious privilege is to change that system to make that less and less the case. And because of the things that we have been thinking about over the last couple of years, really coming to see the injustice of the system—it is systemic. So I feel like this is our role—is to point out the systemic injustice and to change that. Because the guys on the bottom—no one is going to do that—no one is going to listen to them, I feel like really needs to come from the place of privilege—we need to be exposing our privilege—because this stuff doesn't do anything—it perpetuates*

in my mind all of it . . . (I)t feels really slow and I can't imagine my involvement in seeking justice and seeking change in the system is going to have a huge impact." [1]

And then there is SoJ co-founder Dave Diewert's testimony. Justice is basically

[. . .] to do with distribution of power and resources in a community—(and) how that is so central to biblical vision. And think of the prophetic tradition and then seeing ways to participate and so I think in many ways that is where I am particularly interested in pushing that dimension of the issue because I think it is kind of downplayed in significance. I think we need to understand why it is—why the response to social issues is mostly at the charity and advocacy level—and approaching the need for systemic change—there is real reticence and reluctance and less enthusiasm. The thing about the charity and advocacy is that it responds to immediate needs and there needs to be some of that obviously—[. . .] people are cold or hungry—there needs to be some immediate response so I am not downplaying that but if those responses are not done within the larger movements towards justice then it feels really futile. [2]

Another of Dave Diewert's statements expresses:

Real estate companies make money from gentrification and profit from an escalating housing market, now turn around and gather blankets and clothes for people they help to make homeless. This is such a clear example of charity that perpetuates the injustice and inequality of the status quo upon which such charity is predicated. Why not build homes for people instead of giving out blankets and socks? Homes actually last longer than blankets and offer much better protection against poor mental and physical health. It is also less expensive and more humane.[3]

---

1. Teresa Diewert in Dickau's personal interview with her, from transcribed notes for Dickau's D.Min. Thesis research for *Pursuing practices of the Kingdom at Grandview Calvary Baptist Church*, 7–8. (used with permission).

2. Ibid, 8–9.

3. 40 E-mail communication, November 19, 2009

From Metro Vancouver Alliance (MVA):

Deborah Littman, the lead organizer of the Metro Vancouver Alliance (MVA)[4] emphasized a disconnect between dominant values and community values. She comments that often people are ashamed of trying to assert community values at a structural level and so these values often get suppressed in favor of commercial development. She states that there is *"a real hunger for people to say that that isn't right,"* but that *"somehow to express it and to demand that be the dominant reason for things to be done or not done seems like something [people] are reluctant to do."* She sees community-based organizations as playing an important role in helping prioritize community values, putting those values *"front and centre"* in order to *"help people [. . .] find practical ways to assert community values as opposed to just longing for [them] in secret."* These member organizations of the MVA can provide a platform from which to engage societal structures and to show how community values can operate at government or city-wide levels. Deborah states that although those are *"the values of a very large proportion of people, when you have a govern[ment] that doesn't operate on those values and those impulses are consistently frustrated, people just come to think about those values as [. . .] operat[ing] on a family level,"* and as being incapable of operating city-wide. She points to broader organizational initiatives, such as MVA, as being able to emphasize the need to *"be making choices for community over commercial development"* and strategizing as to various ways to begin to do that.

Deborah calls attention to the fact that certain communities are *"harder to crack [and are] quite self-contained."* In such cases, if you do not have a point of contact that is already established, it can be difficult even to begin the process of relationship building. She states that, *"most organizations have their own dynamics and status quo and are fearful of trying something new."* This reticence is only exacerbated in the circumstances of limited and often declining resources and funding, which can sometimes create a competitive environment that impedes the establishment of real relationships between organizations, each organization struggling just to meet the needs of their specific constituencies. This is particularly problematic with regards to partnerships with Aboriginal organizations. Achieving and maintaining Aboriginal involvement in some of the dominant partnerships has been identified as challenging by several MVA participants. One participant has clarified that it is not that Aboriginal organizations do not want to be involved in partnerships but that they are simply too overwhelmed, and

---

4. A broad-based organization aimed at bringing people and organizations into relationship with one another to work on issues for the common good. See also Chapter 7.

"because of their (limited) capacity, they're not able to get involved in partnership meetings [in order to] bring their ideas" to the table.

The MVA adopts a stance of empowerment and capacity-building. Deborah explains the theory behind the organization, stating that, *"people are already organized but frequently people, particularly low-income people or people that are more on the margins, are shut out of the democratic process."* The MVA aims to *"strengthen those civil society organizations that are really the core of how these groups participate and which sustain them in many ways"* as well as *"bring those organizations together to have the power to get to the negotiating table."*

The MVA believes that *"you're not doing for people, you're doing with them and, you are, through their participation, building their strength, [. . .] their skills, and their power to act in a democratic environment"* (Deborah). Through various courses and initiatives such as leadership training and community-mapping projects—to identity neighborhood resources and their strengths—people are able to learn some of the core principles of community organizing and are able to then implement these principles in various spaces in accordance with community needs. Community walks are one such example, whereby people can go out and engage the community in both exploratory and issue-oriented ways. For example, Deborah elaborates that, *"you could do a community walk in the area about how safe people feel in the neighbourhood and what they would be willing to do about it."* Community walks are only one example of the many ways organizations such as the MVA are providing people with the tools to enable them to think about the ways in which such projects could work in different areas, while also giving them a chance to connect with one another through the projects themselves.

From A Community Aware (ACA) by way of co-founder Terry Patten, with Mary Etey and Ken Lyotier:

Terry Patten, who is one of the founding members of the group called A Community Aware (ACA)—that again facilitates a series of courses and discussions centered around specific issues such as hope and despair, aging, and the impacts of neo-liberalism—talks about the extent to which ACA has impacted him:

> When I started to work with [ACA] then I began to substantially change and began to look at society in an entirely different way and see what the free market system, in particular, had done to

society and what we had become as a civilization in the Western world. So my whole world is upside down from 2000.

Terry talks about the fact that he walks away from every ACA event with a different perspective and is constantly amazed by people and their struggles.

An examination of the workshops and discussion forums facilitated by ACA reveals the sense of connection that can be achieved through discussion and by providing the opportunity for individuals to express themselves and get to know each other on a deeper level. Terry remarks that they get constant feedback from the participants that *"this is what they want to talk about"* and that the meetings have really *"changed the way they think."* Mary Etey, also a member of ACA, describes the ways in which the discussions have contributed to her intellectual development and the benefits of *"having the ideas to work with and talk about."* In this way, ACA can also be seen as an "alternative to university," that is accessible to all and stimulates thought and growth. She describes ACA as providing a context in which people can *"talk about [their] values and maybe be inspired to know how [they] want to live with them."* Mary expressed an appreciation for the open nature of the forums facilitated by ACA, stating that they are *"open to all kinds of people and ideas [. . .] mak[ing] it a nice community."*

Groups such as ACA are extremely effective at bridging the gap between the theoretical and personal aspects of community, providing a space for intellectual development in the context of very real personal experiences and emotions. Ken Lyotier, who is also involved with ACA and brings to bear his several other community-based initiatives, comments on the necessity of engaging both the personal and the theoretical:

> There's this theoretical discussion about concepts, which is very interesting, and then there's these personal experiences that people have that need to be somehow woven into what this discussion is about. And I guess that's part of what the point of [ACA] is, a community being aware of these conceptual things and, at the same time, recognizing one another as part of how we're expressing these concepts in reality.

In outlining a brief history of the development of ACA, Terry describes its progression from an almost exclusive focus on the economic and systemic aspects of our society, particularly the detrimental effects of the free market system, to one that expands to incorporate the more spiritual components of community and connection. By listening to the needs of the participants and bringing in new individuals and perspectives, ACA has merged the personal with the theoretical, providing people with the opportunity to gain a better understanding of broader systemic and structural issues through their everyday experiences and struggles. The personal can never be fully disconnected from the structural and the ways in which dominant systems serve to impose constraints on the ways in which our daily lives and identities are able to be expressed in the world. Having an understanding of the ways in which those forces can shape our lives' interactions as well as a safe space in which to explore the consequences of those systemic effects is important, and it can help to bring about more supportive and inclusive communities.

A Concluding Note from FNSP Student Researcher Andrea Reid:

What I have learned about community over the course of this project has been both humbling and inspirational. For me, this is not a project that ends with the completion of this paper. What I have learned about community and all of its creativity and possibilities has deeply shaped the ways in which I engage with the world and will serve to inform all of my actions in the future, prompting me to remain even more conscious of those values and attitudes I am communicating through my everyday engagements and practices. This journey, although challenging at times, has been incredibly rewarding. I can personally attest to the transformative potential identified by many of the participants throughout this project. This practicum project has provided me with the opportunity to engage with many groups and individuals that I most likely would not have had the opportunity to interact with otherwise, and has made me more conscious of the subtle assumptions I have learned and adopted over the course of my life and that are reinforced by even the most mundane aspects of society. Everything that I have learned over the course of this year would not have been possible had I not been willing to engage with some of my own assumptions and stereotypes that I had held onto for most of my life.

Although I was immediately drawn to the projects outlined by the Longhouse Council of Native Ministry, I was initially hesitant about working with them due to their religious affiliation. I had always held a somewhat negative view of religion and had stereotyped organized religion as perpetuating judgment and espousing dogmatic ideals. That is one of the ironic and paradoxical things about those kinds of assumptions. I had categorized organized religion as judgmental and dogmatic, while I was perpetuating and communicating those exact same characteristics through those assumptions. While I am still not a religious person, working with the Longhouse Council of Native Ministry has helped me to engage with some of my own deep-seated assumptions to better understand the ways in which those function and get communicated in dysfunctional ways, serving to keep parts of myself closed off and foreclosing opportunities to connect with others that could, and did, enrich my life in truly incredible ways. *It is so easy to judge someone based on the way that they look or come across, without considering that person as a unique human being with an amazing set of experiences, struggles, and insights that you could not have previously imagined.* Although this is something that I have always known on a theoretical level, I am now incorporating that realization into my life more fully and consciously. *I am truly humbled and amazed by people and their struggles. Often, people do not realize how much they have to share and offer based on their unique life experiences. Through our relations with others, we have the possibility to open up to so much more than is possible in isolation. Together, we can work to realize a world that is rich in diversity, creativity, and compassion.* [5]

Inducing a Compact Story-line via Application of Grounded Theory

Grounded theory can be described as an inductive or bottom-up method of comparing two or more cases or situations for the purpose of formulating an overview of "what is happening", how, and why? The "grounding" accounts for what appears to make sense with and out of the observed and/or reported data of the cases. The data or testimony is consistently and constantly compared for check-and-balance purposes and to formulate categories—and ultimately a central category—that describe important activities, even the origins to a network's existence or urban ministry project.[6]

5. Reid, unpublished First Nations Studies Program research paper. (italics added)

6. Grounded theorists and practitioners define grounded theory more formally: "[It is a] qualitative research method that uses a systematic set of procedures to develop an inductively derived grounded theory about a phenomenon", Strauss and Corbin, *Basics of Qualitative Research*, 24. Cf., " . . . '(G)rounded theory' refers to both a method of inquiry and to the product of the inquiry [. . .] (It) encourages researchers to remain close to their studied worlds and to develop an integrated set of theoretical concepts from their empirical materials that not only synthesize and interpret them but also show processual relationships [. . .] Not only are justice and injustice abstract concepts,

One of the gifts of grounded theory is to discern and summarize the story line of a body of material. In the cases of the three networks described in Chapter 7—Streams of Justice, A Community Aware, and Metro Vancouver Alliance—grounded theory can, through a discernment of the story line, reveal the *raison d-etre* of each of the networks. These story lines contribute clues to the origins of the networks or alliance (MVA) and thus how best to summarize what is going on herein (story line). Grounded theory representatives express it thus:

> (Central category) consists of all the products of analysis condensed into a few words that seem to explain what all this research is about [. . .] findings should be presented as a set of interrelated concepts [. . .] an analyst reduces data from many cases into concepts and sets of relational statements that can be used, in a general sense, to describe what is going on [. . .] (T)here is always more than one way of expressing relational statements.[7]

I invite the reader to trust that a participant-observer of these networks can induce a central category or phrase to account for each network's story line or core reason for being and continuing. I call this story line a "theme focus". A story line of each of the networks may be expressed as follows: for ACA, the theme focus is awareness and organizing; for SoJ, the theme focus is justice; and, for MVA, the theme focus is power. All three have in common the discipline task of organizing—organizing awareness, stimulating justice advocacy, and finally organizing power to take action for the sake of justice. For the story line for all three networks/alliances, a valuable lead arises from Schillebeeckx's helpful interpretive category of a *contrast-awareness*. This concept is developed in Chapter 1 where the literature on urban ministry and theology there may supplement the story line induced by grounded theory. The contrast-awareness category helps to account for what motivates each of the networks' founders to become aroused to take action for social justice. An emotional arousal is more than a mere abstract, cerebral experience. When social justice issues and actions are considered, as they are mandated for ACA, SoJ and MVA, animation can meaningfully be added. Evoking a phrase for each from above, there is SoJ's *"to point out the systemic injustice and to change that"* as well as to *"expose privilege"*. For ACA, there is "*I began to substantially change and began to look at society in an entirely different way and see what the free market system, in particular,*

---

but they are, moreover, enacted *processes*, made real through actions performed again and again", Charmaz, "Grounded Theory in the 21st Century," 204.

7. Strauss and Corbin, *Basics of Qualitative Research*, 2nd edition, 146, 145.

had done to society and what we had become as a civilization in the Western world." And, for MVA, there is *"a real hunger for people to say that that isn't right,"* in order to *"help people [. . .] find practical ways to assert [them] as opposed to just longing for [them] in secret."*

Then an *animated contrast-awareness,* the action-taking stage, accounts for how the above agents have been moved to become involved in seeking justice and, in turn, how they contribute at least so far to their respective networks. Put otherwise, this is what Fred White calls "discontent as inspiration": "It's a delicate balance: wait too long and you'll 'cool off', to the point of losing the motivation; don't wait long enough and the red you see will transfer onto the page."[8] This action implies a disciplined commitment, more than an initial and enthusiastic level of involvement. The commitment extends to a long-term dedication where ever again discipline is less a ready-made road map than what arises by virtue of living out one's convictions[9] and hence sharing them with others. Such a level of commitment affords an adequate renewal for when weariness sets in and the temptations to self-righteousness or despair loom large. Thus, finally, a central category is that of an *animated and disciplined contrast-awareness.* This awareness recalls the mission purpose of urban ministries of and for this book—that there be a faithful public and prophetic witness for the long haul.

---

8. White, *The Daily Reader,* 112. See also Hessel, *Time for Outrage Indignez-vous!,* especially 26–29, combining hope and justice via resistance and finally, see Keating, *The Power to Make It Happen,* on when community organizing needs a "hot gut" but with "cool anger," 234.

9. See again, Merton: "The real function of discipline is not to provide us with maps but to sharpen our own sense of direction, so that when we really get going we can travel without maps", *Contemplation in a World of Action,* 126–27.

Bibliography

Adam, Margaret B. *Our Only Hope: More than We Can Ask or Imagine*. Distinguished Dissertations in Christian Theology 12. Eugene, OR: Pickwick, 2013.
Alcoholics Anonymous. 3rd edition. New York: Alcoholics Anonymous World Services, 1976.
Alexander, Bruce K. "The Dislocation Theory of Addiction." In *The Globalisation of Addiction: A Study in Poverty of the Spirit*, 57–84, New York: Oxford University Press, 2008.
Alicea, Benjamin. *Christian Urban Colonizers: A History of the East Harlem Protestant Parish, 1948 to 1968*. PhD diss., Union Theological Seminary, 1989.
Alinksy, Saul D. *Rule for Radicals: A Practical Primer for Realistic Radicals*. New York: Vintage, 1989.
———. *John L. Lewis: An Unauthorized Biography*. N.Y.: G. P. Putnam's Sons, 1949.
Allen, Diogenes. *Traces of God in a Frequently Hostile World*. New York: Cowley, 1981.
Allen, Joseph. *Love and Conflict: A Covenantal Model of Christian Ethics*. Nashville, TN: Abingdon, 1984.
Althouse, Peter. "In Appreciation of Jürgen Moltmann." *The Journal of the Society for Pentecostal Studies*. Spring Studies 28 1 (2006) 21–32.
Alves, Ruben. "Christian Realism: Ideology of the Establishment." *Christianity and Crisis* 33 (1973) 173–76.
Anderson, Bernard. *Out of the Depths: The Psalms Speak for Us Today*. Revised and expanded edition. Philadelphia, PA: Westminster, 1983.
Anderson, Terence R. "The Thought of Reinhold Niebuhr and the Twilight of Modernity in Canada." In *Reinhold Niebuhr (1892–1971): A Centenary Appraisal*, eds. Gaudin and D. Hall, 7–28, Atlanta, Georgia: Scholars, 1994.
———. *Walking the Way: Christian Ethics as a Guide*. Toronto: United Church, 1993.
Anholt, Dennis. "A Hub of Hope and Belonging" *Victoria Times-Colonist Supplement*, November 2009, D5. <www.ourplacesociety.com/print/media_articles/279>
Ansell, Nicholas. *The Annihilation of Hell: Universal Salvation and the Redemption of Time in the Eschatology of Jürgen Moltmann*. Eugene, Oregon: Wipf and Stock, 2013.
Answers in the Heart. Anonymous. Hazeldon Publishing: Central City, MN, 1989.
Arendt, Hannah. *On Violence*. London, England: Penguin, 1970.
Aristotle. *Nichomachean Ethics*. Translated by M. Oswald. Indianapolis: Boobs-Merrill, 1962.
Athanasiadis, Harris. *George Grant and the Theology of the Cross: the Christian foundations of His Thought*. University of Toronto Press, 2001.
(St.) Augustine. "Charity is no substitute for justice withheld" <http://thinkexist.com/quotation/charity_is_no_substitute_for_justice_withheld/340942.html>
Austin, Reverend Juanita. "Hastings Street." In *The Word on the Street*, edited by B. Morris, H. Stevens, and A. Urquhart, 121. Winfield, British Columbia: Wood Lake, 1991.

Badertscher, John. "Letter to B. K. Morris." In *Engaging Urban Ministry*. Master of Theology Thesis, Vancouver School of Theology, 1999, Appendix C-3.
Bakke, Ray. *Signs of Hope in the City: Ministries of Community Renewal*. Valley Forge, PA: Judson, 1997.
———. *A Theology as Big as the City*. Downer's Grove, IL: Inter-Varsity, 1997.
Baldwin, Lewis V. and Rufus Burrow, Jr., eds. *The Domestication of Martin Luther King: Clarence B. Jones, Right-Wing Conservatism, and the Manipulation of the King Legacy*. Eugene, Oregon: Cascade, 2013.
Barth, Karl. *Church Dogmatics*, eds. G.W. Bromiley and T.F. Torrance. Translated by Bromiley. Vol. IV Part 2. Peabody, MA: Hendrickson, 2010 (orig. 1958).
———. *Church Dogmatics*, Volume III/Part 4. "The Doctrine of Creation", eds. Bromiley and Torrance. Peabody, Mass: Hendrickson, 2010 (orig. 1961).
Bellah, Robert et al. "Individualism and the Crisis of Civic Membership." *Christian Century* (1996) 510–13.
Bellett, Gerry. "Recovery Centre Takes a Tough Love Approach to Addiction." *Vancouver Sun*, May 5, 2011, A10.
Bendroth, Norman B. "Designing the City: Reflections on the New Urbanism." *Christian Century* 118 (2001) 15, 19.
Benedict, Donald L. *Born Again Radical*. N.Y.: Pilgrim, N.Y, 1982.
———. "Structures for the New Era." In *Who's Killing the Church*, edited by S. Rose. 42–48. Renewal/Chicago City Missionary Society, 1966.
Benesh, Sean. *View from the Urban Loft*. Eugene, OR: Wipf and Stock, 2011.
Bennett, John C. *Christian Realism*. London: SCM, 1941.
———. "Greetings to the Niebuhr Symposium at McGill University, September 1992." In *Reinhold Niebuhr [1892–1971]: A Centenary Appraisal*. McGill Studies in Religion. eds. by G. Gaudin and D.J. Hall, vii. Atlanta, Georgia: Scholars, 1994.
———. *The Radical Imperative: From Theology to Social Ethics*. Philadelphia, PA: Westminster, 1975.
———. "Reinhold Niebuhr's Social Ethics." In *Reinhold Niebuhr: His Religious, Social and Political Thought* eds. C. W. Kegley and R. W. Bretall, 45–78. N.Y.: Macmillan Paperback, 1961.
Berger, Peter L. *The Sacred Canopy: Elements of a Sociological Theory of Religion*. Garden City, New York: Doubleday Anchor, 1969.
Bergman, Carla. "Taking Care of Each Other." *The Thistler*, 18 (2011).
Bethge, E. *Friendship and Resistance: Essays on Dietrich Bonhoeffer*. Word Council of Churches/Wm B. Eerdmans, 1995.
———. *Prayer and Righteous Action*. Belfast, Ireland: Christian Journals, 1979.
Beverley, John. "Testimonio, Subalternity, and Narrative Authority." In *Strategies of Qualitative Inquiry*, eds. Norman K. Denzin and Y. S. Lincoln. 257–69. San Francisco: Sage, 2008.
Bingham, June. *The Courage to Change: An Introduction to the Life and Thought of Reinhold Niebuhr*. N.Y.: Scribner's Sons, 1972 (orig. 1961).
Blaikie, Bill. *The Blaikie Report: An Insider's View of Faith and Politics*. Toronto, Ontario: United Church, 2011.
Blomley, Nicholas. *Unsettling City: Urban Land and the Politics of Property*. London: Routledge, 2004.
Bochen, C. and William Shannon, eds. *Cold War Letters Thomas Merton*. Maryknoll, New York: Orbis, 2006.

Bonhoeffer, Dietrich. *Letters and Papers from Prison*. Enlarged edition. Edited by E. Bethge. New York: Macmillan/Collier, 1971.

———. *Life Together*. Translated by John W. Doberstein. San Francisco, CA: Harper and Row, 1954.

———. "The Secret of Suffering." In *A Testament of Freedom*, eds. Kelly & Nelson, 289–303. HarperSanFrancisco, 1995.

Bosch, David J. *Transforming Mission: Paradigm Shifts in Theology of Mission*. American Society of Missiology Series No. 16. Maryknoll, N.Y.: Orbis, 1991.

Boulton, Matthew Myer. "The City of God/ The City of Cain: How Taking it to the Streets Is Changing Theological Education." *Sojourners*. (2013) 34–37.

Bourgeois, Michael. "*What's in a Name?*" n. p., n. d., Committee Report of Toronto Christian Resource Centre, Personal Correspondence with B. Morris (Jan. 28, 2011).

Bourne, Richard. *Seek the Peace of the City: Christian Political Criticism as Public, Realist and Transformative*. Eugene, Oregon: Cascade, 2009.

Brach, Tara. *Radical Acceptance: Embracing Your Life with the Heart of a Buddha*. Toronto: Bantam, 2003.

Brashear, Bob. "The Church in the City/The Future Is Already Here." In *Seeking the Peace of the City: The Next Decade in Urban Ministry* issue of *Church and Society*, Presbyterian Church (USA), (1995) 15–16.

Bretherton, Luke. "A Postsecular Politics? Inter-faith relations as a Civic Practice." *Journal of the American Academy of Religion*, (2011) 79 2 346–77.

Brown, Raymond E. *The Gospel According to John XIII–XXI*. Volume 29A The Anchor Bible. Garden City, New York: Doubleday, 1970.

Brueggemann, Walter. *Awed to Heaven, Rooted in Earth: Prayers of Walter Brueggemann*, ed. by Edwin Searcy. Philadelphia: Fortress, 2003.

———. *The Church in Joyous Obedience: Biblical Expositions*. Disc 5/6: "Receiving Salvation and Doing Justice: From Vision to Imperative in Isaiah". Regent College Audio, Vancouver, B.C., 2008.

———. *Journey to the Common Good*. Louisville, KY: Westminster John Knox, 2010.

———. "Justice: the Earthly Form of God's Holiness." In *The Covenanted Self: Explorations in Law and Covenant*, 48–58. Minneapolis, MN: Augsburg Fortress, 1999.

———. *Mandate to Difference: An Invitation to the Contemporary Church*. Louisville, KTY: John Knox Press, 2007.

———. *The Practice of Prophetic Imagination: Preaching an Emancipating Word*. Minneapolis: Fortress Press, 2012.

———. *The Prophetic Imagination*. Second edition. Minneapolis: Augsburg/Fortress, 2001.

———.*Truth Speaks to Power: The Counterculture Nature of Scripture*. Louisville, KY: Westminster John Knox, 2013.

———. *Truth-Telling as Subversive Obedience*, edited by K.C. Hanson. Eugene, OR: WJK, 2013.

Brueggemann, Walter, et al. *To Act Justly, Love Tenderly, Walk Humbly: An Agenda for Ministers*. N.Y.: Paulist, 1986.

Bucher, Glenn R. "Christian Political Realism after Niebuhr: The Case of John C. Bennett." *Union Seminary Quarterly Review* 41 1 (1986) 43–58.

Buckland, Jerry. *Hard Choices: Financial Exclusion, Fringe Banks, and Poverty in Urban Canada* Toronto, Ontario: University of Toronto Press, 2012.

Burrows, Bob. *Hope Lives Here: A History of Vancouver's First United Church*. Madeira Park, B.C.: Harbour, 2010.

Byassee, Jason. "The New Monastics: Alternative Christian Communities" In *Discerning the Body: Searching for Jesus in the World*, 51–60. Eugene, Oregon: Cascade, 2013.

Camacho, Daniel Jose. *God Loves Gentrification: Taking Jesus Seriously*. July 9 2015. http://www.christiancentury.org/blogs/archive/2015-07/god-loves-gentrification.

Cameron, Sandy. *Sparks from the Fire*. Vancouver, British Columbia: Lazara, 1998.

———. *Taking Another Look at Class: Reflections from the Carnegie Community Centre's Newsletters*. Vancouver, B.C.: Canadian Centre for Policy Alternatives & Carnegie Community Centre Association, 1999.

Campbell, Bart. *The Door is Open: Memoir of a Soup Kitchen Volunteer*. Vancouver, BC: Anvil Press, 2001.

Campbell, Cathy C. *Stations of the Banquet: Faith Foundations for Food Justice*. Collegeville, MN: Liturgical, 2003.

Camus, Albert. *Notebooks 1935–1942*. Translated by Philip Thody. New York: Modern Library, 1965, (orig. 1963).

Caputo, John. *The Weakness of God*. Bloomington, IN: Indiana University Press, 2006.

———. *What Would Jesus DECONSTRUCT? The Good News of Post-Modernism for the Church*. Grand Rapids, MI: Baker Academic, 2007.

Carse, James. *After Atheism: New Perspectives on God and Religion*. Part 4, May 3, 2012. http://www.cbc.ca/books/2012/05/after-atheism-ideas-explores-new-perspectives-on-god-and-religion.html.

Chambers, Ed. *Roots of Radicals: Organizing for Power, Action and Justice*. New York: Continuum, 2003.

Chan, Cheryl. "Shelters Turn Away Homeless." *Vancouver Province*, Jan. 14, 2013, A 4.

Charmaz, Kathy. "Grounded Theory in the 21st Century: Applications for Advancing Social Justice Research" In *Strategies of Qualitative Inquiry*, eds. by Denzin and Lincoln, 201–41. Thousand Oaks, CA: Sage, 2008.

Chittister, Joan. *In the Heart of the Temple: My Spiritual Vision for Today's World*. Ottawa: Novalis, 2004.

———. *Scarred by Struggle, Transformed by Hope*. St. Paul University, Ottawa: Novalis, 2003.

Chudnovsky, David. *The Way Home, a Documentary about Homelessness and its Solutions*. Organic Films @yahoo.com.

Clark, Henry B. *Serenity, Courage, & Wisdom: The Enduring Legacy of Reinhold Niebuhr*. Cleveland: The Pilgrim, 1994.

Clements, Keith. "Ecumenical Witness for Peace." In *The Cambridge Companion to Dietrich Bonhoeffer*, ed. by John W. deGruchy. Cambridge, England: Cambridge University Press, 1999.

Coffin, William Sloane. "*Consecration Sermon: The Good Samaritan*" a sermon (listserv.virtueonline.org/pipermail/virtueonline_listserv.virtue).

Cohen, Leonard. "You Have Loved Enough." In *Ten New Songs*. Columbia Records, 2001.

Cole, Yolande, "Food Banks Seek Solutions to End Hunger." *The Georgia Straight*. (December 27/ 2012 – Jan. 3/ 2013) 18.

Coles, Robert. *The Secular Mind*. Princeton University Press, 1999.

Conde-Frazier, Elizabeth. "Participatory Action Research." In *The Wiley-Blackwell Companion to Practical Theology*, ed. Bonnie J. Miller-McLemore, 234–43. Chichester, West Sussex: Wiley-Blackwell, 2012.

The Condition of Jewish Belief. A symposium. Compiled by the editors of Commentary Magazine New York: Macmillan, 1966.

Corbin, Juliet and Anselm Strauss. *Basics of Qualitative Research: Techniques and Procedures for Developing Grounded Theory.* 3rd edition. Thousand Oaks, CA: Sage, 2008.

Cox, Harvey. *Fire from Heaven: The Rise of Pentecostal Spirituality and the Reshaping of Religion in the 21st Century.* Cambridge, MA: Da Capo, 2001 (orig. 1995).

———. *The Future of Faith.* San Francisco, CA: Harper One, 2009.

———. *On Not Leaving It to the Snake.* New York: The Macmillan Co., 1967.

———. *Religion in the Secular City: Toward a Postmodern Theology.* New York: Simon and Schuster, 1983.

———. "The Pull of the Future." In *New Theology No. 5.* eds. M. Marty and D. Peerman, 191–203. New York: Macmillan, 1969.

———. *The Secular City: Secularization and Urbanization in Theological Perspective.* N.Y.: Macmillan, 1965.

———. "The Secular City 25 Years Later." *The Christian Century.* (1990) 107 32, 1029. 32.

Creswell, John W. *Qualitative Inquiry and Research Design: Choosing among Five Traditions.* Thousand Oaks, CA: Sage, 1998.

Crossan, John Dominic. *The Birth of Christianity.* San Francisco, CA: Harper, 1998.

———. *God & Empire: Jesus against Rome, Then and Now.* HarperSanFrancisco, 1997.

———. *The Greatest Prayer: Rediscovering the Revolutionary Message of the Lord's Prayer.* San Francisco: HarperOne, 2010.

———. *Jesus: A Revolutionary Biography.* New York: Harper Collins, 1994.

Crouch, Andy. "A New Kind of Urban Ministry." *Christianity Today* (2011). http://www.christianitytoday.com/et/2011/november/urbanministry.html.

Crysdale, Stewart. *Churches where the Action Is!* Toronto: United Church, 1966.

Dalrymple, T. *Patheos: Life in the Marketplace of Ideas* <http://www.patheos.com/About-Patheos/Timothy-Dalrymple.html>.

Dandelion Society. *Quarterly Community Report.* Fall 2013 issue.

Dart, Ron. *The Beatitudes: When Mountain Meets Valley.* Abbotsford, BC: Freshwindpress, 2005.

———. *The Spirituality of John Cassian.* Dewdney, British Columbia: Synaxis, 2006.

Davey, Andrew. "Being Church as Political Praxis." In *Liberation Theology UK*, eds. Chris Rowland and John Vincent, 55–74. Sheffield, England: Urban Theology Unit, 1995.

———. "Christ in the City: The Density of Presence." In *Crossover City: Resources for Urban Mission and Transformation*, ed. A. Davey., 84–96. London, UK: Mowbray Continuum, 2010.

———. ed. *Crossover City: Resources for Urban Mission and Transformation.* N.Y.: Mowbray/Continuum, 2010.

———. *Urban Christianity and Global Order: Theological Resources for an Urban Future.* Peabody, Massachusetts: Hendrickson, 2002.

Davis, Ellen. "*The Prophetic Interpreter.*" (Chapter I of an unpublished manuscript shared with Biblical Prophecy and Ministry class of July 1–5th, 2013). Vancouver School of Theology.

Davis, H.R. and R. C. Good, eds. *Reinhold Niebuhr on Politics: His Political Philosophy and its Application to Our Age*. New York: Scribner's and Sons, 1960.

Davis, Mike. *Planet of Slums*. Brooklyn, New York: Verso, 2006.

Delbrel, Madeleine. *We, the Ordinary People of the Streets*. Translated by D.L. Schindler, Jr. and C.F. Mann. Grand Rapids, MI: Eerdmans 2000, (orig. 1966).

The *Devil Plays Hard-ball* (DVD).The Passionate Eye CBC Documentary. https://youtu.be/wZdfQFvNCyE.

Dickau, Timothy Reid. *Plunging into the Kingdom: Practicing the Shared Strokes of Community, Hospitality, Justice, and Confession*. Eugene, OR: Cascade, 2010.

———. *Pursuing practices of the Kingdom at Grandview Calvary Baptist Church: Radical Hospitality, Integrated Multicultural Living, Justice for the Least, and Repentance of Idolatry*, D. Min. Thesis. Vancouver, B.C.: Carey Theological College, 2008.

Diewert, Dave, "Religion and Citizenship" Address, Simon Fraser University, Vancouver, British Columbia, (Spring 2010) unpublished.

———. "White Christian Settlers, the Bible and (De)Colonization." In *Buffalo Shout, Salmon Cry: Conversations on Creation, Land Justice, and Life Together*, ed. S. Heinrich, 127–137. Waterloo, Ontario: Herald, 2013.

Dorrien, Gary. "Society as the Subject of Redemption: Washington Gladden, Walter Rauschenbusch, and the Social Gospel." In *Economy, Difference, Empire: Social Ethics for Social Justice*, 3-28, N.Y: Columbia University Press, 2010.

———. *The Making of American Liberal Theology: Idealism, Realism and Modernity, 1900–1950*. Louisville, KY: Westminster John Knox, 2003.

———. *Social Ethics in the Making: Interpreting an American Tradition*. West Sussex, England: Wiley-Blackwell, 2009.

———. "Society as the Subject of Redemption: The Relevance of the Social Gospel." *Tikkin Magazine*, (November/December, 2009) www.questia.com/magazine/1P3-1896963031/society-as-the-subject-of-redemption-the-relevance.

Doucet, Clive. *Urban Meltdown: Cities, Climate Change and Politics as Usual*. Gabriola Island, British Columbia: New Society, 2007.

Douglas, Gordon. "Poisonous Inequality." In *Resistance: the New Role of Progressive Christians*, ed. John Cobb, Jr., 75–96. Louisville, KY: Westminster John Knox, 2006.

Douglas, Stan, ed. *Every Building on 100 West Hastings*. Vancouver, B.C.: Contemporary Art Gallery & Arsenal Pulp, 2002.

Douglas-Klotz, Neil. *Prayers of the Cosmos: Meditations on the Aramaic Words of Jesus*. Translated with commentary. San Francisco, CA: Harper 1990, 1991.

Dykstra, Laurel. "Riff, Bedbugs, and Signs: Reading the Plague Narratives from Vancouver's Downtown Eastside." In *Liberating Bible Study: Scholarship, Art and Action in Honor of the Center and Library for the Bible and Social Justice Service*, eds L. Dykstra and C. Myers, 50–59. Eugene, OR: Cascade, 2011.

———. *Set Them Free: the Other Side of Exodus*. Maryknoll, N.Y.: Orbis, 2002.

Eisen, Arnold. "The Spirituality of Abraham Joshua Heschel." *On Being with Krista Tippet*. Dec. 8, 2012. http://onbeing.org.

Elliot. T.S. "East Coker, Part III. In *Four Quartets*. http://www.coldbacon.com/poems/fq.html.

Fabello, Danny. "Always, There is Hope" In *War & Roses*. Musikang Buyan Productions, 2001.
Fackre, Gabriel. *The Promise of Reinhold Niebuhr*. Third Edition. Grand Rapids, MI: Eerdmans, 2011.
Fainstain, Susan S. *"Planning and the Just City"* April 29, 2006 lecture for the Conference on Searching for the Just City, Graduate School of Architecture, Planning and Preservation of Columbia University <http://www.avaaz.org/en/stop_the_quarry/97. php?cl_tta_sign=2d87086572f377eba7190ed2264728f6>.
Farley, Gary. "Poverty: The Urban-Rural Linkages." In *Envisioning the City: A Reader on Urban Ministry*, ed. by E. S. Meyers, 109–24. Louisville, KY: Westminster John Knox, 1992.
Farley, Wendy. *The Wounding and Healing of Desire: Weaving Heaven and Earth*. Louisville, KY: WJK books, 2005.
Fawkes, Deb Cameron. *"There Is a Power not Ourselves, That makes for Righteousness" Tommy Douglas: Political Life as Religious Vocation*. Master of Theology Thesis, Vancouver School of Theology, 2011.
Fineman, Martha Albertson. "The Vulnerable Subject and The Responsive State." *Emory Law Journal* (2010) www.emory.edu/vulnerability. via papers.ssrn.com/sol3/papers.cfm?abstract_id=1694740.
———. "The Vulnerable Subject: Anchoring Equality in the Human Condition." *Yale Journal of Law and Feminism* (2008) www.ucd.ie/esc/html/vulnerable subject – clean version . . .
Finger, Reta Halteman. "Paul's Letter to the 1%." *Sojourners*. (2012) 41 6, 26–29.
———. *Roman House Churches for Today: A Practical Guide for Small Groups*, 2nd edn. Grand Rapids, MI: Eerdmans, 2007.
Finn, Ed. "Shortcomings of Philanthropy: Bigger Crumbs from the Tables of the Elite Are Not Enough." *The CCPA Monitor: Economic, Social, and Environmental Perspectives*, (2012) 18 84-5.
Fishburn, Janet. *Confronting the Idolatry of Family: A New Vision for the Household of God*. Nashville, TN: Abingdon, 1991.
Fox, Richard. *Reinhold Niebuhr: A Biography*. N.Y.: Pantheon, 1985.
Frankl, Victor. "The Case for a Tragic Optimism." In *Man's Search for Meaning: An Introduction to Logotherapy*, revised and updated, 161–79. M.Y.: Simon & Schuster, 1970.
———. "Finding Meaning in Difficult Times: Interview with Victor Frankl." http://youtu.be/LlC2OdnhIiQ.
Freudenberger, Herbert J. *Burn Out: The High Cost of High Achievement*. Toronto, Ontario: Bantam, 1981.
Fujiyoshi, Ronald S. *A Comparison of Action Theory: Saul Alinsky and Reinhold Niebuhr*. BD Thesis, Chicago Theological Seminary.
Fule, A. T. "Being Human Before God: Reinhold Niebuhr in Feminist Mirrors." In *Reinhold Niebuhr [1892–1971]: A Centenary Appraisal. McGill Studies in Religion*. eds. by G. Gaudin and D.J. Hall, 55–78. Atlanta, Georgia: Scholars, 1994.
Fung, Raymond. "Compassion for the Sinned Against." *Theology Today* (1980) 37 162–69.
Ganz, Marshall. *Why David Sometimes Wins: Leadership, Organization, and Strategy in the California Farm Worker Movement*. New York: Oxford University Press, 2009.

Gathje, Peter R., ed. *A Work of Hospitality: The Open Door Reader 1982–2002*. Atlantic: The Open Door Community, 2002..
Gench, Roger J. *Theology from the Trenches: Reflections on Urban Ministry*. Louisville, Kty: Westminster John Knox, 2014.
Gilkey, Langdon. *On Niebuhr: A Theological Study* .University of Chicago Press, 2001.
Glaser, Barney G. and Anselm L. Strauss. *The Discovery of Grounded Theory: Strategies for Qualitative Research*. Chicago, IL: Aldine, 1967.
Gornik, Mark R. *To Live in Peace: Biblical Faith and the Changing Inner City*. Grand Rapids, MI: Eerdmann's, 2002.
Grant, George P. *English-Speaking Justice*. The Josiah Wood Lectures. Sackville, NB: Mt. Allison University, 1974.
———. *George Grant in Conversation, with David Cayley*. Toronto: Anansi, 1995.
Graves, Mark. *Insight to Heal: Co-creating Beauty Amidst Human Suffering*. Eugene, OR: Cascade, 2013.
Green, Clifford, ed. *Churches, Cities, and Human Community: Urban Ministry in the U.S.A. 1945–1985*. Grand Rapids, MI: Eerdmann's, 1996.
Green, Laurie, "'I can't Go There': The Urban Vocation." In *Crossover City*, ed. by A. Harvey, 11–14. London, England: Mowbray/Continuum, 2010, 11.
Grenz, Stanley J. *Prayer: The Cry for the Kingdom*. Grand Rapids, MI: Eerdmans, 2005, revised edition.
Grimley, A. and J. M. Wooding. *Living the Hours: Monastic Spirituality in Everyday Life*. London, England: Canterbury, 2010.
Groody, Daniel G. *Globalization, Spirituality, and Justice*. Maryknoll N.Y: Orbis Books, 2007.
Gustafson, James M. *Ethics from a Theocentric Perspective*. Vol. 1, "Theology and Ethics." Chicago, IL: University of Chicago Press, 1981.
———. *Ethics from a Theocentric Perspective*. Vol. II "Ethics and Theology". Univ. of Chicago Press, 1984.
———. *A Sense of the Divine: The Natural Environment from a Theocentric Perspective*. Cleveland. OH: Pilgrim, 1994.
Gutierrez, Gustav. *A Theology of Liberation*, rev. edn Maryknoll, NY: Orbis, 1988, orig. 1971.
Hall, Douglas J. *Bound and Free: A Theologian's Journey*. Minneapolis, MN: Augsburg Fortress, 2005.
———. *The Future of the Church: Where Are We Headed?* Toronto, Ontario: The United Church, 1989.
———. *Imaging God: Dominion as Stewardship*. Grand Rapids, MI: Eerdmans, 1986.
———. "'The Logic of the Cross': Niebuhr's Foundational Theology." In *Reinhold Niebuhr Revisited: Engagements with an American Original*, ed. Daniel Rice, 55–74.Grand Rapids, MI: Wm. B. Eerdmans, 2009.
———. *Remembered Voices: Reclaiming the Legacy of 'Neo-orthodoxy'*. Westminster John Knox, 1998.
———. "Theological Education in the Urban Context." In *Seek the Peace of the City*, ed by E. Villanfane, 97–102. Grand Rapids, MI: Eerdmans, 1995.
———. *Thinking the Faith: Christian Theology in a North American Context*. Minneapolis: Augsburg Fortress, 1989.
———. *When You Pray: Thinking Your Way into God's World*. Judson Press, Valley Forge, 1987.

Hammarskjöld, Dag. *Markings*. Translated by L. Sjoberg and W.H. Auden. New York: Alfred A. Knopf, 1965.
Hampshire, Stuart. *Justice is Conflict*. Princeton, NJ: Princeton University Press, 2000.
Hargraves, J. Archie. "The East Harlem Protestant Parish." *Church & Society*. 14 (1949) 9–13.
Hargraves, J. Archie. "The Local Church and Juvenile Delinquency." In *Cities and Churches: Readings on the Urban Church*, ed. R.Lee, 320–25. Philadelphia: Westminster, 1962
Hargraves, J. A. *Stop Pussyfooting Through the Revolution: Some Churches That Did*. Stewardship Council of the United Church of Christ, New York, no date.
Haring, Bernard. *To Do Justice: A Christian Social Conscience*. St. Louis, Missouri: Liguori, 1999.
Harland, Gordon. *The Thought of Reinhold Niebuhr*. N.Y.: Oxford University Press, 1960.
Haroutunian, Joseph. *God with Us: A Theology of Transpersonal Life*, 2nd enlarged edn. Allison Park, PA: Pickwick, 1991.
Harper, Niles. *Urban Churches, Vital Signs: Beyond Charity to Justice*. Eugene, OR: Wipf Stock, 2005.
Harries, Richard, ed. *Reinhold Niebuhr and the Issues of Our Time*. Grand Rapids, MI: Erdmann, 1986.
Harrison, Beverly Wildung, eds Elizabeth M. Bounds et al. *Justice in the Making: Feminist Social Ethics*, Westminster John Knox, 2004.
———. *Making Connections: Essays in Feminist Social Ethics*, ed. Carol S. Robb. Boston: Beacon, 1989.
Hart, Patrick and Jonathan Montaldo, eds. *The Intimate Merton: His Life from His Journals*. San Francisco, CA: Harper, 2001.
Hauck, F. "Koinonia." In *Theological Dictionary of the New Testament*, eds. G. Kittel and G. Friedrich, 447–50. Grand Rapids, MI: Eerdmans, 1985.
Hauerwas, Stanley and Charles Pinches. *Christians Among the Virtues: Theological Conversations with Ancient and Modern Ethics*. Notre Dame, IN: University of Notre Dame Press, 1997.
Haugen, Gary A. *Good News about Injustice: A Witness of Courage in a Hurting World*. Downers Grove, Illinois: InterVarsity, 1999.
———. with Gregg Hunter. *Terrify No More*. Nashville: W. Publishing Group, 2005.
Hemmings, Michael. *On the Merger of Upper Room and The Open Door*. An untitled and unpublished paper for the Public Administration Faculty at the University of Victoria, British Columbia, April 7, 2008.
Hercules, Bob and Bruce Orenstein. *The Democratic Promise: Saul Alinsky and His Legacy*. Chicago, IL: Media Process Educational Films, 1999.
Hern, Matt. *Common Ground in a Liquid City: Essay in Defense of an Urban Future*. Oakland, CA: AK Press, 2010.
Hessel, Stephane. *Time for Outrage: Indignez-vous!* Translated by M. Duvert 2000. London: Twelve Hachette Book Group, 2011.
Higgins, John J. *Merton's Theology of Prayer*. Spencer, Mass.: Cistercian, 1971.
Higgins, Michael W. *Heretic Blood: An Audiobiography of Thomas Merton*. CBC Radio One Tapes, 1998.
———. *Heretic Blood: The Spiritual Geography of Thomas Merton*, Stoddart, 1998.

———. *The Unquiet Monk: Thomas Merton's Questing Faith.* Toronto, Ontario: Novalis, 2015.

Himes, Michael and Kenneth. *Fullness of Faith: The Public Significance of Theology.* Mahwah, NJ: Paulist, 1993.

Hope and Recovery: A Twelve-step Guide for Healing from Sex Additions. Center City, MN: Hazeldon Educational Materials, 1987.

Horton, Myles. *The Long Haul.* West Sussex, England: Columbia University Press, 1998.

Howard, Keith. "The Prophet They Call Rev Al." *The United Church Observer* 64 (2001) 6 28–32.

Hulsether, Mark. *Building a Protestant Left: Christianity and Crisis Magazine, 1941–1993.* Knoxville, TN: University of Tennessee Press, 1999.

Hume, Stephen. "Income Inequality Threatens Our Society." *Vancouver Sun,* September 14, 2013, D5.

Hunt, Albert. *Hopes for Great Happenings: Alternatives in Education and Theatre.* New York: Taplinger Publishing Co., 1976.

Hunter, James Davidson. *To Change the World: The Irony, Tragedy and Possibility of Christianity in the Late Modern World.* New York: Oxford University Press, 2010.

Hurtig, Mel. *Pay the Rent or Feed the Kids: The Tragedy and Disgrace of Poverty.* Toronto, Ontario: McClelland and Stewart, 1999.

Hutchinson, John A. "Two Decades of Social Christianity." In *Christian Faith and Social Action,* ed. J. A. Hutchinson, 1–22. N.Y.: Scribner Son's, 1953.

Hutchinson, Roger. "Education for Social Transformation." In *Action Training in Canada: Reflections on Church-Based Education for Social Transformation,* eds. Ted Reeve and Roger Hutchinson, 5-12 Toronto: Ontario: Centre for Research in Religion Emmanuel College.

The Hymn and Worship Book of the United Church of Canada. *Voices United.* Toronto, Ontario: United Church, 1996.

Isaacs, Anne. *Torn Thread.* London: Scholastic Signature, 2000.

Ivereigh, Austin. *Faithful Citizens: A Practical Guide to Catholic Social Teaching and Community Organising.* London, England: Darton Longman Todd, 2010.

Jacobs, Jane. *Dark Age Ahead.* New York: Vintage Canada/Random House, 2004.

Jacobsen, Dennis A. *Doing Justice: Congregations and Community Organizing.* Minneapolis: Fortress, 2001.

James, William. *The Varieties of Religious Experience: A Study in Human Nature.* N.Y.: Mentor, 1958.

James, William. "The Will to Believe." In *Essays on Faith and Morals,* selected by Ralph Barton Perry. New York: New American Library, 1962, (orig. 1896).

Jevne, Ronna. *It All Begins with Hope: Patients, Caregivers and the Bereaved Speak Out.* San Diego: Lura Media, 1991.

Jevne, Ronna and J. Miller. *Finding hope: Seeing the World in a Brighter Light.* Fort Wayne, Indiana: Willowgreen, 1999.

Jevne, Ronna. *Voice of hope: Heard Across The Heart of Life.* San Diego: Lura Media, 1994.

Johns, Rob. "In Suffering Love." In *Songs of a Gospel People,* #53. Winfield, British Columbia: Wood Lake, 1987.

Johnson, Fenton. *Keeping Faith: A Skeptic's Journey among Christian and Buddhist Monks.* N.Y.: Mariner, 2003.

Jones, Paul D. "Review of Eccentric Existence: A Theological Anthropology by David Kelsey." *Journal of the American Academy of Religion*. (2012) 80 3 787–800.
Kamergrauzis, Normunds."Ronald Preston and the Future of Christian Ethics." *Studies in Christian Ethics*, 17 2 62–86.
Keating, Donald R. *The Power to Make It Happen: Mass-based Organizing What It Is and How It Works*. Toronto: Green Tree, 1975.
Keating, Thomas. *Intimacy with God: An Introduction to Centering Prayer*. N.Y.: Crossroads, 1994/2003.
Keller, John E. *Let Go, Let God: Surrendering Self-Centered Delusions in the Costly Journey of Faith*. Minneapolis, MN: Augsburg, 1985.
Kelly, Geoffrey & Burton Nelson. *The Cost of Moral Leadership: the Spirituality of Dietrich Bonhoeffer*. Grand Rapids, MI: Eerdmans, 2003.
———. "Prayer and Action for Justice." In *The Cambridge Companion to Dietrich Bonhoeffer*, ed. by John W. deGruchy, 246–68, Cambridge, England: Cambridge University Press, 1999.
Kemmis, Stephen and Robin McTaggart. "Participatory Action Research." In *Strategies of Qualitative Inquiry*, eds N. Denzin and Y. Lincoln, 271–330. Thousand Oaks, CA: Sage, 2008.
Kenrick, Bruce. Parish *Come Out the Wilderness: The Story of the East Harlem Protestant*. Harper & Row, N.Y., 1962.
Keshgegian, Flora A. *Redeeming Memories: A Theology of Healing and Transformation*. Abingdon, 2000.
———. *A Time for Hope: Practices for Living in Today's World*. New York: Continuum, 2006.
Kierkegaard, Soren. "The Purity of Heart Is to Will One Thing"; "Soren Kierkegaard quotes." ThinkExist.com Quotations Online 1 January 2012. a href="http://en.ThinkExist.com/quotes/soren_kierkegaard/">Soren Kierkegaard quotes</a.
Kilpin, Juliet. *Urban to the Core: Motives for Incarnational Mission*. Eugene: WIPF & Stock, 2012.
King, Jr., Martin Luther. *The Papers of Martin Luther King, Jr. Volume VI "Advocate of the Social Gospel"*, eds. Susan Carson et al. University of California Press, 2007.
———."A Long Way to Go." NBC News interview with Sander Vanocur 1967.
Klein, Naomi. *This Changes Everything: Capitalism vs. the Climate*. Toronto: Alfred A. Knopf, 2014.
Kneen, Brewster. *Journey of an Unrepentant Socialist*. Ottawa: The Ram's Horn, 2014.
Kolakowski, Leszek. "The Priest and the Jester." *Dissent*, (Summer 1962) 215-35. www.independent.co.uk /news/obituaries/leszek-kolakowski-polishborn.
Kuile, Martha ter. *The Virtues of a Christian Realist: Toward a Niebuhrian Virtue Ethics in Conversation with Martha Nussbaum*. PhD diss., Ottawa: St. Paul University, 2011.
Kurtz and Ketchum, eds. *The Spirituality of Imperfection: Story-telling and the Search for Meaning*. N.Y.: Bantam Dell, 1992.
Labrie, Ross and Angus Stuart, eds. *Thomas Merton: Monk on the Edge*. North Vancouver, B.C.: Thomas Merton Society of Canada, 2012.
Lasn, Kalle. *Culture Jam: How to Reverse America's Suicidal Consumer Binge — and Why We Must*. New York: Quill and HarperCollins, 1999.
Lathrop, Gordon W. *Holy Things: A Liturgical Theology*. Minneapolis: Augsburg Fortress, 1993.

Lederman, Marsha. "This Vancouver Isn't in the Brochures." *The Globe and Mail*. February 13, 2010, R4.

Lee, Jeong-Woo. *Toward a Trinitarian Ecological Theology: A Study in Jürgen Moltmann's Panentheism*. PhD diss., University of Toronto, 2007.

Lee, Robert, ed. *Cities and Churches: Readings on the Urban Church*. Philadelphia: Westminster, 1962.

———. *The Promise of Bennett: Christian Realism and Social Responsibility*. The Promise of Theology series. N.Y.: J. B. Lippincott, 1969.

Leech, Kenneth. *Prayer and Prophecy: The Essential Kenneth Leech*, ed. by David Bunch and Angus Ritchie. New York: Seabury Books, 2009

———. "The Soul and the City: Urban Ministry and Theology 1956–2006" The Samuel Ferguson Lecture 2006.University of Manchester. http://www.anglocatholicsocialism.org /soulandcity.html.

———. *Through our Long Exile: Contextual Theology and the Urban Experience*, London: Darton, Longman & Todd, 2001.

———. *True Prayer: An Introduction to Christian Spirituality*. Toronto, Ontario: Anglican Book Centre, 1980.

———. "Urbanism and its Discontents." In *Through our Long Exile*, 98–112. London, England: Darton Longman Todd, 2001.

Lefevre, Perry D. *Radical Prayer: Contemporary Interpretations*. Chicago: Exploration, 1982.

———. *Understandings of Prayer*. Westminster, 1981.

Lehman, Paul L. "The Foundation and Pattern of Christian Behaviour" In *Christian Faith and Social Action*, ed. John A. Hutchison, 93–116. N.Y.: Scribner's Sons, 1953.

Lind, Christopher and Joe Mihevc. *Coalitions of Justice: The Story of Canada's Interchurch Coalitions*. Ottawa: Novalis, 1994.

Linthicum, Robert. *City of God City of Satan: A Biblical Theology of the Urban Church*. Grand Rapids, MI: Zondervan, 1991.

———. *Transforming Power: Biblical Strategies for Making a Difference in Your Community*. Downers Grove, Ill: InterVarsity, 2003.

Livezey, Lowell. "Church as Parish: the East Harlem Protestant Parish." *The Christian Century* (1998) 1176–1177.

Loring, Ed. "Bringing Love and Justice Together." In *A Work of Hospitality: The Open Door Reader*, edited by P. R. Gathje, 96–100. Atlanta, GA, Open Door Community, 2002.

Lovin, Robin. *Christian Realism and the New Realities*. Cambridge, England: Cambridge University Press, 2008.

———. *Reinhold Niebuhr and Christian Realism*. Cambridge, England: Cambridge University Press, 1995.

Luborsky, Mark E. "The Identification and Analysis of Themes and Patterns" In *Qualitative Methods in Aging Research*, eds. J. Gubrium and A. Sankar, 189–209. Walnut Creek, CA: Sage, 1993.

Lupton, Robert D. *Charity Detox: What Charity Would Look Like If We Cared About Results*. NY: HarperCollins, 2015.

———. *Toxic Charity: How Churches and Charities Hurt Those They Help (and How to Reverse It)*. NY: HarperCollins, 2011.

Lynch, William F. *Images of Hope: Imagination as Healer of the Hopeless*. Toronto, Ontario: Mentor-Omega, 1967 (orig. 1965).
Marcuse, Herbert. *Negations: Essays in Critical Theory*. Boston, MA: Beacon, 1968.
———. *One-Dimensional Man: Studies in the Ideology of Advanced Industrial Society* Boston, MA: Beacon, 1964.
Maté, Gabor. *In the Realm of the Hungry Ghost: Close Encounters with Addiction*. Toronto, Alfred A. Knopf, 2008.
May, Gerald. *Will and Spirit: A Contemplative Psychology*. N.Y.: HarperCollins, 1982.
MacIntyre, Alasdair. *After Virtue*. 3rd edn. Notre Dame, IN: University of Notre Dame Press, 2007.
McAfee Brown, Robert. *Reflections over the Long Haul: A Memoir*. Louisville: Westminster/John Knox, 2005.
McAfee, Lois. "The Strength to Resist: The Life of Prayer." In *Resistance: The New Role of Progressive Christians*, ed. by John Cobb, Jr., 32–54. Louisville, KY: Westminster John Knox, 2008.
McCarroll, Pamela. *Waiting at the Foot of the Cross: Toward a Theology of Hope for Today*; Foreword by Douglas John Hall. Distinguished Dissertations in Christian Theology Book 11. Eugene, OR: Pickwick, 2014.
McClendon, James Wm., Jr. *Biography as Theology: How Life Stories Can Remake Today's Theology*. Nashville, Tennessee, 1974.
McCourt, Kevin. "Homelessness: System Does Not Prepare Youth in Care for Eventualities of Adult Life on Their Own." *Vancouver Sun*. October 19, 2013, C5.
McCullum, Hugh. "No Place to call Home." *The United Church Observer*. (Dec. 1987) 25.
McDonnell, Thomas P., ed. *A Thomas Merton Reader*, rev. edn. New York: Image, 1974.
McDonnell, Thomas P., ed. *Through the Year with Thomas Merton: Daily Meditations from His Writings*. New York: Doubleday Image, 1985.
McEntyre, Marilyn Chandler. *Caring for Words in a Culture of Lies*. Grand Rapids, MI: Eerdmans, 2009.
McGee, Timothy, interview with J. Rieger. "Power, Economics, and Christian Faith from Below." In "Marxism: An Intersection of Theology and Culture." *The Other Journal*. (Presented by Seattle School of Theology & Psychology) 22 72–80. Eugene, Oregon: Cascade, 2013.
McInnes, Craig. "Human Development Index Reinforces Occupy's Mantra." *Vancouver Sun*, November 3, 2011, B1.
McMartin, Pete. "A Tale of Two Cities: One Big, One Small." *Vancouver Sun*, Jan. 5, 2013, A5.
McNamee, John. *Diary of a City Priest*. Kansas City, MO: Sheed & Ward, 1993.
———. *Endurance: The Rhythm of Faith*. Kansas City, MO: Sheed & Ward, 1996.
McQuaig, Linda. "Restraint for Everything But Sports: Canada Spends $6 Billion for Olympics But Budget Holds Line on Health and Education." *Toronto Star*, February 26, 2010. <http://www.straightgoods.ca/2010/ViewArticle.cfm?Ref=263&Cookies=yes>.
Meeks M. Douglas. "Jürgen Moltmann's Systematic Contributions to Theology." *Religious Studies Review* 22 (1996) 95–102.
———. *Love: the foundation of Hope: the theology of Jürgen Moltmann and Elisabeth Moltmann-Wendel*, with Fred B. Burnham and Charles S. McCoy. San Francisco: Harper & Row. 1988.

———. *Origins of the Theology of Hope* (preface by Jürgen Moltmann). Philadelphia: Fortress, 1974.

Meeks, Wayne A. *The First Urban Christians: The Social World of the Apostle Paul*. New Haven, Connecticut: Yale University Press, 1983.

Mercer, Joyce Ann. "Economics, Class, and Classism." In *The Wiley-Blackwell Companion to Practical Theology*, ed. by Bonnie J. Miller-McLemore, 432–42. Chichester, West Sussex, Wiley-Blackwell, 2012.

Merton, Thomas. *The Asian Journal of Merton*, eds. N. Burton, P. Hart and J. Loughlin. New York: New Directions, 1975.

———. "Building Community on God's Love." In *Thomas Merton in Alaska: The Alaskan Conferences, Journals, and Letters*, 100-102. New York: New Directions, 1989.

———. *Cold War Letters Thomas Merton*, eds. C. Bochen and Wm Shannon. Maryland: Orbis, 2006.

———. *Contemplation in a World of Action*. Image/Doubleday, 1973.

———. "Contemplation in a Word of Action." In *Contemplation in a World of Action*, 172–79. Garden City, New York: Doubleday Image, 1973.

———. "Conversion of Life." In *The Monastic Journey*, ed. Br. Patrick Hart., 145–61. New York: Doubleday Image, 1978.

———. "First and Last Thoughts." In *A Thomas Merton Reader*, ed. by Thomas P. McDonnell. rev. edn, 17–19. Garden City, New York: Image, 1974.

———. *Honorable reader: Reflections on My Work*, eds. Robert E. Daggy and Thomas Merton. New York, N.Y.: Crossroad, 1989.

———. *The Intimate Merton: His Life from His Journals*. eds Patrick Hart and Jonathan Montaldo. HarperSanFrancisco, 2001.

———. "Letter to An Innocent Bystander" In *Raids on the Unspeakable*, 53–64. New York: New Directions, 1964.

———. *The Life of the Vows: Initiation into the Monastic Tradition 6*. Selected and edited by Patrick F. O'Connell. Collegeville, Minnesota: Cistercian, 2012.

———. "Marxism and Monastic Perspectives." In *The Asian Journal of Thomas Merton*, eds. Naomi Burton, P. Hart and J. Laughlin. N.Y.: New Directions, 1975.

———. *The Monastic Journey*, ed. Br. Patrick Hart. New York: Doubleday Image, 1978.

———. *New Seeds of Contemplation*. New York: New Directions, 1972.

———. *No Man Is an Island*. New York: Harvest/HBJ, 1955.

———. "Prayer, Tradition, and Experience" In *Thomas Merton in Alaska: The Alaskan Conferences, Journals, and Letters*, 115–17. New York: New Directions, 1989.

———. "The Primitive Carmelite Ideal" In *Disputed Questions*, 218–263. Orlando, Florida: First Harvest edition, 1985, (orig. 1960).

———. "Time of the End Is No Room in the Inn." In *Raids on the Unspeakable*, 65-78. N.Y.: New Directions, 1964.

———. *Seeds of Destruction*. N.Y.: Farrar, Strauss & Giroux, 1964.

———. *The Sign of Jonas*. New York: Harcourt Brace Jovanovich, 1953.

———. *Thomas Merton: A Life in Letters: The Essential Collection*, eds Wm. Shannon and C. Bochen. N.Y.: HarperCollins, 2008.

———. *Thomas Merton: Essential Writings*, edited and selected by C. Bochen. Maryknoll, New York: Orbis, 2005.

———. *Thomas Merton in Alaska: The Alaskan Conferences, Journals, and Letters*. New York: New Directions, 1989.

———. "Toward a Theology of Prayer." *Cistercian Studies Quarterly Review*, Vol. XIII, 3, (1978) 191–99.

———. "Toward a Theology of Resistance." In *Faith and Violence: Christian Teachings and Christian Practice*, 3–13. Notre Dame, IN: University of Notre Dame Press, 1968.

———. *The Wisdom of the Desert*. New York: New Directions, 1970 (orig. 1960).

———. *A Year with Thomas Merton: Daily Meditations from His Journals* selected and edited by Jonathan Montaldo. N.Y.: HarperCollins, 2004.

Michaud, Derek with Hyung-Kon Kim. "Jürgen Moltmann." In *Boston Collaborative Encyclopedia of Western Theology*. http://people.bu.edu/wwildman /bce/ moltmann.htm.

Miller, Patrick D. *They Cried to the Lord: The Form and Theology of Biblical Prayer*. Philadelphia: Fortress Augsburg, 1994.

Moe, Terry A. *O Healing River: Just Prayer and Organizing*. D.Min. doctoral thesis, Wesley Theological Seminary, Washington, DC, 1998.

Moir, John S. *Enduring Witness: A History of the Presbyterian Church in Canada*. Toronto, Ontario: Bryant, 1987.

Moltmann, Jürgen. "The Adventure of Theological Ideas." *Religious Studies Review* 22 (1996)102–5.

———. *A Broad Place: An Autobiography*. Trans. by M. Kohl. Minneapolis, MN: Fortress, 2008.

———. *The Church in the Power of the Spirit*. Trans. M. Kohl. N.Y.: Harper & Row, 1975.

———. *The Coming of God: Christian Eschatology*. Trans. M. Kohl.Minneapolis, Minnesota: Fortress, 2004.

———. *The Crucified God*. Trans. R.A. Wilson and J. Bowden. N.Y.: Harper & Row, 1973.

———. *Experiences in Theology: Ways and Forms of Christian Theology*. Trans. by Margaret Kohl. Minneapolis, MN: Fortress, 2000.

———. *Experiences of God*. Philadelphia: Fortress, 1980.

———. *Ethics of Hope*. Trans. by Margaret Kohl, Minneapolis: Fortress Press, 2012

———. *The Experiment Hope*. ed. Douglas Meeks. Philadelphia: Fortress, 1975.

———. *God in Creation: A New Theology of Creation and the Spirit of God*. Trans. by M. Kohl. Minneapolis, MN: Fortress, 1993.

———. *The Gospel of Liberation*. Trans. by H. Wayne Pipkin. Waco, TX: Word Books, 1973.

———. "Hope and Reality: Contradiction and Correspondence." In *God Will Be All in All: The Eschatology of Jürgen Moltmann*, ed. R. Bauckham, 77–86. Minneapolis: Fortress. 2001.

———. *How I Have Changed: Reflections on Thirty Years of Theology*, ed. Jürgen Moltmann. Trans. by John Bowden. Harrisburg, PA: Trinity International, 1997.

———. *In the End – The Beginning: The Life of Hope*. Trans. M. Kohl. Minneapolis: Fortress, 2004.

———. *Hope for the Church: Moltmann in Dialogue with Practical Theology*, ed. Theodore Runyon. Nashville: Abingdon Press, 1979.

———. "Horizons of Hope: A Review of 'Spe Salvi' Encyclical." *Christian Century*, 125 10 (2008) 31–33.

———. *Jürgen Moltmann Collected Readings.* Edited by M Kohl and introduction Richard Bauckham. Minneapolis, Minnesota: Fortress, 2014.

———. "The Liberation of the Future and Its Anticipations in History." In *God Will Be All in All: The Eschatology of Jürgen Moltmann,* ed. R. Bauckham, 265–90. Minneapolis: Fortress. 2001.

———. "Messianic Atheism." In *On Human Dignity: Political Theology and Ethics.* Translated and introduction by M. Douglas Meeks, 180–86. Philadelphia: Fortress, 1984.

———. with Elisabeth Moltmann-Wendel. *Passion for God: Theology in Two Voices.* Louisville: Westminster John Knox, 2003.

———. "Progress and Abyss: Remembrances of the Future of the Modern World." In *The Future of Hope: Christian Tradition Amid Modernity and Postmodernity,* eds. M. Volf & Wm. Katerberg, 3–26. Grand Rapids, MI: Eerdmans, 2004.

———. *The Source: The Holy Spirit and the Theology of Life.* Trans. by M. Kohl. Philadelphia: Fortress, 1997.

———. *The Spirit of Life: A Universal Affirmation.* Trans. by M. Kohl. Minneapolis, MN: Fortress, 2001.

———. *Theology of Hope: On the Ground and Implications of a Christian Eschatology.* Translated by James W. Leitch. N.Y.: Harper & Row, 1967.

Montreal City Mission Society website <http://www.montrealcitymission.org>.

The Moody Blues. "*The Search for the Lost Chord*". <http://themoodybluesalbum.tripod.com/id7.html>.

Moon, Lawrence. "The Door Is Always Open." *Mandate,* special edition. Toronto, Ontario: The United Church of Canada, Mission and Service Fund, 1989.

———. *History of the Open Door 1986-1996,* September 1996.

Moore, J.J. "Difficult Words." *Sojourners: Living the Word.* (2014) 43 6 49.

Moss, Robert G. *The Neighborhood Church: God's Vision of Success.* Eugene: WIPF & Stock, 2014.

Morris, Barry K. *Engaging Urban Ministry: Embracing the Ministry in the City, and Discerning the City in Ministry.* Th.M. thesis for Vancouver School of Theology, May, 1998.

———. "Hope, Justice and Prayer." *Touchstone.* (2010), 28 2 52–55.

——— and Harvey Stevens and Aileen Urquhart, eds. *The Word on the Street: An Invitation to Community Ministry in Canada.* Winfield, British Columbia: Wood Lake, 1991.

Mowrer, O. Hobart. *New Group Therapy.* Princeton, NJ: Van Nostrand Insight, 1964.

Muller-Fahrenholz, Geiko, *The Kingdom and the Power: The Theology of Jürgen Moltmann,* trans. by John Bowden. Philadelphia: Fortress, 2001.

Myers, Ched. *The Biblical Vision of Sabbath Economics.* Washington. D.C.: Church of the Saviour, 2001.

Myers, Ched and L. Dykstra, eds. *Liberating Bible Study.* Center and Library for the Bible and Social Justice Service Vol. 1. Eugene, OR: Cascade, 2011.

Myers, William R. *Research in Ministry: A Primer for the Doctor of Ministry of Program.* Chicago: Exploration Press, 2000, 3rd edition.

Nabhan-Warren, Kristy. "Embodied Research and Writing: a Case for Phenomenologically Orientated Religious Studies Ethnographies." *Journal of American Academy of Religion,* 79 2, (2011) 378–407.

Neal, Marie Augusta. *A Socio-Theology of Letting Go.* N.Y: Paulist, 1977.

Neyrey, Jerome H., ed. *The Social World of Luke-Acts: Models for Interpretation*. Peabody, MA: Hendrickson, 1991.

Niebuhr, H. Richard. "Center of Value." In *Radical Monotheism and Western Culture*. New York: Harper Torchbooks, 1970.

———. *The Responsible Self: An Essay in Christian Moral Philosophy*. New York: Harper Row, 1963.

Niebuhr, Reinhold. "Augustine's Political Realism." In *Christian Realism and Political Problems*, 119–46. Fairfield, NJ: Augustus M. Kelly, reprint 1977 (orig.1953).

———. *Beyond Tragedy*. New York: Scribner's Sons, 1937.

———. "Christian Faith and Social Action." In *Christian Faith and Social Action*, ed. J.A. Hutchinson, 225–242. N.Y.: Scribner's Sons, 1953.

———. *Christian Realism and Political Problems*. Fairfield, NJ: Augustus M. Kelly P, reprint 1977 (orig. 1953).

———. *Christianity and Power Politics*. Archon Books, 1969, (orig. N.Y.: Scribner's Sons, 1940).

———. "Development of a Social Ethic in the Ecumenical Movement." In *Faith and Politics; A Commentary on Religious, Social and Political Thought in a Technological Age*, ed. by R.H. Stone, 165–84. N.Y. George Braziller, 1968.

———. *Discerning the Signs of the Times*. N.Y.: Charles Scribner's Sons, 1946.

———. "Double love commandment" No. 3 of *The Reinhold Niebuhr Audio Tape Collection*. Union Theological Seminary, Richmond, Virginia.

———. *Essays in Applied Christianity*, ed. D.B. Robertson. N.Y.: Meridian, 1959.

———. "The Ethic of Jesus and the Social Problem." In *Love and Justice: Selections from the Shorter Writings*, ed. D.B. Robertson, 29-39. New York: Meridian, 1957.

———. "Intellectual Autobiography." In *Reinhold Niebuhr: His Religious, Social and Political Thought*, ed. by C.W. Kegley and R. W. Bretall. Library of Living Theology. Vol. 11. 3–7. New York: McMillan, 1961.

———. *Justice & Mercy*, ed. by Ursula Niebuhr. N.Y.: Harper & Row, 1974.

———. *Leaves from the Notebook of a Tamed Cynic*. Chicago: Willett, Clark & Colby, 1929.

———. *Love and Justice: Selections from the Shorter Writings*, ed. D.B. Robertson. New York: Meridian, 1957.

———. *Moral Man & Immoral Society*. Louisville, Kty: Westminster John Knox, 1932, repr. 2001.

———. *The Nature & Destiny of Man*. Volume I "Human Nature". N.Y.: Charles Scribner's Sons, 1964 (orig. 1941).

———. *The Nature & Destiny of Man*. Volume II "Human Destiny". N.Y.: Charles Scribner's Sons, 1964 (orig. 1943).

———. *On Man's Nature and His Communities*. N.Y.: Charles Scribner's Sons, 1965.

Niebuhr, Reinhold. *The Reminiscences of Reinhold Niebuhr*. Columbia Oral Research Project, 1957 [microfilm].

———. "'Reply to Interpretation and Criticism." In *Reinhold Niebuhr: His Religious, Social, and Political Thought*, eds. Charles Kegley and R. Bretall, 429–52. N.Y.: Pilgrim, 1956.

———. *The Self and the Dramas of History*. New York: Charles Scribner's Sons, 1955.

———. "View from the Sidelines." In *The Essential Reinhold Niebuhr Selected Essays and Addresses*, ed. Robert Mcfee Brown, 250–58. Yale University Press, 1987.

Niebuhr, Ursula, ed. *Remembering Reinhold Niebuhr: Letters of Reinhold and Ursula Niebuhr*. San Francisco, CA: Harper, 1991.
Norris, Kathleen. "Of Poets and Monks." *Christian Century*. (1994) 722.
———. *On Acedia and Me: A Marriage, Monks, and a Writer's Life*. New York: Riverhead, 2008.
Northcott, Michael. "Toward an Urban Theology 1960–1990s." *Crucible*. Part I (1990) 161–70.
———. "Toward an Urban Theology 1960s–1990s." *Crucible*. Part II (1991) 17–23.
Northcott, Michael, ed. *Urban Theology: A Reader*. London, UK: Cassell, Wellington House, 1998.
Nouwen, Henri. *The Return of the Prodigal Son: A Story of Homecoming*. N.Y.: Image/Doubleday, 1992.
O'Connell, Patrick. Selected and edited. *Cassian and the Fathers: Initiation into the Monastic Tradition*. Kalamazoo, MI: Cistercian, 2005.
———. *An Introduction to Christian Mysticism: Initiation into the Monastic Tradition 3* Kalamazoo, MI: Cistercian, 2008.
Oates, Stephen. "Let the Trumpet Sound", http://racism.org/index.php?option=com_content&view=article&id=1109.
Ogletree, Thomas W. "Facilitating Freedom and Constraining abuses of Power: Reinhold Niebuhr's Quest for Balance in the Public Oversight of Market Economies." Niebuhr Society Address at the 2011 American Academy of Religion. n. p.
———. *Hospitality to the Stranger: Dimensions of Moral Understanding* Philadelphia, PA: Fortress, 1985.
———. *The Use of the Bible in Christian Ethics: A Constructive Essay*. Philadelphia: Fortress, 1983.
Osborn, Bud. *Hundred Block Rock: Poems of Lament*. Vancouver, BC: Arsenal, 1999.
———. *Oppenheimer Park*: Prints by Richard Tetrault. Vancouver, British Columbia, n.d.
Osborn, Bud and Richard Tetrault. *Signs of the Times*. Vancouver, BC: Paneficio Studios and Anvil, 2005.
Ottati, Douglas F. *Hopeful Realism: Reclaiming the Poetry of Theology*. Cleveland, OH: Pilgrim, 1999.
The Overnighters: We Are the American Dream. Drafthouse Films. DVD directed by Jesse Moss, 2014. http://drafthousefilms.com/film/the-overnighters.
Owen, H. P. *The Basis of Christian Prayer*. Vancouver, B.C.: Regent College Publishing, 2005.
Oyer, Gordon. *Pursuing the Spiritual Roots of Protest: Merton, Berrigan, Yoder and Muste at the Gethsemane Abbey Peacemakers Retreat*. Eugene, OR: Cascade, 2014.
Paeth, Scott R. *The Niebuhr Brothers for Armchair Theologians*. Louisville, KY: Westminster John Knox, 2014.
Palmer, Parker J. *The Active Life: A Spirituality of Work, Creativity and Caring*. San Francisco: Harper & Row, 1990.
———. *A Hidden Wholeness: The Journey Toward an Undivided Life*. San Francisco: Jossey-Bass, 2004.
Pannenberg, Wolfhart. "Appearance and the Arrival of the Future." In *Theology and the Kingdom of God*, edited by R. J. Neuhaus, 127–43. Philadelphia, PA: Westminster, 1975.

Paul, Greg. *God in Alley: Being and Seeing Jesus in a Broken World*. Shaw Books of Water Brook, 2004.
Pauw, Amy Plantinga. "Attending to the Gaps between Beliefs and Practices." In *Practical Theology: Beliefs and Practices in Christian Life*, eds. M. Volf and D.C. Bass, 33–50. Grand Rapids, MI: Eerdmans, 2002.
Peters, Ronald. *Urban Ministry: An Introduction*. Nashville, TN: Abingdon, 2007.
Phipps, Bill. "Social Justice and a Spirituality of Transformation." In *The Emerging Christian Way*, ed. M. Schwartzentruber, 155–67. CopperHouse/WoodLake, 2006:
Pohl, Christine D. "A Community's Practice of Hospitality: The Interdependence of Practices and of Communities." In *Practical Theology: Beliefs and Practices in Christian Life* eds. M. Volf and D.C. Bass, 121–36. Grand Rapids, MI: Eerdmans, 2002.
Porter, J.S. *Thomas Merton: Hermit at the Heart of Things*. Toronto: Novalis, 2008.
Putman, Robert. *Bowling Alone in America: The Collapse and Revival of American Community*. New York: Simon and Schuster, 2000.
Ramsey, Paul. *Who Speaks for the Church*. Nashville, TN: Abingdon, 1967.
Rasmussen, Larry. *Earth Community Earth Ethics*. Maryland: Orbis, 1998.
———. "Ethics of Responsible Action." In *The Cambridge Companion to Dietrich Bonhoeffer*, ed. by John W. deGruchy Cambridge, 206–25. England: Cambridge University Press, 1999.
———. *Moral Fragments & Moral Community: A Proposal for Church in Society*. Minneapolis, MN: Augsburg Fortress, 1993.
Reeves, Ted and Roger Hutchinson, eds. *Action Training in Canada: reflections on Church-based Education for Social Transformation*. Toronto, Ontario: Emmanuel College's Centre for Study of Religion, 1997.
Reynolds, Anna Maria. "Woman of Hope." In *Julian Woman of Our Day*, ed. R. Llewellyn, 11–26. New London, CT: Twenty-Third, 1987.
Rice, Daniel F. *Reinhold Niebuhr and His Circle of Influence*. Cambridge, England: Cambridge University Press, 2012.
———, ed. *Reinhold Niebuhr Revisited: Engagements with an American Original*. Grand Rapids, Michigan: Wm. B. Eerdmans, 2009.
Rice, Joshua. *Paul and Patronage: The Dynamics of Power in I Corinthians*. Eugene, OR: Pickwick, 2013.
Rieder, Barry. *Energy from the Edges: Historical Study of the Biennial United Church Outreach Workers Consultation Events*. Comprehensive Paper for Master of Theological Studies, Waterloo Lutheran Seminary, Ontario, Canada, 2003.
Rieger, J. and Kwok Pui-Ian. *Occupy Religion: Theology of the Multitude*. Rowman & Littlefield, 2013.
———. *Religion, Theology and Class: Fresh Engagements after Long Silence*, ed. J. Rieger. N.Y.: Palgrave Macmillan, 2013.
Riessman, Catherine K. *Narrative Analysis*. Qualitative Research Methods Series 30. Newbury Park, CA: Sage, 1993.
Ringma, Charles R. *Seek the Silences with Thomas Merton: Reflections on Identity, Community, and Transformative Action*. Vancouver, British Columbia: Regent College, 2003.
Roberts, J. Deotis. *Bonhoeffer and King: Speaking Truth to Power*. Louisville, Kty: WJK, 2005.
Robinson, John A. T. *Honest to God*. London, England: SCM, 1963.

Roche, Douglas. *Justice Not Charity: A New Global Ethic for Canada.* Toronto: McClelland & Stewart, 1976.

Roddan, Andrew. *The Church in the Modern City: The Story of Three Score Years of Practical Christian Service 1885–1945.* Dunsmuir: First United Church, no date.

Roddan, Sam. *Batter My Heart.* Vancouver, British Columbia: United Church of Canada BC Conference, 1975.

Rolheiser, Ronald. *The Holy Longing: The Search for a Christian Spirituality.* New York: Doubleday, 1999.

Rose, Stephen, ed. *Who's Killing the Church?* Chicago City Missionary Society, 1966.

(The) Roundtable Association of Diocesan Social Action Directors. *Living God's Justice: Reflections and Prayers.* Cincinnati: St. Anthony Messenger, 2006.

Ruether, Rosemary Radford. "Spirituality for New Communities of Life." In *My Quests for Hope and Meaning: An Autobiography,* 153–57. Eugene, Oregon: Cascade, 2013.

———. "A US Theology of Letting Go" In *The Emergence of Liberation Theologies: Models for the Twenty-First Century,* ed. Thia Cooper, 43–48. N.Y.: Palgrave Macmillan, 2013.

Ruiz, Pablo. "Cry! Presente! Now and Forever." In *Bury the Dead: Stories of Death and Dying, Resistance and Discipleship,* ed. L. Dykstra. Eugene, 147–54. Oregon: Cascade, 2013.

Russell, Letty M. *Christian Education in Mission.* Philadelphia: Westminster, 1967.

The Rutba House, eds. *School(s) for Conversion: 12 Marks of a New Monasticism.* Eugene, OR: Cascade, 2005.

Sample, Tex. *The Future of John Wesley's Theology: Back to the Future with the Apostle Paul.* Eugene, OR: Cascade, 2012.

———. *Hard Living People & Mainstream Christians.* Nashville: Abingdon, 1993.

Saunders, Stanley and Charles Campbell. *The Word on the Street: Performing the Scriptures in the Urban Context.* Grand Rapids, MI: Eerdmans, 2000.

Schillebeeckx, Edward. *Christ: the Experience of Jesus as Lord.* Translated by John Bowden. N.Y.: Crossroads, 1981.

———. *God the Future of Man.* Translated by N.D. Smith. New York: Sheed and Ward, 1968.

Schipani, Daniel S. "Case Study Method" In *The Wiley-Blackwell Companion to Practical Theology,* ed. by Bonnie J. Miller-McLemore, 91–101. Chichester, England: Wiley-Blackwell, 2012.

Schreiter, Robert J., ed. *The Schillebeeckx Reader.* New York: Crossroad, 1984.

Schwartzentruber, Michael, ed. with photographer Bob Ballantyne and preface by Allen Tysick. *Out in the Open: Life on the Street.* Kelowna, B.C.: Northstone, 1997.

Schweitzer, Don. *Jesus Christ for Contemporary Life: His Person, Work, and Relationships.* Eugene, OR: Cascade, 2012.

Searle, Mark, ed. *Liturgy and Social Justice.* Collegeville, Minnesota: Liturgical, 1980.

Sennett, Richard with J. Cobb. *The Hidden Injuries of Class.* N.Y.: Vintage, 1973.

———, ed. "Introduction." In *Classic Essays on the Culture of Cities,* 13–19. New York: Meredith Corporation, 1969.

———. *Respect in a World of Inequality.* N.Y.: W. W. Norton, 2003.

Sensing, Tim. *Qualitative Research: A Multi-methods Approach to Projects for Doctor of Ministry Theses.* Eugene, Oregon, Cascade, 2011.

Sex Addicts Anonymous (Green Book). Houston, TX: International Service Organization of SAA, 2005.

Shannon, Wm. and C. Bochen, eds. *Thomas Merton: A Life in Letters: The Essential Collection.* New York: HarperCollins, 2008.

Shearer, J. G. "The Redemption of the City" (Pre-Assembly Toronto 1913 Congress Addresses). In *John Muir. Enduring Witness: A History of the Presbyterian Church in Canada.* Toronto: Presbyterian Church in Canada, 1987.

Sherman, Amy. *Restorers of Hope: Reaching the Poor with Church-based Ministries that Work.* Wheaton, IL: Crossway, 1997.

Shinn, Roger. *Forced Options: Social Decisions for the 21st Century.* New York: Harper and Row, 1982.

Shroyer, Danielle. *The Boundary-Breaking God: An Unfolding Story of Hope and Promise.* San Francisco: Jossey-Bass, 2009.

Sifton, Elisabeth. *The Serenity Prayer: Faith and Politics in Times of Peace and War.* N.Y.: W.W. Norton, 2003.

Silone, Ignazio. *Emergency Exit.* Translated by Harvey Fergussion II. New York: Harper and Row, 1968.

Smith, Gary N. *Street Journal: Finding God in the Homeless.* N.Y.: Sheen & Ward, 1994.

Smith, Graeme. "Being a Christian Socialist: Problems of What to Say, When and How to Say It." *Studies in Christian Ethics.* (2004) 17 2 134–39.

Smith, James K. A. "Determined Hope: A Phenomenology of Christian Expectation." In *The Future of Hope: Christian Tradition amid Modernity and Postmodernity,* 200–27.Grand Rapids, MI: Eerdmans, 2004.

Soelle, Dorothee. *The Silent Cry: Mysticism and Resistance.* Translated by Barbara and Martin Rumscheidt. Minneapolis, MN: Fortress, 2001.

Somerville (Margaret) in Conversation with James K. A. Smith. "'Healthism' and a Healthy Society." *Comment: Public Theology for the Common Good.* (2015) 46–52.

Somerville, Margaret. *The Ethical Imagination: Journeys of the Human Spirit.* Toronto: Ontario, House of Anansi, 2006.

Songs of a Gospel People, eds Gerald Hobbs et al. Winfield, B.C.: Wood Lake, 1987.

Spivy, Ed Jr. "The Church of No Lost Causes: A Little Methodist church (Rising Hope) Has a Big Heart for the Left Out and the Lonely in the Shadow of the Nation's Capital." *Sojourners: Faith in Action for Social Justice,* 40 6 (2011) 22–25.

Spurgaitus, Kevin. "Global Crisis, Urban Answers." *The United Church Observer.* (2012) 76 1 30–31.

Stackhouse, John. *Making the Best of It: Following Christ in the Real World.* Oxford University Press, 2008.

Stake, Robert E. "Qualitative Case Studies." In *Strategies of Qualitative Inquiry,* editors N. Denzin and Y. Lincoln, 119–149. Thousand Oaks, CA: Sage, 2008.

Stebner, Ellie. GEM: *The Life and Work of Sister Mac.* Ottawa: Novalis, 2001.

Steffenhagen, Janet. "'From Bombs to Books' Indomitable Spirit of ESL Students Inspired Principal to Write Book." *Vancouver Sun.* November 19, 2011, A2.

Stendahl, Krister. *Energy for Life: Reflections on the Theme 'Come, Holy Spirit—Renew the Whole Creation.'* Geneva, Switzerland: World Council of Churches, 1990.

———. "Your Kingdom Come: Notes for Bible Study." In *Your Kingdom Come: Mission Perspectives, Commission on World Mission and Evangelism,* 72–82. Geneva, Switzerland: World Council of Churches, 1980.

Stetzer, Ed. "The World as God Intends: New Survey Data on Pastors and Social Justice." *Sojourners*. (2013) 42 9 30–37.

Stewart, Robert B., ed. *The Resurrection of Jesus: The Crossan-Wright Dialogue*. Minneapolis, MN: Fortress, 2006.

Stock, J. with T. Otto and J. Wilson-Hartgrove. Inhabiting the Church: Biblical Wisdom for a New Monasticism. Eugene, OR: Cascade, 2007.

Stone, Ronald H. *Professor Reinhold Niebuhr: A Mentor to the Twentieth Century*. Louisville, KY: Westminster John Knox, 1993.

Stout, Jeffery. *Blessed are the Organized: Grass-roots Democracy in America*. Princeton, NJ: Princeton University Press, 2010.

Strauss, Anslem and Barney Glaser. *The Discovery of Grounded Theory: Strategies for Qualitative Research*. N.Y.: Aldine/Atherton, 1967.

Strauss, Anselm with Juliet Corbin. *Basics in Qualitative Research: Grounded Theory and Techniques*. Thousand Oaks, CA: Sage, 1990.

Streams of Justice.org website, February 20, 2007.

Stringfellow, William. *An Ethic for Christians and Other Aliens in a Strange Land*. Waco, TX: Word, 1973.

———. *My People Is the Enemy: An Autobiographical Polemic*. New York: Holt, Rinehart and Winston, 1965.

———. *A Simplicity of Faith: My Experience in Mourning*. Nashville, TN: Abingdon, 1986.

———. 'Through Dooms of Love' In *New Theology No. 2*, M. Marty and D. Peerman, eds., 288–96. N.Y.: Macmillan Co., 1965.

Stubbs, V. J. "Toward a New Paradigm for Specialized Urban Ministry." Unpublished essay, Saskatoon, SK: circa 1990.

Suchocki, Marjorie. In *God's Presence: Theological Reflections on Prayer*. St. Louis, MO: Chalice Press, 1996.

Sullender, R. Scott. *Ancient Sins . . . Modern Addictions: A Fresh Look at the Seven Deadly Sins*. Eugene, OR: Cascade, 2013.

Swanson, Jean. *Poor-Bashing: The Politics of Exclusion*. Toronto: Between the Lines, 2001.

Task Group on the Church in the Metropolitan Core. *A Dream Not for the Drowsy*. United Church of Canada publication of the 1980 Division of Mission in Canada. Toronto, Ontario.

Tattersal, Amanda. *Power in Coalition: Strategies for Strong Unions and Social Change*. Ithica, New York: Cornell University Press, 2010.

Taylor, Barbara Brown. "Looking for God in the City: A Meditation." In *Envisioning the New City: A Reader on Urban Ministry*, ed. by Eleanor Scott Meyers. 182–89. Louisville, KY: Westminster/John Knox, 1992.

Taylor, Charles. *The Malaise of Modernity*. Concord, Ontario: House of Anansi, 1991.

———. *A Secular Age*. Harvard University Press, 2007.

Thistlethwaite, Susan. *Occupy the Bible: What Jesus Really Said (and Did) About Money and Power*. New York: Astor and Blue Editions, 2012.

Tillich, Paul. *Love, Power and Justice*. New York: Oxford University Press, 1960.

Tinder, Glen. *The Fabric of Hope: An Essay*. 2nd edn Grand Rapids, MI: Eerdmans, 2001.

Todd, Doug. "Diversity's 'Inconvenient Truths.'" *Vancouver Sun*. Feb. 8, 2014, C5.

———. "How Can We Help the Poor: Religious Leaders Debate the Charity Model... Discourage Effective Income Redistribution." *Vancouver Sun.* June 22, 2013, C5.
Tracey, David. *The Earth Manifesto: Saving Nature with Engaged Ecology.* Toronto: Rocky Mountain, 2013.
Trothen, Tracy J. *Winning the Race? Religion, Hope, and Reshaping the Sport Enhancement Debate.* Macon, Georgia: Mercer University Press, 2015.
Troyer, Marty. "Subverting the Myth: A Pastor's Experiment in Unmasking White Privilege." *Sojourners.* 41 11 (2013) 28–31.
Turner, Robert S. *Our Father Who Aren't in Heaven: Subversive Reflections on the Lord's Prayer.* Eugene. OR:WIPF & Stock, 2015.
Tutu, Desmond. *No Future Without Forgiveness.* New York: Image, 1999.
Twelve Steps and Twelve Traditions. New York: Alcoholics Anonymous World Services, 1987.
Tysick, Al. "We're All Panhandlers Here.'" *The United Church Observer.* January 2007, 21.
Valentine, Charles. *Culture of Poverty: Critique and Counter-proposals.* Chicago, IL: University of Chicago Press, 1968.
Vandergrift, K. "CRA Audits: Six Questions." *The Catalyst.* Citizens for Public Justice, (2014) 37 3 10.
Vennard, Jane. *Embracing the World: Praying for Peace and Justice.* San Francisco: Jossey-Bass, 2003.
———. *Praying for Justice and Peace: Participating in the Reign of God* (sound recording). V.S.T. Chalmers Institute, 2001.
Villafane, Edan. *Seek the Peace of the City: Reflections on Urban Ministry.* Grand Rapids City, MI: Eerdmans, 1995.
Vincent, John. "*The Radical Tradition*." 2005. http://www.radical christianity.org.uk.
Voices United: The Hymn and Worship Book of The United Church of Canada. Toronto: United Church, 1996.
Volf, Miroslav. *A Public Faith: How Followers of Christ Should Serve the Common Good.* Grand Rapids, MI: Brazos, 2011.
Volf, Miroslav and Dorothy C. Bass, eds., *Practical Theology: Beliefs and Practices in Christian Life.* Cambridge, UK: Eerdmans, 2002.
Waldron, Robert. *Thomas Merton: Master of Attention.* Ottawa, Ontario: Novalis, 2007.
Wallis, Jim. "From a Shoebox to a Movement: for 40 yrs, Sojourners Has Been Fighting the Good Fight. Where Do We Go from Here?" *Sojourners* (2011) 40 10 15–20.
———. *On God's Side: What Religion Forgets and Politics Hasn't Learned about Serving the Common Good.* Grand Rapids, MI: Brazos Press, 2013.
Warf, Brian, ed. *Community Work in Canada.* Toronto, Ontario: McClelland and Stewart, 1979.
Warren, Donald L. *Helping Networks: How People Cope with Problems in the Urban Community.* University of Notre Dame Press, 1981.
Wartenberg-Potter, Barbel von. *We will not Hang our Harps on the Willows: Global Sisterhood and God's Son,* N.Y: Crossroad, 1990.
Webber, George W. 'The Christian Minister and the Social Problems of the Day' in *New Theology No.3,* eds. M. Marty and D. Peerman, 149–55. N.Y.: Macmillan, 1966.
———. *God's Colony in Man's World.* Nashville, TN: Abingdon, 1960.
———. *Today's Church: A Community of Exiles and Pilgrims.* Nashville, TN: Abingdon, 1979.

Wells, Samuel. *Improvisation: The Drama of Christian Ethics*. Grand Rapids, MI: Brazos Press, 2004.
Welton, Michael. *Unearthing Canada's Hidden Past: A Short History of Adult Education*. Toronto, Ontario: Thompson, 2013.
West, Cornel. "Prisoners of Hope." In *The Impossible Will Take a Little While: A Citizen's Guide to Hope in a Time of Fear,* ed. Paul Rogat Loeb, 293–97. Cambridge, Mass.: Basic, 2004.
White, Fred. *The Daily Writer*. Cincinnati: Writers Digest, 2008.
Whitehead, Alfred North. *Adventures of Ideas*. New York: Free Press, 1977.
———. *Process and Reality* (corrected edition by D. Griffin and D. Sherburne). N.Y.: Free Press, 1978.
Whyte, William F. *Participant Observer: An Autobiography*. Ithaca, New York: ILR, 1994.
———. *Street Corner Society: The Social Structure of an Italian Slum*, 4th edition. University of Chicago Press, 1993.
Wills, Gary. *Saint Augustine's Childhood. Confessiones Book 1*. London, England, Penguin, 2001.
Wilson, David. "No One Ever Said Remaking Regent Park Would Be Easy." *The United Church Observer* (June 2006) 22.
Wilson, Jonathan R. *Gospel Virtues: Practicising Faith, Hope & Love in Uncertain Times*. Eugene, OR: WIPF and Stock, 2004.
———. *Living Faithfully in a Fragmented World*, 2nd edn. Cambridge, England: Lutterworth, 2010.
Wilson, Robert. *Prophecy in Ancient Israel*. Philadelphia: Fortress, 1980.
Wilson-Hartgrove, Jonathan. *The Awakening of Hope: Why We Practice a Common Faith*. Grand Rapids, Michigan: Zondervan, 2012.
———. *New Monasticism: What It Has to Say to Today's Church*. Grand Rapids, MI: Brazos, 2008.
———. *The Wisdom of Stability: Rooting Faith in a Mobile Culture*. Brewster, MA: Paraclete, 2010.
Wink, Walter. *The Powers that Be: Theology for a New Millennium*. New York: Random House, 1998.
Winter, Gibson. *Being Free: Reflections on America's Cultural Revolution*. New York: Macmillan Co., 1970.
———. *The New Creation as Metropolis: A Design for the Church's Task in an Urban World*. New York: The Macmillan Co., 1963.
Winter, Gibson with Lawrence Witmar. "The Problem of Power in Community Organizing: An Essay in Parapolitics." A Research Paper for the Conference on Community Organizing, (April 12–13) 1968. The Centre for Urban Studies, the University of Chicago.
Wirth, Louis. "Urbanism as a Way of Life." In *Cities and Churches: Readings on the Urban Church,* ed., Robert Lee, 21–33. Philadelphia, PA: Westminster, 1962.
Wogaman, Philip. *The Great Economic Debate: An Ethical Analysis*. Philadelphia, PA: Westminster, 1977.
Wolfteich, Claire E. *Lord, Have Mercy: Praying for Justice with Conviction and Humility*. San Francisco: Jossey-Bass, 2006.
Wolterstorff, Nicholas. "The Contours of Justice: An Ancient Call for Shalom." In *God and the Victim: Theological Reflections on Evil, Victimization, Justice, and*

Forgiveness, eds. Lisa Barnes Lampman and Michelle D. Shattuck, 107–30. Minneapolis, MN: Eerdmans, 1999.

———. *Hearing the Call: Liturgy, Justice, Church and World*, eds. Mark Gornik and G. Thompson. Grand Rapids, MI: Eerdmans, 2011.

———. "How I Got to Justice and What Keeps Me There." *Journal of the American Academy of Religion*, 76 3 664–79.

———. *Justice in Love*. Grand Rapids, MI: Eerdmans, 2011.

———. "*Love and Justice*" Lang Lectures, Regent College, Regent Audio Compact Disc, 2007. http://www.regentbookstore.com.

———. "Seeking Justice in Hope." In *The Future of Hope: Christian Tradition Amid Modernity and Postmodernity*, eds. by M. Volf and William Katerberg, 77–100. Grand Rapids, MI: Eerdmans, 2004.

———. *Until Justice and Peace Embrace*. Grand Rapids, MI: Eerdmans, 1980.

(The) Women's Collective of St. Columba House. *Hope Is the Struggle: A Community in Action*. Toronto: United Church, 1996.

Wright, N.T. "The Lord's Prayer as a Paradigm of Christian Prayer." In *Into God's Presence: Prayer in the New Testament*, ed. by Richard N. Longenecker. 132–54. Grand Rapids, MI: Eerdmans, 2002.

———. *Surprised by Hope: Rethinking Heaven, the Resurrection, and the Mission of the Church*. New York: HarperOne, 2008.

Wright, Robert. "Generational Angst." *Vancouver Sun*, February 11, 2012, C1.

Wuthnow, Robert. "Spiritual Practice." *Christian Century*. (1998) 855.

Yin, Robert K. *Case Study Research: Design and Methods*, 4th edn. Los Angeles, CA: Sage, 2009.

Yuile, L. "Snowden Did Citizens a Service Leaking Surveillance Secrets." *24 Hours*, (July 22, 2013) 4.

Index

A Community Aware, xiii, xix, 12, 30–32, 80n36, 103, 108, 133, 146
Alexander, Bruce K., xix, 25n28, 31, 34n2, 67n2, 84n3, 96n3, 103, 146, 159
Alves, Rubin, 69, 159.
Alinsky, Saul, 62
Augustine, St., 3n7, 14n42, 56n6, 70n9, 74, 79n35, 89, 105, 132, 135n25, 136
Anderson, Terence, xix, 5n16, 6n21, 16, 20, 32n41, 41n17, 65n28, 77n30, 79n34, 98n46, 18n33
animate, animation, xv, 12, 20n15, 30, 43, 50, 53, 56, 62, 66, 68, 92, 106, 109, 112, 114, 126, 128, 130–31, 134, 137–38, 158
Ansell, Nicholas, 138n32
Answers in the Heart, 98n44, 134n18

Badertscher, John, 16n1, 17n4, 48
balance, vital balance, xvi, 3, 6, 9–11, 29, 31, 47–48, 52, 61–62, 68, 70, 73, 76, 78–79, 82, 84, 91, 95, 97, 105, 112–14, 116, 119–121, 123, 128, 130–32, 136, 139–40, 145, 156, 158
Barth, Karl, 120n32, 160
BC Conference of the United Church, 140n37
Bennett, John C., 6, 10, 11n36, 30, 140n37
Bethge, Eberhard, 32, 61n18, 130n7, 160
Biblical writings
  Amos, 51, 90, 126
  I Corinthians, 5n20, 56, 77n32
  Genesis, 93n28
  Hebrews, 110n18, 138
  Hosea, 90
  Jeremiah, 41, 47–48, 51, 90, 119, 128;
  John, gospel of, 93n28
  Luke, 62, 91
  Matthew, 90
  Proverbs, 87 and n12
  Psalms, 52, 93n28, 127
  Revelation, 52
  Romans, 77n32, 93n28–29, 124, 137
Blaikie, Bill, 26n21, 160
Bochen, Christine, 88n14, 89n15, 96n38, 98n43
Bonhoeffer, Dietrich, 4n12, 18, 32, 40n14, 60n16, 71, 80n38, 101n4, 123, 130n17, 143
Bosch, David, 118, 161, 119n27
Bretherton, Luke, 133n13, 161
Brueggemann, Walter, 10n29, 117, 122n34, 161
Burrows, Bob, 26n32, 41

Canadian Urban Training Centre, 23
(St.) Columba House (Montreal), 45n23
Caputo, John, 4n15, 22, 39n9, 49n33
Chittister, Joan, 22n21, 130–31n7
community organizing, xix, 12, 14, 19n12, 29, 32, 41, 50, 62n21, 73–74, 79, 80n36, 102, 113, 115, 133, 147, 153, 158n8
compassion, xiv, 14, 30, 50, 69–70, 72, 84, 88, 91, 124, 156
contrast-awareness, 8, 14, 30, 49, 66, 114, 126, 157–58
covenant, covenant-making, 40, 41n17, 42, 51, 56, 70n9, 78, 86, 99, 125, 128, 143n11
Corbin, Juliet, 156n6, 157n7
cross, theology of, xviii, 5, 45–46, 56, 58–59, 62, 65n27, 84n3, 86, 89

INDEX

Cox, Harvey, 3n6, 17, 18n5, 18n8, 19n10, 20n15, 20n16, 25, 27, 35, 58n12, 129
Chambers, Ed, 102, 103n5, 108n16, 147n21
Coles, Stuart, 129
Crossan, John Dominic, 149n27
Crysdale, Stewart, 13n40, 26n29

Dandelion Society, 41, 63, 121
Dart, Ron, 22n41, 32n40, 83, 93n28
Diewert, Dave and Teresa, xix, 104, 150, 151
Dorrien, Gary, 51n36, 68n4
Dykstra, Laurel, 37n6, 117n23
Dyson, Arnold, 125n44

East Harlem Protestant Parish, xiii, 12–3, 21–2, 24–25, 32, 38, 75, 93, 125, 145
endurance, 4, 82, 112, 123, 127, 138n33
eschatology, eschaton, 55, 120n32, 138–9n32, 149n27
evil, 15n42, 23n23, 35, 65–6, 86, 104, 135

faith, faithfully, xiii, xiv, xv, xvi, xviii and n6, 1–2, 6, 13, 16–18, 25, 48, 50–51, 55–57, 59, 61, 63, 70, 77, 80–82, 85, 90–91, 93, 98n44, 113, 116, 118–19, 120n31, 121, 123, 129–130, 132n12, 135, 140, 147–48
failure, 2, 31, 73
faithful public witness, faithful public-prophetic witness, 9–10, 17–18, 47, 51, 62, 84, 90, 92, 99, 101, 124, 126
Farley, Wendy, 4n15, 14n, 49, 50n34
Fawkes, Deborah, xix, 26n31, 75n22
First United Church, 26n32, 30, 37, 40–41, 46, 49, 81n44, 120
fulfillment, 6, 66, 76, 130, 139
Fineman, Martha, xivn4, xviiin9, 2n4, 7n25
finis (mortality), xv, 130. 138, 140
Fule, A.T., 69n5

Fox, Ed, 71n13, 72, 73n17, 75n21, 76n25
grace, grace-based, xvi, xviii, 9, 51, 53, 55, 57, 59, 64, 70, 76, 78, 80–81n40, 85–6, 98 n44, 109, 128, 130–31, 134–39

Grandview Calvary Baptist Church, 12, 105, 121, 151n1
Gilkey, Langdon, 77n30
Gornick, Mark, 40, 47n31, 119n28
grounded theory, xv, 12, 30, 129n3, 150, 156n6, 157
Green, Clifford, 22n, 22n22, 24, 24n25, 25n27
Green, Laurie, 46n27, 108n15
Grimley, A., 39n10
Gustafson, James, 16, 16n1, 32n42, 137n31
Gutierrez, Gustav, 91n22

haiku, 53, 88, 131 and n9, 140
Hall, Douglas J., xviii, 19n4, 61, 81n41, 125n44
Hammarskjold, Dag, 5n20, 60n17, 77, 77n32, 93n27
Hargraves, J.A., 25
Harrison, Beverley Wildung, 14, 16, 16n1, 68, 68n4
Harper, Niles, 37n6, 132n12
Hart, Patrick, 86n8, 90n18, 94n32, 144n11, 148, 148n25
Hili, Carmel, 99n34, 95 and n35
Hemmings, Michael, 62n21
Hessel, Stephanie, 9n27, 155n28
Higgins, John J., 93n27
Higgins, Michael W., 90n18
hope, hopeful,1–2, 4–7n22, 9 n25, 9n27, 10–17, 22–3, 25n28, 26, 28–29, 31–32, 35, 37, 39, 41, 43, 45n25, 53–71, 76–82, 83–7, 90, 92, 94–9, 100, 103, 105, 107, 109–14, 116–29, 130–37, 139–41, 143, 145n15, 148–49n28, 153, 158n8;
as goad, incite, 56, 99, 124, 130–31n8
as horizon(s), 11, 52–55, 59n15, 81–82, 87, 97–98, 123–24, 131

as relative term, helper, 4, 66n32, 139
tension with despair, xiv, xvi, 4–5, 14, 27, 30, 57, 62–64, 66, 68, 73, 80, 86, 92, 94, 98n46
virtue, xiv-xvii, 5n16, 14, 37, 41, 43, 47, 53–54, 56, 60, 68–69, 90, 98n 46, 119, 120n31, 122, 128, 130–31, 149, 158
with waiting, xviii, 6n22, 51, 119–20
Houston, Jim, 28n36
Hulsether, Mark, 75n21
Hume, Stephen, 36n5

Industrial Areas Foundation, xvii, 12, 14, 29, 32, 79, 102, 133, 147n21

Jevne, Ronna, 123n37
Johns, Rob, 81n44
Johnson, Fenton, 142n5, 144n12
justice, injustice, xi-xii, xiv-xix, 3, 9–15, 17n3, 18, 20–24, 27–32, 34, 37–44, 46–53, 56, 60–63, 65n27, 66, 67–82, 85–88, 89n15, 90–93n 27, 94–95, 97n42, 99, 120–136, 138, 140–43n11, 144n12–13–14, 145–49, 150–58;
covenant(s) of loyalty 70n9, 78
as equality, 2n14, 12, 20, 36n5, 38, 41n16, 42, 52, 69, 70, 72–73, 78, 88, 114, 135, 138n33, 151
as liberty (and equality), 63, 70, 72–73, 78, 88
as order, 51, 67, 69–70n9, 72, 78, 88
tension with charity, xvii-xviii and n7, 3, 31, 37n6, 38–39, 42, 48, 50, 64, 68, 73–74, 78–79, 87, 92, 105, 108, 112–13, 116, 119–21, 125, 132n12, 133, 136, 144 n14

Kamergrauzis, Normunds, 126n47
Kiplin, Juliet, 108n15, 109n17, 119n28, 127n2
King, Jr. Martin Luther, 1, 42, 46, 104
Klein, Naomi, xviii
Kneen, Brewster, 69, 69n6
Kuile, Martha, 5n16, 69n4n7
Kurtz, Ernest, 96n37

Just Society Movement, 26n30, 120
kairos, 81, 108, 110, 114–15, 138
Kingdom, Kingdom of God, 51, 63, 71n12, 72, 149
koinonia, 27, 62, 85

Lederman, Martha, 49n30
Leech, Kenneth, xviii, 16, 16n1, 21, 21n18–19, 22, 22n20, 25n20, 84
Lehman, Paul L., 137n31
Lind, Christopher, 28n37
Linthicum, Robert, 35
Lindsey, Bob, xvin5, 129
Lovin, Robin, 11, 11n14, 67n1, 75n22, 79n35
liberation, liberation theology, 18, 20, 56, 62–63, 65n29, n30, 69, 90n18, 91, 120, 138
Longhouse Ministry, xi-xiii, xvi, xix, 35–6, 43, 45, 47n31, 100–26, 153, 128–9, 133, 137–39, 140n37, 155–6
Lupton, Robert D., xviii, 3n8
love
with justice, xii, 10n29, 14, 48, 50–51, 62, 67, 69n8, 70n9, 71–3, 74n19, 76, 78, 79n19, 82, 90n19, 135, 143;
tension with charity, xvii-xviii, 3, 31, 37–9, 42, 48, 50–51, 62, 67, 69n8, 70n9, 71–73, 74n19, 76, 78, 79n34, 82, 90n19, 120–21, 132–33n12, 135–36, 143, 144n14, 150–51;
mature, true love, 74, 78–79, 91n23, 133, 137, 144n11;
hope nourished, 149n28 (see also hope and triad)
Lynch, William F., 4n13, 66, 66n32, 120n31
Lyotier, Ken, xix, 153–54

Marcuse, Herbert, 62n22
MacIntyre, Alasdair, 119n29, 141, 141n2
McAfee, Lois, 97n13
McCarroll, Pamela R., xviii, 5, 6n22, 11, 11n33, 19n11, 65n28, 120n31
McCourt, Kevin, 50

INDEX

McDonnell Thomas P., 86, 89n15, 90n18, 93n26, 122n35
McEntyre, Marilyn Chandler, 125n41
McInnes, Craig, 41n16
McQuaig, Linda, 49n32
meditation, xviii, 4, 29, 31–32n 40, 56, 64, 89, 91–92, 93n28, 103n6, 104, 125, 130, 134
Meeks, M. Douglas., 54n2, 55n3, 61, 61n19
McNamee, John, 22, 39n9, 82n45, 127n1, 138n33
mercy, 34, 63, 85, 135, 137n28, 144
Merton, Thomas, viii, xivn3, xvi, xix, 3, 3n6n10, 13, 22, 30, 32, 40, 40n13n21, 47n30, 54, 56, 59, 63, 65, 66, 68, 68n3, 83, 84, 84n3, 85, 85n4, 86, 86n6, 86n7, 86n8–9, 87, 87n11, 87n13, 88, 88n14, 89, 89n15, 89n16n17, 90, 90n18, 90n19–20, 91, 91n23–24, 92, 92n25, 92n26–27, 94, 94n32–33, 95, 95n9, 96, 96n38–39, 97, 97n41, 98, 98n43, 99, 117, 117n23, 121, 122, 122n35, 124, 124n42, 125, 126, 128, 130, 130n7, 134, 134n16–17, 136, 136n26, 139, 141, 142n5, 143, 143n10–11, 144, 144n12–13, 145n15–16, 147, 147n23, 148, 148n23, 148n24, 148n25–26, 149, 149n28, 158n9
Metro Vancouver Alliance, xix, 12, 29–30, 32, 36, 41, 79, 80n36, 101, 108, 110, 121, 123, 133, 136, 146, 147n21, 152, 157
Michaud, Derek, 58, 58n11
Mission, mission of the church, xvi, 1, 10n30, 12, 30, 39, 40–48, 55, 68, 100, 108–9, 111, 113, 118–19, 121, 126, 128–29, 140, 146, 158
Moir, John, 23n23
Moltmann, Jurgen, vii, xi, xvi, 5, 5n19, 6, 20, 30, 52n38, 54, 54n2, 55, 55, 56n7, 57, 57n8, 58, 58n12, 59, 59n13n15, 60, 60n16, 61, 61n20, 62, 63, 63n23–24, 64, 65, 65n27n30, 66, 66n31n34, 68, 86, 87, 97, 98, 98n44–46, 99, 120, 120n32, 122, 122n36, 124, 124n39, 125n43, 128, 130, 131n8, 134, 137, 137n30, 138, 138n32, 139, 145n15

Montreal City Mission, 40, 42n20
Moon, Lawrence, 123
Moore, J.J., 106n9
Morris, Barry K., 9n27, 12n37, 16n1, 17n4, 28n36, 43n22, 49n32, 81n44, 94n34, 95n35, 108n15, 110n19
Moss, Robert G., 106n10, 108n15, 137n30

Neal, Marie Augusta, xviii
Niebuhr, H. Richard, 6, 135n20
Niebuhr, Reinhold, viii, xi, xviii, xix, 2, 2n5, 3, 3n6, 6, 6n24, 9, 10n31, 11n34 and 35, 13, 14n42, 30, 51, 54, 59, 66, 67, 68, 68n4, 69, 69n5, 69n8, 70, 70n9n10, 71, 71n12n13, 72, 72n14, 73, 73n14, 74, 74n18–19, 75, 75n21–23, 76, 76n24–28, 77, 77n30–31, 78, 79, 79n35, 80, 81, 81, 81n43–44, 82, 85, 87, 88, 90 94, 97, 98, 102, 105, 109, 120, 121, 128, 130, 132, 133, 133n13–14, 135, 135n20, 135n22–24, 136, 136n28, 137, 137n31, 139, 139n37, 139, 139, 139n37, 144n14, 145n15
Norris, Kathleen, 4n14, 18, 18n7, 66n32, 120n30, 145n17
Northcott, Michael, xix, 22, 22n22
Nouwen, Henri, 90n19

Ogletree, Thomas W., 10n32, 16, 16n1, 41n18, 110, 120n18, 138n33, 139, 139n34
Ottati, Douglas, 7, 7n25, 75n22
Oyer, Gordon, 90n1
organize, organizer, 26, 30, 37, 41, 61, 74, 79, 80, 90, 115, 121, 123, 133n13, 141, 152–53

paceful, pacefulness, xviii, 4, 32, 136

INDEX

Pannenberg, Wolfhart, 120n4
Parallel Institute, 26, 120
patience, 4, 14, 48, 63–64, 79–80, 96, 98n44n46, 109, 145n16
Patten, Terry, xix, 103, 104n7, 153, 156n5
peace, 5, 40n14–15, 41, 52, 60–62, 65n27, 77, 81n44, 85–6, , 89, 92, 93n27, 109, 119, 130, 131n8, 143, 147
Phipps, Bill, 125n22
Pohl, Christine D., 125n22
prayer, prayerful, xi-xii, xiv-xviii, 4–5, 8–9, 13–15, 21–22, 31–32, 35, 37–40n13, 43, 47, 50–54, 55–56, 60–64, 66, 68, 70, 76n24, 77–8, 80n38, 81n42 n44, 82, 83–99, 121, 127–40, 145–46, 148n25, 149n27;
    as attention, 34, 44, 64, 68, 81, 89n15, 117n23, 143;
    as engagement, 6, 13, 21, 48, 52, 104, 131, 135, 155;
    as grounding, xviii, 5, 29, 39, 47, 81, 91n24, 134, 137;
    tension with self-righteousness/weariness, xiv, 60–61n18, 76, 87, 91, 120, 125, 140, 158

Rasmussen, Larry, 1, 1n4
realism, Christian realism, xvi-vii, 1–3, 5–12,, 14–15n42, 16, 22, 32–3, 50–53, 66–67, 69, 70n9, 71, 74–76, 78–79, 82–84, 96, 107, 111, 119, 122–24, 128–131, 134, 136–37, 139, 144
reconciliation, 8, 41, 55, 60, 95n36, 101
Reid, Andrea, xiii, xivn2, 103, 104n7, 150, 155, 156n5
Reider, Barry, 108
response ethics, 10, 16, 109–110, 127
rest, restlessness, 3n6, 4–5, 20, 36, 51, 60, 66, 77, 89n17, 93n27n28, 124, 134n15, 135
resurrection, cross-resurrection, 57–59n15, 62n27, 77, 86, 93n29
Ringma, Charles R., 89, 90, 90n2, 91
Ruether, Rosemary Radford, xviii

Serenity Prayer, xviii, 9n28, 51, 53, 78, 81n40, 85, 98, 109, 128, 129n4
Saunders, Stanley, xix Bill
Schillebeeckx, Edward, 8, 9n27, 120n2, 140n38, 157
Schipani, Daniel S., 107, 107n14
Schreiter, Robert J., 9n27, 140n, 140n38
Sennet, Richard, xviii, 27n4
Shannon, William, 68n43
Shearer, J.G., 24n24
Sherman, Amy, 43n21, 46n28
Shinn, Roger, 1n2, 27n7
Sifton, Elizabeth, 9n28, 81, 81n40n42, 129n34n35
silence, silenced, 93n27, 94, 116
Silone, Ignazio, 21n18
sin, sinned-against, 2–3, 7, 11, 18–19, 33, 35, 52, 59, 63, 69–71, 78–9, 86n7, 92, 95, 97n42
Soelle, Dorothee, 87n13, 90, 90n19
social ethics, xix, 9–10, 29, 41–42, 48, 68, 77, 113, 144n14
Stake, Robert E., 107, 107n13
steadfast, steadfastness, 2, 4–5, 14–15, 30–33, 35, 38, 41, 48, 50, 53, 60, 62,70, 73–76, 84–85, 88, 94, 96, 99, 102, 107–9n17, 113, 119, 123, 131, 136–37, 140, 147
Steffhagen, Janet, 45n26
Stetzer, Ed, 17n3
Stone, Ronald H., 75n23
Strauss, Anselm, 56, 57n7
Stringfellow, William, 22, 22n13, 93, 94n3, 95n45, 129, 146, 146n19
Stubbs, Valerie J., 44n23
struggle, xi-xv, 14, 19, 21, 30, 44–45, 47, 51, 55, 57, 62–3, 68–69n4, 72–74, 84, 86, 96–97, 98–9n46, 105, 125n44, 126n47, 142n4,147, 154–56
Streams of Justice, xix, 12, 29–30, 32, 38, 41–42, 52n37, 80n36, 83, 104, 108, 110, 113, 121, 123, 126, 132n12, 133, 146, 150–51, 157
success, successful, xvii, xviiin6, 1, 28, 42, 67, 87n12, 100, 117, 127
Suchocki, Marjorie, 87

Swanson, Jean, 38

telos, xv, 112, 130, 138, 140, 142n4
Tillich, Paul, 6, 6n23, 71, 90, 90n19
Tinder, Glen, 66, 66n32, 120n31
Toronto Christian Resource Centre, xiv, 12, 25, 41, 46, 75, 94n34, 113, 123–24
Tracey, David, 8n9, 121n33, 144n13
triad: praying justice hopefully, hoping justice prayerfully, xv-xviii, 5, 10, 14–15, 35, 37, 47, 50–53, 60–64, 66–70,76, 78–81, 83–84, 93–99, 106, 109, 111–12, 119–26, 128, 130, 139–40, 145–46, 149n27
Trothen, Tracy J., 8n6, 49n3
Tutu, Desmond, 95n36
Twelve-Step Fellowship, 81, 96n40, 132, 135n19
Tysick, Al, 108n15

Valentine, Charles, 48
Vandergrift, K., 52n39, 118n25
Villifane, Edan, 47, 119n28
Vincent, John, 20, 20n17, 22

Waldron, Robert, 89n15, 117n23
Wallis, Jim, 17, 17n21 22n34
Wartenberg-Potter, Barbel von, 61n18
Warf, Brian, 26
Webber, George W., 146n8
Wells, Samuel, 35n4
Welton, Michael, xix, 106, 106n11 n12
Whitehead, Alfred North, 62n22, 101n4, 138n32
Wills, Gary, 89n17
Wilson- Hartgrove, Jonathan, 80n37, 124n18, 141, 141n2–3, 142n6, 143, 143n7, 147n23
Wink, Walter, 35, 87n13
Wirth, Louis, xviii
wisdom, xvi, 9, 53, 71n13, 72, 80n36, 81n40, 86–87, 134, 137, 139

www.ingramcontent.com/pod-product-compliance
Lightning Source LLC
Chambersburg PA
CBHW071442150426
43191CB00008B/1207